The
Liberal Self

The
Liberal Self

JOHN STUART MILL'S MORAL
AND POLITICAL PHILOSOPHY

Wendy Donner

CORNELL UNIVERSITY PRESS

Ithaca and London

First published 1991 by Cornell University Press.

International Standard Book Number 0-8014-2629-4
Library of Congress Catalog Card Number 91-55065

Printed in the United States of America

Librarians: Library of Congress cataloging information appears on the last page of the book.

⊗ The paper in this book meets the minimum requirements of the American National Standard for Information Sciences— Permanence of Paper for Printed Library Materials, ANSI Z39.48-1984.

To the memory of my father,
DAVID DONNER

Contents

Acknowledgments   ix

Introduction   I

1 Mill and Bentham: The Nature of Pleasurable   8
Experience
Associationist Psychology 10
Bentham's Dominant and Secondary Accounts 23
Objectivity and Moral Theory 26
Mill's Objections to Intuitionism 28

2 Qualitative Hedonism   37
Quality as a Good-Making Characteristic 37
Reaction of Critics 41
False Friends 46
A False Start 52
Critique of Bentham's Dominant Account 57
Critique of Bentham's Secondary Account 60

3 Models of Utility   66
Mental-State Accounts 67
Desire-Satisfaction Accounts 79

4 The Sensory Evaluation of Wines   83

5 The Doctrine of Development   92
   Affective Development 97
   Intellectual or Cognitive Development 107
   Moral Development 112

6 From Development to Self-Development   118
   Mill's Conception of Happiness 118
   The Role of the State and Neutralism 125
   The Moral Arts and Sciences 131

7 Liberalism and Individualism   141

8 Liberty of Self-Development   160
   Harm and Rights 161
   Self-Development vs. Autonomy: In Defense of Mill 165
   Elaborations on Self-Development 183

9 Liberty and Harm to Others   188

10 Applications of the Theory   198
   Representative Government 198
   Economic Democracy 208

    Bibliography   218

    Index   226

Acknowledgments

I owe a great debt to Wayne Sumner, my teacher at the University of Toronto, who provided a wonderful balance of support and rigorous critical feedback for my work there. When I turned my attention to writing this book, he continued to be a source of encouragement and stimulation. I am also grateful to David Lyons and Don Brown, the readers for Cornell University Press, whose suggestions were very helpful in my final revisions.

While I was writing much of this book I was leading the life of the philosophic nomad. I encountered many friends and colleagues who helped me in various ways. I thank Ross Andaloro, David Gauthier, Richard Hare, Ellen Haring, Michael Kubara, Douglas Den Uyl, Fred Wilson, Ray Frey, Jan Narveson, Roger Paden, Henry West, Arthur Ripstein, Winnie Tomm, Wesley Cooper, Martin Tweedale, Peter Vallentyne, Helen Cullen, Trish Blackstaffe, Andrea Kristof, Catherine Hopwood, Etta Donner-Rosen, Albert Rosen, Ruby Donner, Gail Donner, Arthur Donner, Arthur Schaffer, and Michael McDonald.

I was fortunate to receive a research grant from the Social Sciences and Humanities Research Council of Canada which allowed me to devote time in 1985 and 1986 to work on the book. Work on this book was also supported by a postdoctoral fellowship at the University of Florida. I am grateful for the research support I received from the University of Regina President's SSHRC Research Fund.

Finally, I thank Roger Haydon of Cornell University Press and John Thomas, my copy editor, for their wonderful assistance.

Portions of Chapter 8 appeared as "Gray's Autonomy: In Defence of Mill," in *Ethics and Basic Rights*, ed. Guy Lafrance (Ottawa: University of Ottawa Press, 1989). A portion of Chapters 1 and 2 appeared as "John Stuart Mill's Concept of Utility," *Dialogue* 22 (September 1983); and part of Chapters 7 and 8 as "Mill on Liberty of Self-Development," *Dialogue* 26 (Summer 1987).

W. D.

Ottawa, Ontario

Introduction

In this book I offer an interpretation and defense of John Stuart Mill's conception of the good, and thus my discussion follows a theme that runs through and links Mill's ethics and political philosophy. In ethics, I examine Mill's qualitative hedonism against the background of the orthodox Benthamite quantitative hedonism, which Mill rejects. Mill's critics have argued that, when he enlarged his concept of utility, he relinquished the consistency and objectivity of Benthamite utilitarianism along with its weaknesses. I argue on the contrary that Mill's enlarged concept of utility overcomes the limitations of Bentham's theory without sacrificing its strengths and that the objectivity and consistency of his theory are not undermined by his recognition of quality as contributing to value.

Alan Ryan has noted that "Mill's concern with self-development and moral progress is a strand in his philosophy to which almost everything else is subordinate."[1] Mill's utilitarian philosophy unifies his ethics and his liberal political philosophy, and these aspects form a unified whole with a view of the good for humans as its foundation. A central constituent of the most valuable forms of happiness for humans is the development and active use of our higher human capacities. In Mill's moral philosophy, the principle of the

[1] Alan Ryan, *The Philosophy of John Stuart Mill,* 2d ed. (New York, 1988), 255.

good is logically prior to the principles of right. As Mill explains in *A System of Logic*, the principle of utility functions as the foundation for all our practical reasoning and is the controller of all the practical arts.[2]

My aim is to set out and defend an interpretation of Mill's views on value which resolves some traditional puzzles and presents Mill's views in a light and with a unity and plausibility that is their due. Mill holds complex views on the good. In the recent past, new approaches to his thought have been gaining currency, and several writers have presented revisionary interpretations of his philosophy which attempt to do credit to the depth, complexity, and subtlety of his work. Previous critics had subjected Mill to a good deal of unsympathetic and unsound interpretation and assessment. In the past twenty years his views have been regarded in a more sympathetic and realistic light as reflecting the complexity and richness of the domain of moral and political philosophy and as attempting to balance conflicting tendencies of a complex moral and social reality. The recent reinterpretations and explorations of his philosophy by writers such as Alan Ryan, David Lyons, Don Brown, John Gray, Henry West, and Fred Berger have been attempts to redress past unsympathetic interpretation and present Mill more accurately. These writers have, however, concentrated on principles of the right or obligation within Mill's philosophy. I contend that revisionary work on Mill's principle of the good has lagged behind work on his principles of right, and we have not yet been presented with a complete and adequate account of his complex views of the good and how these unify diverse elements of his moral and political philosophy.

Mill was educated by his father, James Mill, to be the intellectual heir to the utilitarian philosopher Jeremy Bentham. Like so many educational experiments, this one did not quite go the way its planners intended, and the young Mill instead used his educational foundation in critical thinking to transcend and reject key elements of his predecessors' thought. He is regarded as a revisionary or rebel utilitarian and liberal, a transitional figure who made the breakthrough in the movement from classical to contemporary utilitarian and liberal theories.

[2]John Stuart Mill, *A System of Logic*, in *The Collected Works of John Stuart Mill*, 33 vols., ed. John M. Robson (Toronto, 1974–91), 8:951. Mill's *Collected Works* hereafter cited by volume and page only.

Mill's early education had other unexpected results as well. In early adulthood, he suffered acute depression, which he describes in his *Autobiography*, and he later traced this problem to certain deficiencies in his education and in the philosophy on which it had been based. He then went on to redesign and expand his philosophy to overcome what he saw as crucial shortcomings of classical utilitarianism. This revision can be viewed from different perspectives, but I contend that the fundamental redesign and expansion centered on Mill's conceptions of human nature and of the good or happiness for humans with this nature. Mill's most fundamental commitment, the driving force of all his thought and writing, is the promotion of human self-development and the happiness involved in the development and exercise of our higher human faculties. He thought that the conception of the good, or quantitative hedonism, used by his utilitarian predecessors had been far too narrow and had exposed its proponents to the charge that they were promoting "a doctrine worthy only of swine" (10:210). If we focus our attention, as Bentham and James Mill did, on the simple psychological sensations of pleasure and pain which are the earliest constituents of our mental life, and if we build value only on the quantity of these elements of experience, then we may well be open to such charges. If instead we focus our attention on complex experiences that are generated out of these simple elements in the course of psychological development, and if we broaden the basis on which we measure the value of these experiences to encompass their quality or kind as well as their quantity, we can meet the charge head on and defeat it. Mill's qualitative hedonism leaves a path for assessing complex experiences, which are the bearers of value in his theory, according to their worth as kinds of experiences. The value of forms of happiness depends on their good-making characteristics, properties of the experiences that are the basis of their worth or produce their value. Mill thinks that the most basic good-making features of experiences are quantity and quality or kind, and he further maintains that the most valuable kinds are those that involve the development and active use of the human intellectual, affective, and moral capacities.

When Mill broadened the basis of the value of pleasurable experiences or satisfactions, he needed to work out a new method of measuring value, because Bentham's simple felicific calculus does not apply to the expanded and more complex terrain. He turned to measuring value by eliciting the preferences of competent agents. Thus, like many contemporary moral philosophers, Mill gives a key role in his moral theory to judgments of rational moral agents. The competent agents who play this role in Mill's theory are those who have undergone a process of development that has transmuted into self-development. His discussions of the doctrine of development and self-development are rooted in his conception of human nature as naturally seeking to nurture, expand, and use its higher capacities.

In Chapter 1, I map out the common ground of Bentham's and Mill's concepts of the good and begin to explore their differences. Mill, like Bentham, builds his moral theory around the single ultimate standard of utility and sees utilitarianism as the rational, objective alternative to intuitionism. Both philosophers are also associationists and hold a mental-state account of utility. But their accord over the question of what has value—pleasurable experiences and the absence of painful ones—starts to break down over the issue of the nature of these valuable objects. I claim that Mill's theory is a sophisticated form of hedonism, but the use of this term is simplistic and could be misleading. I call Mill's views hedonistic because their theoretical associationist psychological foundation is set out in terms of pleasures and pains.

Chapter 2 is concerned with the crux of Mill's break with orthodox Benthamism, his view that both the quantity and the quality of pleasurable experiences contribute to their value. I set out several standard objections to Mill's inclusion of quality in utilitarian calculations. I examine two attempts by false friends to provide alternative interpretations of Mill which aim to circumvent these criticisms, and I look at one false start in the right direction. I argue that these attempts all fail. I provide a critique of Bentham's account, showing that it does not meet his own standards of objectivity.

In Chapter 3 I examine Mill's conception of utility in the context of current controversies about the nature of the good, particularly the debate between the mental-state or experience model and the desire-satisfaction model of utility. Some twentieth-century theorists, following one direction in Bentham's thought, see utility in terms of choice, desire-satisfaction, or giving people what they prefer. Others view utility along more classical Millian lines, in terms of psychological states such as pleasure, happiness, or satisfaction.

Chapter 4 is devoted to an analogy between Mill's position on the assessment of the value of pleasurable experiences and the sensory evaluation of wines, including a comparison of the role of Mill's competent judges and that of expert wine tasters.

In contrast to Bentham's felicific calculus, Mill's method of measuring value uses the judgment of competent agents. The preferential ranking of pleasures by knowledgeable judges is the foundation of Mill's measurement of value. Part of what is required for a judge to be competent, or in a position to know, is that the judge undergo a process of development that transforms into self-development. In Chapter 5 I discuss Mill's doctrine of development, and in Chapter 6 I examine the transition from development to self-development. Mill's doctrine of development lays out the broad socialization program by which agents' generic human cognitive, affective, and moral capacities are nurtured to reach the stage at which the agents themselves take control of the developmental process. At this juncture the process of self-development continues with the development of the higher-level capacities of individuality, autonomy, and sociality being constructed on the groundwork of the generic capacities. In this chapter I also set out the final version of Mill's conception of happiness at play in both his ethics and his political philosophy. Since humans have these capacities, certain enjoyments involving the use, fulfillment, and activity of these faculties are essential components of their happiness. Self-development is thus both an indispensable condition for and an essential element of happiness.

Self-developed moral agents become the pivot of the whole system. We use their preferences as the best indicators of the value of various forms of happiness. They are both the best judges of value and the source of value. Agents must develop in order to become competent judges of value, but the most valuable forms of happiness are those that involve the development and use of the capacities promoted and nurtured by development. Some commentators have used this point to propose an elitist interpretation of Mill, but I argue instead that Mill's position is correctly seen as a springboard to an egalitarian form of liberalism. We must also view human self-development in the context of Mill's utilitarian rights theory. This is but one example of a key notion within Mill's system playing multidimensional roles. Mill's ability to see the richness of crucial concepts and the interconnections among key elements of an interwoven and dynamic system accounts for much of the intricacy and interest of his theory. Recent commentators have noted Mill's talent for such intricacies. Fred Berger, for example, notes that "Mill began his account and defense of individuality with his claim that it is both an *ingredient* of the good life and a *necessary condition* for the achievement of the other components of well-being."[3] So it is with self-development: the development and use of our human capacities is both a crucial component of the most valuable forms of happiness and an essential precondition for the ability to judge and appreciate these forms of happiness. We thus see why self-development so occupied Mill's attention. We also begin to see why Millian liberalism has such a different face from forms of liberalism that have been built on a conception of possessive individualism. Possessive individualism regards humans as seeing their good in terms of property acquisition, and this value is tied to a need to control others. Mill sees the good for humans as essentially that of self-development, and this value is antagonistic to a need or desire to control others.

In the remaining chapters I look at the implications for Mill's political philosophy of his conception of the good; the use of preferential rankings by competent agents to measure value has profound social and political implications. These chapters offer an examination, from the vantage point of his views on value, of some of the tensions manifested in Mill's liberalism. There is a basic tension between that thrust of his theory which seems to demand equality of opportunity for all members of society to develop the entire spectrum of their human capacities and the inequitable, debilitating social and economic conditions of his time, which he accepted at least in the short term. As well, Mill is often accused of being a liberal ideologist. Left-wing critics are skeptical about the claims of objectivity made on behalf of these social standards, arguing that they are merely the standards of the upper middle class of Mill's day cloaked as objective judgments.

This challenge is indeed serious because Mill's theoretical commitment to self-development is fundamental. Judgments of utility are the evaluative basis of all our practical reasoning about the ends of the art of life. But agents cannot fully or accurately assess value unless they have reached a certain level of development and become competent judges. Thus Mill's theory requires developed agents even to get off the ground and to be able to do the evaluations on

[3]Fred Berger, *Happiness, Justice, and Freedom: The Moral and Political Philosophy of John Stuart Mill*, (Berkeley, Calif., 1984), 233.

which the theory rests. As well, to deny people the opportunity of development is to deny them the status of full moral agency. From this perspective I argue that Mill's form of utilitarianism, with essential dependence on developed moral agents to measure value and with self-development at the core of human happiness, pushes his political philosophy in the direction of radical egalitarianism. I also argue that according to the fundamental tenets of Mill's theory people have a right to liberty of self-development—that they are harmed and their rights infringed if their social circumstances bar them from developing themselves. I claim that Mill intends to exclude as harmful not only active interference with this liberty but also the failure of society to provide people with reasonable social conditions and resources to allow them to attain and exercise their liberty of self-development. In this context, I review John Gray's recent libertarian interpretation of Mill's right to autonomy and argue that it is seriously mistaken and violates the spirit of Mill's liberalism. In Chapter 9 I examine the relation of Mill's principle of liberty to this framework.

In the final chapter I test the consistency of Mill's theoretical commitment to liberty of self-development by examining his views on representative government and economic democracy. In the political realm, Mill's *Considerations on Representative Government* is a masterful balancing act in which he tries to equilibrate, with questionable success, the goals of participation and political development against those of competent government. His faith in the wisdom of the bureaucratic elite clashes with his aim of developing people's potential through participation in the democratic political process. In the sphere of economics, Mill the liberal economic theorist who respects the workings of the free market strains against Mill the utopian socialist theorist who values worker-run collective industrial enterprises, in part because of the developmental impact of involvement in such activities. The commitment to self-development shapes the discussion of these applied issues.

I

Mill and Bentham: The Nature of Pleasurable Experience

John Stuart Mill and Jeremy Bentham are the two great classical utilitarian thinkers, yet Mill's radical divergences from his predecessor's thought are as marked as his agreements. Mill was groomed to be the intellectual heir of Bentham. His father, James Mill, carefully planned and supervised his education so that he would carry on as the next utilitarian torch bearer. But instead of playing out his intended part, Mill rejected much of Bentham's thought and radically redefined and reinterpreted utilitarianism, expanding and enriching the conception of the good at its core. This reaction came about partly because Mill suffered a serious mental crisis in his youth, which he traced to weaknesses in his education and its underlying philosophy. Much of the impetus for the change and growth came from insights Mill gained through his crisis, and the most notable changes in Mill's thought are manifested in his transformed conceptions of human nature and the good appropriate for creatures with this nature.

One of the results of Mill's well-known mental crisis in his youth was a concept of utility substantially different from the orthodox Benthamite conception, which Mill came to regard as deficient. Mill saw that Bentham's concept was excessively narrow, and he sought to overcome its limitations by enlarging his own concept. The result is a complex mental-state account of utility which includes the quality of pleasurable experiences along with the quantity in the estimation of their worth. At the same time, Mill was highly critical of his major philosophical opponents, the intuitionist ethical theorists of his day, and he propounded utilitarianism as the rational, objective alternative. If Mill's enterprise of countering the subjectivity of intuitionism while avoiding the pitfalls of Benthamite utilitarianism is to be successful, he must retain the objectivity of Benthamism while repudiating and overcoming its narrowness. Mill's critics have argued that, when he expanded his concept of utility to include quality as well as quantity, he modified his theory so radically that he could no longer correctly be called a hedonistic utilitarian, and that he relinquished the consistency and objectivity of Benthamite utilitarianism along with its weaknesses. I argue here that Mill does not abandon utilitarianism and that the objectivity and consistency of his theory are not undermined by his recognition of quality as contributing to value of experience. In contemporary terms, Mill's account is a mental-state account of utility, as is Bentham's. Although I have reservations about calling Mill's views hedonistic, for reasons I take up shortly, there is no easy alternative, and so I continue to use this terminology. The problem is terminological, not substantive.

Mill and Bentham are both regarded as classical utilitarian theorists, yet Mill rejects Bentham's version of utilitarianism and develops his own. Although the philosophical break with Bentham occurs most strikingly over the concept of utility, Mill still has many fundamental agreements with Bentham about moral theory. Like his predecessor, Mill builds his moral theory around the principle of utility, which is the principle governing all areas of practical reasoning, including moral reasoning: "The creed which accepts as the foundation of morals, Utility, or the Greatest Happiness Principle, holds that actions are right in proportion as they tend to promote happiness, wrong as they tend to produce the reverse of happiness" (10:210). Thus Mill's theory provides a single standard for morality. The principle of utility, as the ultimate principle for morality as well as for the other departments of the art of life, provides the fundamental grounding for the evaluation of actions morally.[1]

---

[1]Whether the principle of utility is maximizing, directly or indirectly, in the light of much of the recent literature is a controversial topic—one I do not enter. In recent scholarship many points of the traditional interpretation of Mill's philosophy have been revised; of interest is whether the principle of utility is best seen as a moral

ASSOCIATIONIST PSYCHOLOGY

Both the large common core and the major divergences in Mill's
and Bentham's concepts of utility start to emerge in their views of
the nature of pleasurable and painful mental states. Their accord
over the question of what has value—pleasurable mental states and
the absence of painful ones—starts to break down over the issue of
the nature of these valuable states and the question of which properties make them valuable. These are quite separate issues, and the
failure of many critics to understand this distinction has led to
numerous mistaken objections to Mill's arguments. Even when we
have settled a position on the question of what things have value, we
have still left entirely open the question of what properties of those
things produce their value.

Mill's and Bentham's agreements carry them a long way together
in ethical theory and psychology, for they share both a utilitarian
ethic and an associationist psychology. Not only do they both posit
utility at the center of their systems, they also both define utility
and happiness in terms of pleasurable and painful states of consciousness. In both Mill's and Bentham's theories utility is a causal
property of actions—that property that produces pleasure and ex-
emption from pain (10:209). In the *Theory of Legislation* Bentham
says, "*Utility* is an abstract term. It expresses the property or tendency of a thing to prevent some evil or to procure some good. *Evil* is
pain, or the cause of pain. *Good* is pleasure, or the cause of pleasure."[2]

Bentham holds that only pleasures and pains are real psychological entities, whereas other entities such as happiness and desire are

principle or rather as a principle of the good setting out the end for all domains of the
art of life. I take this point up briefly later. On both questions, see David Lyons,
"Mill's Theory of Morality," *Nous* 10 (1976): 101–20; "Human Rights and the Gener-
al Welfare," *Philosophy and Public Affairs* 6 (1977): 113–29; D. G. Brown, "Mill on
Liberty and Morality," *Philosophical Review* 81 (1972): 133–58; "What Is Mill's Prin-
ciple of Utility?" *Canadian Journal of Philosophy* 3 (1973): 1–12; "Mill's Criterion of
Wrong Conduct," *Dialogue* 21 (1982): 27–44; L. W. Sumner, "The Good and the
Right" in *New Essays on John Stuart Mill and Utilitarianism*, ed. Wesley Cooper, Kai
Nielsen, and Steven Patten, *Canadian Journal of Philosophy, Supplementary Volume*
5 (1979): 99–114.

[2]Jeremy Bentham, *The Theory of Legislation* (London, 1931), 2. In these sections on
Bentham I have been greatly helped by my reading of L. W. Sumner's unpublished
manuscript on Bentham, in particular, Chapter 4, "Utility," and Chapter 5, "The
Principle of Utility."

fictitious entities.[3] Mill does not subscribe to Bentham's theory of fictions, but he does also reduce utility to pleasures and pains. Both philosophers also reduce happiness to pleasures and pains. For Bentham, happiness is not a sensation like pleasure and pain; it is more appropriately seen as a "state of mind."[4] As Mill puts it, "by happiness is intended pleasure, and the absence of pain; by unhappiness, pain, and the privation of pleasure" (10:210). People are said to be happy if their pleasures outweigh their pains fairly heavily over time. The degree of one's happiness depends on the extent to which these pleasurable experiences outbalance painful ones.

The associationist theory of psychology Mill and Bentham share also lays the groundwork for Mill's departure from Benthamism. The point of their divergence is a disagreement about what constitutes the good-making properties of pleasurable experiences. Since pleasures and pains are the basic elements of their moral theories, a difference on this point is a harbinger of far-reaching philosophical disagreements. An understanding of the rudiments of associationist psychology leads us to the focal point of difference— Mill's introduction of quality as a good-making characteristic of pleasurable experience.[5]

Mill's empiricist opposition to intuitionism appears in his repudiation of innate structures of the mind. The content of our minds is created entirely from the basic data of our sense experience. The basic elements of associationist psychology are sensations. James Mill defines these as "the feelings which we have by the five senses—Smell, Taste, Hearing, Touch, and Sight."[6] These sensations are the original mental entities, and after they are received "ideas are perpetually excited of sensations formerly received; after

---

[3]John Bowring, ed., *The Works of Jeremy Bentham*, 10 vols., (New York, 1962), 1:211; 8:196–97.

[4]See Bowring, ed., *Works of Bentham*, 1:206.

[5]John Stuart Mill edited the 1868 edition of James Mill's *Analysis of the Phenomena of the Human Mind*, 2 vols. (rpted. New York, 1967), adding numerous lengthy editorial notes and thereby further clarifying and developing the theory or setting out disagreements. John Stuart Mill did not set out a complete and systematic exposition of associationist psychology; he considered his father's *Analysis* a classic in its field with which he found himself in substantial agreement. I assume that the text of *Analysis* indicates John Stuart Mill's own views unless one of his editorial notes states otherwise. For Mill's attitude toward his father's book, see Mill, *Collected Works*, 16:1506, 1526, 1533; 17:1602; 1:287–88.

[6]James Mill, *Analysis*, 1:3.

those ideas, other ideas: and during the whole of our lives, a series of those two states of consciousness, called sensations, and ideas, is constantly going on."[7] Ideas are the subsequent mental copies of sensations, fainter than the originals but available to experience even when the originals are no longer present.

Sensations and ideas occur according to a certain order. Sensations occur according to the order among external objects that give rise to them. James Mill claims that there are two kinds of order—synchronous order, or order of simultaneous existence, and successive order, or order of antecedent and consequent existence.[8] Because ideas are copies of sensations, their order is derived from the order of sensations: "Our ideas spring up, or exist, in the order in which the sensations existed, of which they are the copies. . . . This is the general law of the 'Association of Ideas'; by which term . . . nothing is here meant to be expressed, but the order of occurrence."[9] Accordingly, when sensations occur synchronically, their ideas also arise synchronically; the same is true in the case of successive sensations and ideas. Thus ideas are associated if they have been connected through the synchronous or successive occurrence of the original sensations.[10]

The strength of association of ideas depends on frequency of association and vividness of the associated feelings. The vividness of feelings in turn varies according to several factors, two of which are the presence of pleasure and of pain. Pleasurable or painful sensations (and their ideas) are more vivid than indifferent ones, and a more pleasurable or painful feeling is similarly more vivid than one less so. Beyond these cases, James Mill contends that sensations are more vivid than ideas, and that recent feelings are more vivid than remote ones. But repetition is more important than vividness as a producer of strong associations.[11] The younger Mill agrees with his father on the most significant point. He says that

[7]Ibid., 1:70.
[8]Ibid., 1:71.
[9]Ibid., 1:78.
[10]See, e.g., Mill, 8:852.

[11]John Stuart Mill does not entirely agree with his father's deliberations here. He discusses approvingly Bain's distinction "between the attributes which belong to a sensation regarded in an intellectual point of view, as a portion of our knowledge, and those which belong to the element of Feeling contained in it." Vividness can only be applied appropriately to the feeling aspect, while the intellectual aspect can only be "distinct or indistinct"; Ibid., 1:86n.

"it is in any case certain, that the property of producing a strong and durable association without the aid of repetition, belongs principally to our pleasures and pains. The more intense the pain or pleasure, the more promptly and powerfully does it associate itself with its accompanying circumstances, even with those which are only accidentally present."[12]

Thus he agrees that pleasures and pains are important in producing strong associations. This fact has important implications, because education and development to a large extent consist in creating the right associations, to build first the right mental states and then the right character. It is in this way that development rests on the foundation of associationism.

Keeping in mind this background of associationist theory and the role of pleasures and pains in creating and strengthening associations, we can pinpoint the differences between Mill and Bentham. In Bentham's system, as we have seen, pleasures and pains are real psychological entities whereas utility and happiness are fictions. Pleasures and pains, the ground-level elements of his theory, are basic to our phenomenal experience and are commonly experienced by everyone. They are separate and distinct mental units and not properties of other mental states. Bentham makes the claim in several places that pleasures and pains are basic psychological entities. In *A Table of the Springs of Action* they are the "roots," the "main pillars or foundations," and "the matter of which all the rest are composed," and their "existence is a matter of universal and constant experience."[13] Although, according to Bentham, pleasures and pains are types of sensation or feeling, he includes quite a variety of sensations under this head. In the *Rationale of Judicial Evidence* he groups them under the heading of sensations, which are feelings arising from the five senses.[14] Here he classifies sensations into three groups: pleasurable ones; painful ones; and indifferent ones. In another place he classifies them into two types: pathematic, those consisting of or accompanied by pleasure or pain; and apathomatic, those not having any such connection with pleasure or pain.[15]

Since pleasures and pains are the basics of the theory, they are

[12]Ibid.
[13]Bowring, *Works of Bentham,* 1:211.
[14]Ibid., 6:217.
[15]Ibid., 8:196n; but at 8:288 Bentham says that this distinction is very difficult to draw in practice.

directly known and experienced but cannot be defined. Bentham
does, however, have some suggestions about their nature. In *Theory
of Legislation* he differentiates pleasures and pains from "sensations
which do not interest us, and which glide by without fixing our
attention." Pleasures and pains, on the other hand, are "sensations
which attract our attention," and "of which we desire the continu-
ance or the end."[16] In *Rationale of Judicial Evidence* those sensations that are not pleasures or pains are "indifferent."[17] And in *Introduction to the Principles of Morals and Legislation*, pleasures
and pains "may be called . . . interesting perceptions."[18] Even
though no definition of them is possible, Bentham is confident that
pleasures and pains are sensations known by all.

Bentham maintains that there are many different kinds of simple
pleasures and pains as opposed to the complex ones compounded
out of them. He does not classify these different kinds on the basis of
phenomenal differences, although these differences are taken into
account to some extent in the measurement of value of pleasures. In
the two main sets of classification offered by Bentham in *Introduction to the Principles of Morals and Legislation* and *Theory of Legislation*, source is the main basis of difference among kinds of pleasures and pains, with some minor exceptions.[19]

Bentham's psychology is associationist, but given his ideas about
the nature of pleasures the following picture emerges. When a pleasure or pain becomes attached to other sensations or ideas, it remains a distinct mental entity. Relational properties connecting
pleasure to other mental states in accordance with the laws of association, that is, relational properties such as "being a pleasure of
listening to Beethoven" or "being a pleasure of watching a soap
opera," are irrelevant to the measurement of value of the pleasure.
For Bentham the only good-making characteristics of pleasures are
intensity and duration, and thus only these properties are considered in the measurement of value. In his view, the sorts of things
people take pleasure in are not relevant to the measurement of value
of pleasures. All that counts is the pleasure's intensity and duration.
Bentham goes as far as to maintain that even sadistic pleasures have

[16]Bentham, *Theory of Legislation*, 21.
[17]Bowring, *Works of Bentham*, 6:217.
[18]Jeremy Bentham, *The Collected Works of Jeremy Bentham: An Introduction to
the Principles of Morals and Legislation*, ed. J. H. Burns and H. L. A. Hart, (London,
1970), 42.
[19]Ibid., 42–50; Bentham, *Theory of Legislation*, 21–27.

some value: "Now, pleasure is in *itself* a good: nay, even setting aside immunity from pain, the only good: pain is in itself an evil; and, indeed, without exception, the only evil. . . . And this is alike true of every sort of pain, and of every sort of pleasure." He includes specifically, "the pleasure he takes at the thought of the pain which he sees, or expects to see, his adversary undergo. Now even this wretched pleasure, taken by itself, is good: it may be faint; it may be short: it must at any rate be impure: yet while it lasts, and before any bad consequences arrive, it is as good as any other that is not more intense."[20]

Although John Stuart Mill agrees with his father and Bentham that pleasures and satisfactions have intrinsic properties and also relational properties, including causal and intentional properties, he differs with them in regarding these latter as relevant to the evaluation of pleasurable experiences. The implications of this difference emerge only gradually in my discussion. Put simply, the things that are sources of pleasure and more significant to Mill than to Bentham. It matters a great deal to Mill what sort of things people enjoy.

[20]Bentham, *Collected Works*, 100. James Mill's comments on the nature of pleasures and pains often parallel Bentham's. But since Mill does not adhere to the theory of fictions, it is not clear whether he holds that pleasures are sensations, that is, distinct mental entities. His remarks are compatible with Bentham's position that pleasures and pains are sensations, but they are also compatible with the position that pleasures and pains are properties of sensations. John Stuart Mill certainly seems to think that his father holds the latter view, for in an editorial note he refers to his father's belief that a pleasure or pain is "merely a particular aspect or quality of the sensation." (James Mill, *Analysis*, 2:185n). In any case, James Mill agrees with Bentham that the differences among pleasures and pains are directly experienced and cannot be defined. He provides the same indication of their nature as Bentham, namely, that some are such that we do not care if they are of long or short duration (indifferent), some are such that we would end them if we could (painful), and some are such that we would lengthen them if we could (pleasurable); (ibid., 2:184).

John Stuart Mill is of divided mind over whether some pleasures and pains are sensations or properties of sensations. He toys with the idea that some may be distinct sensations rather than properties, but he does not come to any definite conclusion: "In the case of many pleasurable or painful sensations, it is open to question whether the pleasure or pain . . . is not something added to the sensation, and capable of being detached from it, rather than merely a particular aspect or quality of the sensation. It is often observable that a sensation is much less pleasurable at one time than at another, though to our consciousness it appears exactly the same sensation in all except the pleasure" (ibid., 2:185n). Mill does not come out solidly on one side of the question or the other. But these remarks are overshadowed by the importance of his views on "mental chemistry" which set the stage for the evaluation of our more complex mental experiences.

Although some pleasures may remain as fairly simple mental states, in many cases they come to be surrounded by bundles of other mental entities through association and develop into rather complex states of experience. Pleasures become linked to other feelings until it is difficult to separate the elements that originally composed the complex. Suppose, for example, that I enjoy reading feminist fiction. In the first instance, my pleasure is caused simply by the book or the activity of reading it, apart from any associations I have formed about the activity of reading. In experiential terms, this can be pictured as a relation between my experience of reading the book and my sensation of pleasure, and the resulting unity can be called the pleasure of reading or taking pleasure in reading. And so the causal source of my pleasure is the book, and the phenomenal object is my experience of reading it. But over time, if the experiences of reading and of pleasure are linked often or intensely, new associations are created between these two elements, transforming what was originally a relatively simple mental state into a more complex unity with these added dimensions. As Mill says, "when two impressions have been frequently experienced (or even thought of) either simultaneously or in immediate succession, then whenever one of these impressions, or the idea of it, recurs, it tends to excite the idea of the other" (8:852). Eventually, when I enjoy a good book, my inner state contains not only the newly aroused pleasures related to my reading experience but also pleasures stimulated by the presentation of an object that has been associated with so much enjoyment in the past. And the feminist content of the book may inspire numerous other pleasurable trains of thought concerning life changes, growth, love, strength, autonomy, and so on. So what can still be called my experience of reading a feminist book is actually composed of a multitude of ingredients, including pleasures of diverse strength and nuance, related in manifold ways to other ideas and feelings.

But these rich experiences do not often occur in a vacuum, which is why sources of pleasure are so important for Mill; they are the usual spurs to these satisfying states of consciousness (although these mental states can be recalled without their occurrence).[21] This

---

[21]An interesting discussion of the connections among pleasures and their causes and objects is found in Rem Edwards, *Pleasures and Pains: A Theory of Qualitative Hedonism* (Ithaca, 1979), 86–92.

is how we form attachments to things that habitually cause us pleasure: "... those persons, things, and positions become in themselves pleasant to us by association; and, through the multitude and variety of the pleasurable ideas associated with them, become pleasures of greater constancy and even intensity, and altogether more valuable to us, than any of the primitive pleasures of our constitution."[22]

Mill draws a distinction between mechanical and chemical union of elements related through association. In the former, which Bentham thinks covers all cases of mental association, the components are connected but also keep their distinct characters. But in chemical combination, which Mill thinks happens in many cases of association, the original items are amalgamated into a new whole— the old parts do not retain their individual character but merge as in a chemical reaction into a synthesis that can have quite different features:

> Reverting to the distinction which occupies so prominent a place in the theory of induction; the laws of the phenomena of mind are sometimes analogous to mechanical, but sometimes also to chemical laws. When many impressions or ideas are operating in the mind together, there sometimes takes place a process of a similar kind to chemical combination. When impressions have been so often experienced in conjunction, that each of them calls up readily and instantaneously the ideas of the whole group, those ideas sometimes melt and coalesce into one another, and appear not several ideas, but one . . . it appears to me that the Complex Idea, formed by the blending together of several simpler ones, should, when it really appears simple, (that is, when the separate elements are not consciously distinguishable in it,) be said to *result from*, or *be generated by*, the simple ideas, not to *consist* of them. . . . These therefore are cases of mental chemistry: in which it is proper to say that the simple ideas generate, rather than that they compose, the complex ones. (8:853–54)

That association and the resulting complexes and relations are important for Mill is evident in many of his discussions. In speaking of the lower pleasures, he says,

> To them there is a fixed limit at which they stop: or if, in any particular case, they do acquire, by association, a power of stirring up ideas greater than themselves, and stimulate the imagination to en-

large its conceptions to the dimensions of those ideas, we then feel that the lower pleasure has, exceptionally, risen into the region of the aesthetic, and has superadded to itself an element of pleasure of a character and quality not belonging to its own nature.[23]

Mill's recognition of the importance of association and the resulting relations and new unities allows him to take full account of the complexity of our mental experiences. The pleasurable experiences his theory assesses for worth are not the original simple elements, lost through the "quasi-chemistry"[24] of association, but the compounds born of the workings of association. Thus, in his view, the relations produced by association are critical to the value of pleasurable experiences.

Mill's theory can be considered a sophisticated form of hedonism because its theoretical associationist psychological foundation is set out in terms of pleasures and pains. But it is distorting to give the impression that Mill is primarily interested in evaluating human pleasure, for he views pleasures as only the starting point in studying what has value. Out of the building blocks of pleasures are built human happiness and satisfaction, and on this base of pleasures is erected the edifice of developed humans of character freely choosing the projects and activities of a meaningful life. Mill's most fundamental commitment is to encourage people to fulfill their life plans and engage in active, worthwhile lives. For these reasons, it often seems appropriate to speak of happiness, enjoyment, and satisfactions as well as pleasures in his theory, and in fact I use all these expressions to refer to the complex mental experiences that are the focus of his concern. It is because Mill moves beyond claiming that the things of value are just these simple pleasures that some have argued that he is not a hedonist. His theory is a complex hybrid, and so it is difficult to settle on a name for it. But the label "hedonist" has a certain attractiveness because of the role of pleasures in the formation of the complex mental states.

Questions still remain about the phenomenal status of pleasures within these complex experiences that result from association and are the most likely candidates for serious value assessment. In some places Mill seems to maintain that we experience simple sensations

[23]Ibid., 2:255n. For further discussion of this issue, see ibid., 2:217–18n, 241–42n, 246–47n, 252–55n, 278–79n, 295–96n, 297n, 307–309n.
[24]Ibid., 2:235n.

as distinct and separate entities fairly infrequently and most often in the early stages of our psychological development. I have explained how pleasurable and painful sensations become associated with ideas to form the complex experiences that are evaluated. But Mill is maddeningly unclear about the phenomenal status of pleasures at the end of these processes. It is questionable whether simple sensations of pleasure are the objects of evaluation; because of the "quasi-chemical" effect of association, such pleasures are not always distinct and discernible elements of mental states. Alternatively, they may be phenomenally present but too mixed with other aspects of the experience to be evaluated separately. We must ask whether pleasure is present only as generative cause of the desirable mental complex, because of the workings of association, or whether it is also phenomenally present in the complex experience. If the latter, we must not assume that its phenomenal presence manifests itself as a uniform, distinct element, for it could take different forms like glows, tinges, or intense sensations, related through family resemblance. It may not even be possible to pick it out as a distinct component.

The textual evidence here is mixed and open to different interpretations. Initially, there seems to be evidence that pleasure is not always present to experience in valuable mental complexes—specifically, on a particular interpretation of "quasi-chemistry." If it is the case that Mill thinks that such experiences can be valuable even though pleasure is not present, the desirability would seem to rest on the causal role pleasures play in generating the resultant experiences. But there is also powerful textual evidence that pleasure has to be present in the final product complex or the complex loses its claim to value in itself.

Mill's discussion of the proof of the principle of utility gives much of the evidence that pleasure must not only play a causal role but must also be phenomenally present if the final product of association is to be a bearer of value. I take up this proof in more detail shortly, but here I focus on a narrow point. There is solid evidence, contrary to another popular misconception, that Mill maintains that people can desire many things other than pleasures.[25] My concerns, however, are about mental states that are desirable or valu-

<hr>

[25]See Berger, *Happiness, Justice and Freedom*, 12–17. Berger criticizes this misconception.

able. Mill claims that "the sole evidence it is possible to produce that anything is desirable, is that people do actually desire it" (10:234). He tries to establish that the fact that people can desire such things as virtue and money is not inconsistent with the thesis that "there is in reality nothing desired except happiness" (10:237). His argument rests on the association of the idea of virtue or money with happiness:

> This opinion is not, in the smallest degree, a departure from the Happiness principle. The ingredients of happiness are very various, and each of them is desirable in itself, and not merely when considered as swelling an aggregate. The principle of utility does not mean that any given pleasure, as music, for instance, or any given exemption from pain, as for example health, are to be looked upon as a means to a collective something termed happiness, and to be desired on that account. They are desired and desirable in and for themselves; besides being means, they are a part of the end. Virtue, according to the utilitarian doctrine, is not naturally and originally part of the end, but it is capable of becoming so; and in those who love it disinterestedly it has become so, and is desired and cherished, not as a means to happiness, but as a part of their happiness. (10:235)

Our desires can be the subject of mental chemistry, and so it may be questioned whether pleasures are present to experience in the final product. Mill's comments on acting from habit seem to confirm that they need not be. But my interest here is not about whether these complex experiences phenomenally contain pleasure; it is rather about whether they can be held to be valuable if they do not. In what may come as a surprise to those who interpret Mill as maintaining a simple form of psychological hedonism, Mill comments that not all our actions are motivated by the anticipation of pleasure or pain.[26] The conclusion he reaches about the implications of acting from habit are important but easy to overlook. Some background from the *Logic* clarifies this step in the argument:

> When the will is said to be determined by motives, a motive does not mean always, or solely, the anticipation of a pleasure or of a pain. I shall not here inquire whether it be true that, in the commencement, all our voluntary actions are mere means consciously employed to obtain some pleasure, or avoid some pain. It is at least certain that we gradually, through the influence of association, come to desire the

[26]Ibid., 12–13. Berger explains this point well.

means without thinking of the end: the action itself becomes an object of desire, and is performed without reference to any motive beyond itself. Thus far, it may still be objected, that, the action having through association become pleasurable, we are, as much as before, moved to act by the anticipation of a pleasure, namely, the pleasure of the action itself. But granting this, the matter does not end here. As we proceed in the formation of habits, and become accustomed to will a particular act or a particular course of conduct because it is pleasurable, we at last continue to will it without any reference to its being pleasurable. Although, from some change in us or in our circumstances, we have ceased to find any pleasure in the action, or perhaps to anticipate any pleasure as the consequence of it, we still continue to desire the action, and consequently to do it. . . .

. . . A habit of willing is commonly called a purpose; and among the causes of our volitions, and of the actions which flow from them, must be reckoned not only likings and aversions, but also purposes. It is only when our purposes have become independent of the feelings of pain or pleasure from which they originally took their rise, that we are said to have a confirmed character. (8:842–43)

It may be thought that this is a serious admission; it seems to commit Mill to holding that, since when we act from habit we do not anticipate happiness, such instances contradict the thesis that "happiness is desirable, and the only thing desirable, as an end" (10:234). But, on the contrary, the conclusion he draws from the examination of habit fully supports the thesis that pleasure must be phenomenally present in valuable experiences:

Will, the active phenomenon, is a different thing from desire, the state of passive sensibility, and though originally an offshoot from it, may in time take root and detach itself from the parent stock; so much so, that in the case of an habitual purpose, instead of willing the thing because we desire it, we often desire it only because we will it. This, however, is but an instance of that familiar fact, the power of habit, and is nowise confined to the case of virtuous actions. . . . The distinction between will and desire thus understood, is an authentic and highly important psychological fact; but the fact consists solely in this—that will, like all other parts of our constitution, is amenable to habit, and that we may will from habit what we no longer desire for itself, or desire only because we will it. It is not the less true that will, in the beginning, is entirely produced by desire. . . . How can the will to be virtuous, where it does not exist in sufficient force, be implanted or awakened? Only by making the person *desire* virtue—by making him think of it in a pleasurable light, or of its absence in a painful one. It is by associating the doing right with pleasure, or the doing wrong with pain, or by eliciting and impressing and bringing home to the person's experience the pleasure naturally involved in the one or the pain in the other, that it is possible to call forth that will to be virtuous, which, when confirmed, acts without any thought of either pleasure or pain. Will is the child of desire, and passes out of the dominion of its parent only to come under that of habit. *That which is the result of habit affords no presumption of being intrinsically good;* and there would be no reason for wishing that the purpose of virtue should become independent of pleasure and pain, were it not that the influence of the pleasurable and painful associations which prompt to virtue is not sufficiently to be depended on for unerring constancy of action until it has acquired the support of habit. Both in feeling and in conduct, habit is the only thing which imparts certainty; and it is because of the importance to others of being able to rely absolutely on one's feeling and conduct, and to oneself of being able to rely on one's own, that the will to do right ought to be cultivated into this habitual independence. *In other words, this state of the will is a means to good, not intrinsically a good; and does not contradict the doctrine that nothing is a good to human beings but in so far as it is either itself pleasurable, or a means of attaining pleasure or averting pain.* (10:238–39, emphasis added)

If the absence of pleasure in habitual action cancels the product's claim to intrinsic value, this is strong evidence indeed that pleasure must be present phenomenally in a complex experience for the experience to be valuable.

Mill's conception of utility is a mental-state account. The mental states that have utility are complex experiences rather than simple sensations. These complex states are pleasurable ones, but there are various interpretations of what Mill means by a pleasurable experience: he can be interpreted as arguing one of the following:

(1) Pleasure is not present phenomenally because the sensation of pleasure has been lost through mental chemistry. Pleasure is present only as a formative or generative element or cause of the complex experience.

(2) Pleasure is present phenomenally as a distinguishable element of the complex experience.

(3) Pleasure is present phenomenally as an element of the complex experience, but it is not a distinguishable element of the experience. It is mixed with other aspects of the experience, though not, as in (1), completely lost.

Interpretations (2) and (3) do not require that the pleasurable experience feel the same in all cases. The phenomenal tinge or tone or feel could cover a range of feelings, a family, all of which could be identifiable introspectively as pleasurable. The textual evidence supports interpretation (3) because Mill's comments on habit specifically exclude experiences in which pleasure is not phenomenally present from the class of desirable or intrinsically good experiences. Although (2) is not specifically so excluded, it is hard to see how pleasure could be a distinguishable aspect of the experience because of the mixing or synthesizing effect of association.

Thus (3) stands out as the most plausible candidate. But what is clear from this fact is that the mental complex as a whole has value and not just simple sensations of pleasure "in" the complex. When Mill says, for example, that "all desirable things (which are as numerous in the utilitarian as in any other scheme) are desirable either for the pleasure inherent in themselves, or as means to the promotion of pleasure and the prevention of pain" (10:210), he intends to argue that the complex as a whole has value. The things that have value are complex mental experiences, not simple sensations of pleasure. Some of the value-making properties of these complexes are grounded specifically in pleasure, but this fact is consistent with my previous argument that we must distinguish between questions of what things have value and of what the good-making characteristics of these valuable things are.

BENTHAM'S DOMINANT AND SECONDARY ACCOUNTS

Both Mill and Bentham require methods of measuring the value of mental states. If Bentham's theory is to meet his own standards of objectivity, he needs to be able to measure objectively the overall utility of different actions and to discover which action of a group under consideration has the most utility.[27] He does this by applying a method of measuring the total quantity of pleasure and pain caused by an action—the famous felicific calculus. Bentham stipulates that in the employment of the calculus the pleasures and pains

[27]Although Bentham is an act utilitarian, I do not assume that Mill is. Although I discuss this briefly later, I do not take a definite stand on this problem, which is peripheral to my concerns; see ibid., 64–120.

of everyone involved are to be considered equally, and thus his calculus and his concept of utility have equality built into them.[28]

Bentham provides two accounts of the measurement of value of pleasures and pains. The account that uses the calculus strongly dominates his discussions of this matter and is the one most developed in his writings. Its best-known statement occurs in *Introduction to the Principles of Morals and Legislation* (39–40), where Bentham states that there are seven "circumstances," or dimensions, that must be considered in measuring the value of a pleasure or pain:[29]

(1) intensity
(2) duration
(3) certainty or uncertainty
(4) propinquity or remoteness
(5) fecundity, or "the chance it has of being followed by sensations of the *same* kind: that is, pleasures, if it be a pleasure: pains, if it be a pain."
(6) purity, or "the chance it has of *not* being followed by sensations of the *opposite* kind: that is, pains, if it be a pleasure: pleasures, if it be a pain."
(7) extent, or "the number of persons to whom it *extends*."

These seven elements or dimensions are to be calculated in general as follows: (a) calculate the total quantity of each pleasure and pain of every person whose interests are affected; (b) sum the values of all the pleasures on the one hand, and of all the pains on the other; (c) calculate the balance between the pleasures and the pains, "which, if on the side of *pleasure*, will give the general *good tendency* of the act, with respect to the total number or community of individuals concerned; if on the side of pain, the general *evil tendency*, with respect to the same community."

The method outlined in the calculus quantifies each of the elements and their combination. Bentham regards this quantification as essential to the objectivity and precision of the theory.[30] The calculation is actually considerably more complicated than it first

[28]Bowring, *Works of Bentham*, 2:271; 9:6; Bentham, *Collected Works*, 38–41.
[29]Bentham, *Collected Works*, 39–40.
[30]Bentham, *Theory of Legislation*, 32; see also Bowring, *Works of Bentham*, 1: 304–5; 2:442; 3:286.

appears. The dimensions fall into two groups, and only two dimensions are measures of the value of pleasure or pain. The first two dimensions—intensity and duration, or magnitude jointly—are measures of the value of pleasure or pain. Certainty, which involves the likelihood that a pleasure or pain will exist, is not a mark of the value of pleasure and pain.[31] Propinquity is disregarded; it is evident that Bentham is committed to maintaining that whether a pleasure or pain occurs now or tomorrow does not affect the overall value. Fecundity, purity, and extent introduce other pleasures and pains into the account, but they merely extend intensity and duration to these other pleasures and pains.

The only part of the process strictly relevant to the measurement of value involves the calculation of the magnitude of a single pleasure or pain: "The magnitude . . . of a pleasure, is composed of its intensity and its duration; to obtain it, supposing its intensity represented by a certain number of degrees, you multiply that number by the number expressive of the moments or atoms of time contained in its duration."[32] For this calculation to work, units that can be added and multiplied are required for each of the dimensions. There is no problem with duration, since units of time are readily available. Intensity is another matter. It is premature here to criticize Bentham's position, but it is appropriate to mention that Bentham does not provide an explanation of how units of intensity are to be obtained. At least some of the time, however, he does believe that intensity can be calculated and thus that a measure of magnitude can be obtained.

In his secondary account, which is not developed, Bentham suggests measuring the overall value of happiness by measuring the amount of a clearly quantifiable source of happiness, namely, money.[33] That Bentham introduces this account at all is evidence that he was aware of the defects of parts of his dominant account. He offers the following general procedure. If an agent, offered a choice between a pleasure and a certain amount of money, is indifferent be-

[31]Probability is a highly questionable item, and I have dropped it from the discussion for two reasons: it is not relevant to my purposes since it is not an aspect of the quality of a single pleasure or pain, and its introduction raises problems outside the scope of this discussion.

[32]Bowring, *Works of Bentham*, 4:540.

[33]Jeremy Bentham, *Jeremy Bentham's Economic Writings*, 3 vols., ed. W. Stark, (London, 1954), 3:437–38.

tween the two, then that amount of money can be considered the measure of the value of that pleasure. That amount of money can then be used as a measure against other amounts of money obtained through similar choices.

Bentham never develops this approach in depth, probably because he realizes the problems it faces. One he notes is the problem of diminishing marginal utility: whether a given amount of money is correlated with the same quantity of pleasure for two people depends on their wealth; if one person is wealthier than another to begin with, providing that person with a given amount of money produces a smaller increase in the quantity of pleasure than it does for the poorer person.[34] Bentham recognizes other problems: that the value of many pleasures and pains cannot be measured in terms of money; that wealth and happiness are not strictly correlated but have only "a certain chance of being so connected"[35] and that different people value similar pleasures differently. For all these reasons, Bentham's remarks remain speculative and tentative.

OBJECTIVITY AND MORAL THEORY

Mill is quite critical of subjective intuitionist ethical theories and propounds utilitarianism as the rational, objective, and scientific alternative. Yet Mill himself is often accused of forsaking objectivity by introducing quality into his own theory. But several related issues are often confused in evaluations of the objectivity or lack of it in moral theories.

A moral theory has one or more moral principles that assert that actions are right if and only if they possess one or more right-making properties. The objectivity of a theory depends on the objectivity both of its moral principle and of its right-making property, and so the two most basic requirements of objectivity are that the moral principle be objective and that the right-making property it specifies be objective. We cannot properly evaluate the objectivity of a theory without appraising both of these elements. The right-making property (utility in the case of utilitarianism) includes three require-

---

[34]Bowring, *Works of Bentham*, 3:229; see also Wesley C. Mitchell, "Bentham's Felicific Calculus," in *Jeremy Bentham: Ten Critical Essays*, ed. Bhikhu Parekh (London, 1974), 168–86.
[35]Bowring, *Works of Bentham*, 1:305.

ments that license judgments about the degree of objectivity of a moral theory. The *independence* requirement has two parts. First, the right-making property must be independent of people's uncritical opinions about *what* is right; so a theory that decides what is right according to majority opinion without setting out the characteristics of the agents that would give weight to their choices is not objective. Second, the *estimation* or measurement of the right-making property must be independent of people's opinions; thus there must be a public procedure for measuring the right-making property and a method setting out procedures to ensure that our value measurements have the best chance of being correct. The second objectivity requirement is that the measure of the right-making property be *empirical*. The third objectivity requirement, which concerns the personal versus *interpersonal* dimension of the right-making property, stipulates that a measure of this property be applicable to different people. In the case of utilitarianism, this means that interpersonal comparison of utilities must be possible. The degree of objectivity of a theory partially depends on the extent to which it fulfills these conditions. There is no single objectivity requirement, and one theory can be weaker than another with respect to one of these requirements but stronger with respect to another.

Beyond these three strands of objectivity, there are other dimensions which strictly should not be labeled as elements of objectivity but which are closely connected to it. One of these is the *precision* of a theory, or the extent to which the measurement procedure provided by the theory produces an exact result. In Bentham's felicific calculus, for example, one can ask whether definite units are available for the elements of the calculus, or whether these units are commensurable. Another related dimension is the *strength* of a theory. The strongest theory in this respect is one that produces a unique result if the measurement procedure is carried out correctly; the weakest theory is one that produces an ordinal scale. Between these two are theories of intermediate strength.

Requirements of objectivity aimed at the moral principles themselves evaluate the foundations of moral theories. Under this heading, there are two conditions theories must meet if they are to be judged objective. First we must ask whether a theory under review has a rational foundation. Theories can be grounded in different ways, but a common type of rational foundation for moral theories is empirical. In such a case, it is claimed that the fundamental principles of the theory are based on empirical facts, such as facts about human nature. Mill's proof of the principle of utility is an example of an empirical argument for a fundamental principle grounding moral judgments. (Whether the principle of utility is a moral principle itself or a more general principle of the good, it fulfills this former function in Mill's theory.) What is ruled out of court is an appeal to self-evidence. Theorists who resort to arguing that their ultimate moral principles are self-evident supply no rational foundation whatsoever for their theories.

The second condition of objectivity bears on the number of ultimate principles a theory relies on. A theory is defective if it postulates several principles with no rule for ordering them in cases of conflict. Such a theory is unhelpful when conflicts do arise, yet conflict resolution is a major task of moral theories.

Mill's Objections to Intuitionism

Concerns about objectivity are well illustrated in Mill's disputes with intuitionist theorists of his day such as William Whewell.[36] Mill has several related criticisms of intuitionism. Recall that there are two different kinds of objectivity requirements applicable to moral theories: in assessing the objectivity of a moral theory, we must examine both the objectivity of the moral principles and that of the right-making property specified by the principles. On the question of the foundations of a moral theory, Mill finds intuitionism wanting both in its lack of a rational foundation and in its postulation of several basic moral principles.

Mill's first criticism measures the grounds of the principle of utility against those of fundamental intuitionist principles. His verdict is that intuitionism is devoid of a grounding and "hang[s] self-balanced in space" (10:190). Whewell's theory is a rule intuitionism in which the ultimate rules or precepts are intuitively known by our supreme faculty of reason (which despite its name is not our ordinary intellectual faculty but a distinctive faculty that operates intuitively). As Henry Sidgwick puts it in his critique of some forms of intuitionism, according to this theory "it is implied that we have the

36William Whewell, *Lectures on the History of Moral Philosophy* (Cambridge, 1862).

power of seeing clearly that certain kinds of actions are right and reasonable in themselves, apart from their consequences."[37] This postulation of a sovereign faculty of reason as the source and justification of moral principles and judgments is a hallmark of the kind of theory resisted by Mill. In speaking of the intuitionist Adam Sedgwick, in an argument that applies equally to Whewell, Mill says: "To prove that our moral judgments are innate, he assumes that they proceed from a distinct faculty. But this is precisely what the adherents of the principle of utility deny. They contend that the morality of actions is perceived by the same faculties by which we perceive any other of the qualities of actions, namely, our intellects and our senses" (10:61). Mill objects that intuitionist principles are held by their proponents to be self-evident, and thus incapable of being doubted, and so they are not given a rational foundation. Intuitionist theorists neither appeal to empirical facts or arguments to form a base for their principles nor provide any alternative convincing arguments for these principles. Since they claim that ultimate moral principles are self-evident, they do not believe that arguments are necessary to prove their truth, and any arguments they do advance turn out to be repetitions, disguised in different language, of the statement that the fundamental principles are true.

In contrast, Mill thinks that the principle of utility can be supported by facts and reasons. It is to make good the part of his claim that the ultimate principle of his theory is objective in being rationally grounded that Mill offers his proof of the principle of utility. In Mill's theory, as in Bentham's, the principle of utility is grounded on empirical facts—the existence pleasures and pains. Although a detailed interpretation and justification of this famous or notorious proof lies beyond the compass of my discussion, a clarification of Mill's method in this proof sheds light on his dispute with intuitionism. It is now generally accepted that Mill's intention, which he states quite explicitly, is not to propose a direct deductive proof of the principle of utility but to present an empirical argument or "considerations . . . capable of determining the intellect either to give or withhold its assent to the doctrine" (10:208).[38] Since the

[37]Henry Sidgwick, *The Methods of Ethics* (London, 1901; New York, 1966), 200. See also Alan Donagan, *The Theory of Morality* (Chicago, 1977), 17–21; and Alan Ryan, *J. S. Mill* (London, 1974), 99–101.

[38]G. E. Moore's castigation of Mill for supposedly committing the naturalistic fallacy is based on the assumption that Mill's argument is a strict deductive proof. E.

principle of utility is the first principle of morality (and of the art of life), it is not derivable from a more basic principle.

In his proof, Mill argues for the principle of utility in the form that "happiness is desirable, and the only thing desirable, as an end" (10:234), or in other words that happiness (pleasure) is the only thing that has value. His argument has two parts, for to reach his conclusion he must show both that happiness is desirable as an end and that nothing else is so desirable. For the part of his argument that each person's happiness is desirable to that individual, he adduces that "the sole evidence it is possible to produce that anything is desirable, is that people do actually desire it. . . . each person, so far as he believes it to be attainable, desires his own happiness" (10:234). Mill here is simply bringing in empirical evidence that bears on the subject. He is saying that only things actually desired by people are plausible candidates for being desirable as ends. Although we cannot deduce normative desirability from empirical facts about desires, the fact that people do actually desire their own happiness builds a strong case that happiness is desirable. One the other hand, people could not be convinced that something is desirable if in fact no one desires it.[39]

One problematic aspect of Mill's argument is what seems to be his leap from individual to general happiness when he concludes that "we have not only all the proof which the case admits of, but all which it is possible to require, that happiness is a good: that each person's happiness is a good to that person, and the general happiness, therefore, a good to the aggregate of all persons" (10:234). Mill has been taken to task for apparently concluding that, because each individual seeks his or her own happiness as an end, therefore the collectivity of all members of a society seeks the general happiness as an end, or that each and every member of a society seeks the happiness of all. Mill is guilty of careless expression here, but his argument is not flawed. Elsewhere he explains this point: "I did not

---

W. Hall correctly interprets and successfully defends Mill against Moore's critique; see G. E. Moore, *Principia Ethica* (Cambridge, 1966), 66–68; and E. W. Hall, "The 'Proof' of Utility in Bentham and Mill," *Ethics* 60 (October 1949):1–18, reprinted in *Mill: Utilitarianism with Critical Essays*, ed. Samuel Gorovitz (Indianapolis, 1971), 99–116.

[39]See Hall, "Proof of Utility," 106–7; Henry West, "Mill's 'Proof' of the Principle of Utility," in *The Limits of Utilitarianism*, ed. Harlan Miller and William Williams (Minneapolis, 1982), 23–34; Berger, *Happiness, Justice and Freedom*, 45–63.

mean that every human being's happiness is a good to every other human being, though I think that in a good state of society and education it would be so. I merely meant in this particular sentence to argue that since A's happiness is a good, B's a good, C's a good, etc., the sum of all these goods must be a good" (16:1414). Mill thinks of society not as an organic collection but as an aggregate of individuals, and thus the general happiness just is the simple sum of the happiness of all its members.[40] This clarification completes Mill's argument that happiness is at least one of the things desirable as an end. Although this part of the proof has been the object of intense discussion, if placed in perspective its claim is not controversial. Almost every list of the good includes happiness, and this is all Mill is trying to establish at this point. The difficult part of the proof is to establish that other things commonly put on lists of the good—virtue, knowledge, or love—are compatible with Mill's theory. From my previous discussion of complex mental experiences, it should be evident how Mill tries to resolve this apparent conflict.

Mill's argument that only happiness is desirable as an end is more detailed, but it appeals to the same kind of experiential facts as does the first part of the proof. He admits that it is commonly thought that things other than happiness, such as virtue and money, are also desired. But the desire for these other things does not conflict with hedonism. His argument here partially rests on his associationist theory of psychology. These other things are desired by us only when they have been so closely associated with pleasure in our minds that the ideas of them are pleasurable, or have become part of some pleasurable mental complex, and we think of them as part of our conception of happiness.[41] It is these compounds, with pleasure as an essential ingredient, that we come to think of as desirable. An example is virtue: "Those who desire virtue for its own sake, desire it either because the consciousness of it is a pleasure, or because the consciousness of being without it is a pain, or for both reasons united" (10:237).

In the context of Mill's dispute with intuitionism, it is notable that Mill's proof is an attempt to ground rationally the basic principle of his system. He tries to base the principle of utility on em-

[40]For more detailed defenses of Mill on this point, which I do not pursue further, see West, "Mill's 'Proof'," 30–32; Hall, "'Proof' of Utility," 107; and Alan Ryan, *John Stuart Mill*, (New York, 1970), 196–210.
[41]See West, "Mill's 'Proof'," 27–30; Hall, "'Proof' of Utility," 108.

pirical facts, the kind of empirical facts that are readily open to scrutiny. He has affirmed that humans are built psychologically so that they desire happiness and only happiness as an end, leaving happiness as the only serious contender in the desirability contest. This claim is actually more complicated than it appears; it does not mean that Mill is a psychological hedonist. Fred Berger summarizes this point well: "It is not difficult to show that Mill rejected the view that all acts are motivated by desires for pleasure as the end or aim of the action . . . he maintained that pleasure and pain are *causally* linked to all voluntary human acts (though sometimes only indirectly, through past associations of the act with pleasure). He did not hold, however, that all acts are done with the thought of gaining a pleasure by means of them."[42] Whether Mill's claim is true can only be decided by empirical observation, and Mill appeals to all interested parties to examine the evidence impartially. Since pleasures and pains are commonly and universally experienced, objectivity is built into the foundation of the theory. He says that the truth of his conclusion "can only be determined by practiced self-consciousness and self-observation, assisted by observation of others" (10:237). On this factual evidence he rests his case. This position has to be taken as a weak link in Mill's theory. If we take seriously his views on "mental chemistry" and the fact that in complex experiences pleasures, though phenomenally present, may be mixed together with other elements, it takes a highly sophisticated introspector to give solid evidence to back his contention. The sophistication of his position on complex mental experience, which undercuts many traditional objections to his mental-state version of utility, works here to undermine the proof. But these weaknesses are venial in comparison with the intuitionist method of arguing their case.

Mill also critically contrasts the multiplicity of principles in many intuitionist systems, including Whewell's, with the monistic structure of utilitarianism; he considers it a major strength of utilitarianism that it has but one basic principle (8:951–52; 10:206–7). Moral theories must be able to mediate moral disputes. Intuitionist systems with a set of moral rules, supposedly known by intuition but with no definite order or ordering principles for resolving con-

---

[42]Berger, *Happiness, Justice and Freedom*, 13.

flicts among them, are of little use if they lead to contradictory solutions or to no solution at all.

These foundational weaknesses of intuitionism are central matters in Mill's critique. But he aims other criticisms at the lack of objectivity of the right-making properties of its moral principles. On these points Mill's criticism turns to derision. Look first at Whewell's explanation of what makes an action right:

> The Definition of *rightful*, or of the adjective *right*, is, I conceive, contained in the maxim which I have already quoted as proceeding from the general voice of mankind: namely this, that we must do what is right at whatever cost. That an action is right, is a reason for doing it, which is paramount to all other reasons, and overweighs them all when they are on the contrary side. It is painful: but it is right: therefore we must do it. It is a loss: but it is right: therefore we must do it. It is unkind: but it is right: therefore we must do it. These are self-evident propositions. That a thing is right, is a *supreme* reason for doing it. *Right* implies this supreme, unconquerable reason; and does this especially, and exclusively.[43]

The scornful reaction of Mill, committed as he is to a scientific approach to ethics, is understandable. To say that right is "that which we must do" is not an answer to the question of what makes an action right but a reformulation of the question itself, or, as Mill puts it, a "vicious circle the first" (10:187). The right-making property is not an empirical property, as in utilitarianism, but a peculiar kind of attribute of certain classes of actions, an attribute our reason sees directly. Another way of putting it, of saying what makes actions right, is that right actions are those conformable to this reason. Whewell says that "Reason alone can see what is right; alone can understand that there is such a character as rightness."[44] But this other way of putting it is equally objectionable to Mill, who rejects a special faculty that directly intuits moral attributes. The moral properties are nonempirical, and the use of a distinct faculty of reason fails the independence requirement of objectivity. This intuitionist theories are found wanting with respect to both the independence and the empirical criteria for objectivity. Using reason to tell us what is right is not an objective decision-making procedure for

[43]Whewell, *Lectures*, 2.
[44]Ibid., 4.

settling disputes, for the well-known reason that when two people disagree about their intuitions an impasse is reached. Since reason is supposed to be the ultimate arbiter, when it fails there is no place to turn. Mill thinks that appeals to reason or intuition are disguised appeals to uncritical feelings or outright prejudices.

Utilitarianism has a public decision-making procedure for attempting to settle cases of moral dispute. This procedure consists in applying an independent and empirical test to put us in the best position to decide which action is right. The theory provides an independent adjudicative standard (the principle of utility) and appeals to empirical facts (pleasures and pains). The principle is applied to acts, or to rules in the case of rule utilitarianism. Utilitarianism requires that the pleasures and pains of all those people with an interest in a particular decision-making situation be taken into account. Although Bentham and Mill have different procedures for measuring the value of these pleasures and pains—the former uses the felicific calculus, the latter the preferences of competent agents—the aim for each is objective ethical decision making. The feelings the intuitionist takes into account are not objective empirical facts. Mill criticizes a theory in which the feelings or sentiments of the judge require no justification outside of themselves; such a theory opens the way to abuse. Whewell and other intuitionists do not allow for rational and open resolution of moral conflict.[45]

[45]Mill defends Bentham against Whewell, and agrees with Bentham's claim that intuitionists "find certain feelings of approbation and disapprobation in themselves, take for granted that these feelings are the right ones, and when called on to say anything in justification of their approbation or disapprobation, produce phrases which mean nothing but the fact of the approbation or disapprobation itself. . . . Dr. Whewell will doubtless say that the feelings they appeal to are not their own individually, but a part of universal human nature. . . . A feeling is not proved to be right, and exempted from the necessity of justifying itself, because the writer or speaker is not only conscious of it in himself, but expects to find it in other people. . . . If it is alleged that the intuitive school require, as an authority for the feeling, that it should *in fact* be universal, we deny it. They assume the utmost latitude of arbitrarily determining whose votes deserve to be counted" (10:178–79). Whewell does in fact put forth another kind of test for determining what is right, but Mill finds this equally unacceptable. Whewell starts from the natural authority of reason over desire and affection. His method is to classify the desires and affections and then seek corresponding conditions of rightness (Whewell, *Lectures*, 4). He finds that the primary desires of people are the desires of personal safety, of having, of family society, and of civil society, and he later adds the desire of a mutual understanding among people. He then asks whether there is a general condition that is required such that these desires and affections may be right, and he answers that, in order for them to be right, "they

Mill faults intuitionism for the lack of objectivity of both its moral principles and its right-making properties, but also for its lack of progressiveness. He claims that such theories have a tendency to preserve the status quo and impede the development of moral science and practice. Utilitarianism, on the other hand, is a progressive theory, continually emphasizing development:

> The context between the morality which appeals to an external standard, and that which grounds itself on internal conviction, is the contest of progressive morality against stationary—of reason and argument against the deification of mere opinion and habit. The doctrine that the existing order of things is the natural order, and that, being natural, all innovation upon it is criminal, is . . . vicious in morals.(10:179)

Mill repeats these themes of the lack of objectivity and the unprogressiveness of intuitionism in other places (e.g., 8:951; 10:206–7, 26). Even after he recasts his theory, he remains firmly in the utilitarian camp, and although he rejects the Benthamite method of measuring the value of pleasure and pain he keeps the goal of objectivity strongly in mind.

---

must conform to this primary and universal Condition, that they do not violate the Rights of others" (ibid., 6). Here are the conditions of rightness corresponding to the desires and affections, for there is a classification of legal rights corresponding to that of desires and affections. The primary rights are, conveniently, the rights of the person, of property, of the family, of contract, and political rights. These existing legal rights can be used as a test for the rightness of actions, although Whewell hedges on the question of just how conclusive a test they provide. Thus Whewell wants to base rightness on existing legal rights, and to use the latter as criteria for the former. So he has provided some sort of test for rightness. But Mill sees this test as objectionable and not credible, a rather blatant attempt to impose the status quo. Whewell supplies no plausible arguments to support his contention that legal rights are a condition of rightness, and it is hard to see how this case could be made (ibid., 8–17). Indeed no sooner does he reach his conclusion than he begins to reverse himself and qualify the argument beyond recognition. Now he bases legal rights on rightness, for he says that "nothing can be a man's [legal] Right but that which is *right* he should have," and it is possible that any particular laws may be "contrary to Morality" (ibid., 7,9). He asserts not that legal rights are a test of moral rightness, but that we "rise" from legal rights to moral rightness by means of the principle that "the Supreme Rule of man's actions must be a rule which has authority over the whole of man; over his intentions as well as his actions; over his Affections, his Desires, his Habits, his Thoughts, his Wishes. The man's being cannot be right, except all these be right" (ibid., 7). To say the least, this is not a helpful test for determining which action is right. By the end of the argument, we are led to symphathize with Mill's exasperation with Whewell's convolutions.

Mill's utilitarian theory has a principle that stipulates the right-making properties of actions. It strongly fulfills the independence and interpersonal requirements. The estimation of the value of pleasures is arrived at through a public procedure that does not rest on people's uncritical beliefs about what is right or good. Mill's measurement procedure does rely on people's opinions and preferences, namely, those of competent agents, but people are developed to make those judgments. Thus, although they can be mistaken, they have the best chance to pick out those pleasures that are more valuable in terms of the ultimate development of human potentiality, and so the objectivity of the position is preserved. Mill's theory fulfills the interpersonal condition in allowing for a measurement of utility that can be applied to different people via the application of interpersonal standards. The theory is somewhat weaker with respect to the empirical condition, for the right-making property is not thoroughly empirical but partly dependent on what is good, or the evaluation of quality of pleasure. Finally, the theory has only one ultimate principle, which is grounded empirically.

Mill substitutes his doctrine of development and self-development for the felicific calculus. He agrees with Bentham that the value of mental states depends on their having certain good-making characteristics, but he parts company with him over the question of which characteristics are good-making. He does not agree with Bentham's claim that the good-making characteristics can be perceived and precisely measured introspectively; rather, he maintains that a process of development and self-development—consisting partly of critically developing certain abilities, partly of learning appropriate standards—is necessary to enable people to pick out accurately and measure the value of pleasurable states.

2

Qualitative Hedonism

Mill's inclusion of quality in the measurement of value of pleasurable experience is the crux of his break with the orthodoxy of Benthamite quantitative hedonism. The relational properties created by association, both causal and intentional, matter to Mill because the quality of pleasurable experience rests largely on them.

QUALITY AS A GOOD-MAKING CHARACTERISTIC

Confusion over what Mill means by quality of pleasurable experience has led to numerous misconstruals and misguided criticisms. The *Logic* is a good source of information for clarifying this issue. There Mill sets out his classification of the "Things Denoted by Names" (7:46–75). The three most general classes of nameable things are feelings or states of consciousness, substances, and attributes. Attributes are of three types: quality, relation, and quantity. The qualities of a body "are the attributes grounded on the sensations which the presence of that particular body to our organs excites in our minds." And "when we ascribe to any object the kind of attribute called a Relation, the foundation of the attribute must be something in which other objects are concerned besides itself and the percipient. . . . whenever two things are said to be related, there is some fact, or series of facts, into which they both enter" (7:67–68).

Mill is much less clear about quantity. He contrasts it with quality, but he explains only that the sensations received in the case of a difference of quality are not exactly the same as those received in the case of a difference in quantity. He uses an example in his attempt to clarify matters. We are first to imagine a gallon of water and ten gallons of water, noting that the difference between the two is one of quantity; then we are to imagine a gallon of water and a gallon of wine, noting that the difference is one of quality. The distinction between the two cases, says Mill, is that the sensations received from the gallon of water and the gallon of wine are different in one way and that the sensations received from the gallon of water and the ten gallons of water are different in another way. "This likeness and unlikeness I do not pretend to explain, no more than any other kind of likeness and unlikeness. But my object is to show, that when we say of two things that they differ in quantity, just as when we say that they differ in quality, the assertion is always grounded on a difference in the sensations which they excite" (7:73). Mill does not attempt to explain what the difference is; he claims that everyone is aware of it and experiences it directly, but that it cannot be defined.

Mill's account reviews attributes of minds as well as of bodies. Attributes of minds are also grounded on states of feeling, and they fall into two classes: those grounded exclusively on their own states of feeling, and those grounded on the feelings they produce in other minds. In the latter case, the feelings are thoughts or emotions rather than sensations. Finally, certain attributes of bodies, such as the beauty of a physical object, can be grounded on thoughts or emotions as well as on sensations (7:74–75).

It is apparent that the most important distinction is that between quality and relation. Mill does not set out any clear difference between quality and quantity, but he does distinguish quality and relation. Attributes of quality (and of quantity) are grounded on feelings received from *one* body, while attributes of relation are grounded on feelings received from more than one. The distinction set out between quality and quantity is less clear. Mill himself did not make this distinction in the beginning. In the early draft of the *Logic*, he sets out only two classes of attributes—quality and relation (8:995). The deviation of the later version from the early draft reveals some change of thought on Mill's part, for originally he classified quantity as just one kind of quality. Even in the final draft he skirts the question of the basic difference between quantity and quality (7:74).[1] There is a certain arbitrariness to the distinction, which emerges when we think about the example of wine and water. The visualization used in the example could just as easily apply to shape and color, or to any two different properties for that matter. The example does not explain why quantity and quality are placed in two different classes of attributes while shape and color are in the same class.

If we assume that there is some connection between what Mill means by quality in the *Logic* and in *Utilitarianism*, we can use these ideas to shed light on his remarks in the latter work. In *Utilitarianism*, he claims repeatedly that pleasures differ in quality as well as quantity:

> It is quite compatible with the principle of utility to recognize the fact, that some *kinds* of pleasure are more desirable and more valuable than others. It would be absurd that while, in estimating all other things, quality is considered as well as quantity, the estimation of pleasures should be supposed to depend on quantity alone. (10:211)

> What is there to decide whether a particular pleasure is worth purchasing at the cost of a particular pain, except the feelings and judgment of the experienced? When, therefore, those feelings and judgment declare the pleasures derived from the higher faculties to be preferable *in kind*, apart from the question of intensity, to those of which the animal nature, disjoined from the higher faculties, is susceptible, they are entitled on this subject to the same regard. (10:213)

> According to the Greatest Happiness Principle . . . the ultimate end . . . is an existence exempt as far as possible from pain, and as rich as possible in enjoyments, both in point of quantity and quality. (10:214)[2]

> If I am asked, what I mean by difference of quality in pleasures, or what makes one pleasure more valuable than another, merely as a pleasure, except its being greater in amount, there is but one possible answer. Of two pleasures, if there be one to which all or almost all who have experience of both give a decided preference, irrespective of any feeling of moral obligation to prefer it, that is the more desirable pleasure. If one of the two is, by those who are competently ac-

---

[1]In his conclusion, Mill groups quality and quantity together but separates them from relation.

[2]For further discussion of Mill's inclusion of quality as well as quantity, see 10:419–20, 484–85; James Mill, *Analysis*, 2:252–55n; J. S. Mill, *Inaugural Address Delivered to the University of St. Andrews* (London, 1867), 44–45. There is a wealth of further discussion throughout Mill's writings.

quainted with both, placed so far above the other that they prefer it,
even though knowing it to be attended with a greater amount of dis-
content, and would not resign it for any quantity of the other pleasure
which their nature is capable of, we are justified in ascribing to the
preferred enjoyment a superiority in quality, so far outweighing quantity as to render it, in comparison, of small account. (10:211)

From this verdict of the only competent judges, I apprehend there
can be no appeal. On a question which is the best worth having of two
pleasures, or which of two modes of existence is the most grateful to
the feelings, apart from its moral attributes and from its consequences, the judgment of those who are qualified by knowledge of
both, or, if they differ, that of the majority among them, must be
admitted as final. (10:213)

. . . the test of quality, and the rule for measuring it against quantity, being the preference felt by those who, in their opportunities of
experience, to which must be added their habits of self-consciousness
and self-observation, are best furnished with the means of comparison. (10:214)

In the final passage above, Mill sets out his criterion for the value
of quality of pleasurable experiences. Although in this context he
speaks only of "experience" and "competent acquaintance," I argue
that he actually needs and works out in some depth a more rigorous
requirement. Competent agents who have undergone development
and self-development are in the best position to make these judgments and express these preferences.

The obstacle to a correct interpretation of what Mill means by
quality is that in both the *Logic* and *Utilitarianism* he uses the term
ambiguously to mean either a kind or a normative property. This
vacillation has made him vulnerable to criticisms and misin-
terpretations. It is useful to bring the *Logic* into the discussion of
this question because by choosing a consistent sense of quality we
can demystify this dimension and put Mill's view of value in clearer
perspective. Many interpretations of Mill place quantity (intensity
and duration) on one side as a straightforward empirical property
and quality on the other side as a mysterious, obscure, normative
property.[3] This interpretation misses the point of what both Mill
and Bentham are doing. Bentham regards the quantities of pleasures
as empirical, but he also regards them as normative, that is, productive of good, or that in virtue of which the pleasures that have them
are good. Mill does not regard only the quality as normative; he

[3] Rem Edwards, for example, makes this error; see *Pleasures and Pains*, 32.

regards both quantity and quality of pleasures and satisfactions as normative or productive of good. He also regards both as empirical. He simply adds one further property, quality, as a normative property. It is often assumed that by including quality as productive of good Mill introduces a radically new and mysterious kind of dimension. This is not the case. In the *Logic*, Mill, far from regarding quality as a radically different kind of property, regards quality and quantity as such similar kinds of property that he has difficulty distinguishing them in the final draft and includes them in the same class in the early draft. In Mill's view, quality is just another ordinary property, and so in all of my discussions of quality of pleasurable experiences I use quality to mean that additional good-making characteristic of pleasures. Quality is thus assigned a consistent meaning, and notions that quality is the only normative aspect of pleasurable experiences should be dispelled. Quality is clearly not synonymous with overall value. Overall value or goodness is produced by quantity and quality, the two basic good-making characteristics. When competent agents express preferences for different pleasurable experiences, they are ranking these experiences on a scale of value. What is being measured is value of experience. The properties that contribute to value are quantity and quality.

In *Utilitarianism*, Mill equates the quality of pleasure with its kind. He says, for example, that "the pleasures derived from the higher faculties [are] preferable *in kind*" (10:213). Thus intellectual pleasures can be a kind. But kinds of pleasure are not categorized solely by the faculty affected; they are also classified by cause and by phenomenal differences in the pleasurable experiences themselves. Thus causal and intentional properties enter the picture. Mill's notion that quality of pleasurable experience is roughly equivalent to kind and his particular view of kind give his view a flexibility Bentham's lacks.[4]

REACTION OF CRITICS

Reactions to Mill's inclusion of quality have not been sympathetic on the whole. Even recent excellent scholarship that has corrected many earlier mistaken interpretations and objections has tended to

[4]Jan Narveson has an interpretation of Mill that is in some respects similar; see *Morality and Utility* (Baltimore, 1967), 79–82.

accept what I argue are distorted views of Mill's arguments on quality. These recent revisionary interpretations have focused on Mill's principles of right and have bypassed the principles of good. Most critics are still particularly scathing in their objections to Mill's inclusion of quality in value assessment, correctly seeing it as the basis of his break with Benthamite utilitarianism. Mill is accused of, among other things, abandoning utilitarianism and hedonism, relinquishing objectivity, maintaining a contradictory position, and talking nonsense.

Several criticisms of Mill's addition of quality must be answered by any plausible interpretation of his theory. But before I turn to these, I examine other closely related but less substantial objections that merely obfuscate the more serious objections. The claim that Mill abandons hedonism by introducing quality into the measurement of the value of a pleasurable experience is one of these. Generally this criticism is simply baldly stated without explanation or argument. For example, F. H. Bradley says, "If you are to prefer a higher pleasure to a lower without reference to quantity—then there is an end altogether of the principle which puts the measure in the surplus of pleasure to the whole sentient creation."[5] But this view simply misinterprets the claims of hedonism. All hedonism holds is that pleasure is good and is the only thing that is good, but hedonists differ over the question of which dimensions or properties of pleasure should be used to measure its overall value. Bradley's criticism defines hedonism very narrowly as maintaining that only quantity of pleasure can be counted in the measurement of value, but this definition straightforwardly begs the question.

Mill is not a hedonist in the narrow central sense assumed by this objection, because he values complex pleasurable experiences rather than sensations of pleasures. On the terminological question, Bradley's reservations about whether Mill is a hedonist may have some basis, for reasons I have noted. But Bradley here does not wish to withdraw Mill from the hedonist camp for the same reasons I offered. I questioned whether Mill can be called a hedonist because he assesses complex pleasurable experiences rather than simple pleasures; Bradley wants to deny Mill this label because Mill considers the kind as well as the amount of the experiences. The objection can be extended to apply to Mill's views, but it has as little force in

[5] F. H. Bradley, *Ethical Studies*, 2d ed. (London, 1962), 119.

the extension. The interesting issue is whether my interpretation of Mill is plausible and consistent. Is it plausible to maintain that only pleasurable experiences are valuable and yet that their quality as well as quantity is to count? Mill maintains that quality is to be included in the measurement of the overall value of pleasurable experience, and this standard criticism offers no argument for excluding this dimension out of hand.

A second shallow criticism is often stated in company with a substantial criticism, which I consider shortly. According to it the "something" that an object of more value has to a greater degree can only be quantity (intensity and duration). This argument regards degree and degree of quantity as identical—it is meaningless to talk about "higher" and "lower" unless we are referring to degrees of quantity. As Bradley puts his version, "so that apart from quantity, apart from degree, there is no comparison, no estimation, no higher and lower at all" (118).

This claim that "higher quality" must be referable to more degrees of something can be understood in a strong or a weak sense. In the weak sense, the claim is that pleasures that are more valuable qualitatively have more degrees of something, namely, whatever quality is. This issue needs examination. In the strong sense, the claim is that pleasures that are more valuable qualitatively have more degrees of quantity, that is, of intensity and duration. The general argument trades on the ambiguity between these two senses. The strong sense is needed to draw the conclusion (if quality is not referable to degrees of quantity, then no measurement of value can be obtained), but the assumption of the strong sense begs the question. On the other hand, the conclusion does not follow from the weak sense (pleasures that are more valuable qualitatively must have more degrees of whatever quality is). And this weak sense is not one that Mill would resist. In fact, this objection again construes the question in a narrow and limiting way. As the work on utility theory and social-choice theory of the past few decades has shown, there is a wide range of possibility about the kinds of scale on which utility is to be measured as well as on what the utility to be measured is. The objection in question assumes that measurement must be on strictly cardinal scales, measuring only quantity (intensity and duration) of pleasure. This assumption also begs the question. Scales of utility can be of many different strengths and can measure utility construed in many different ways.

There is another problem with this second superficial objection. If we take the objection seriously, we accept that *all* comparative qualitative judgments are meaningless; not only qualitative differences among pleasures but also qualitative differences among beautiful objects, or noble characters, for example, must be referable to such quantitative degrees. Acceptance of the objection eliminates the possibility of any comparative purely qualitative judgments. To say the least, this is a very strong position to take, yet its proponents adopt it with regard to quality of pleasurable experience without even the ghost of an argument.

One final weak objection, put clearly by G. E. Moore, accuses Mill of abandoning hedonism in a different way. Moore says that Mill, in speaking of different kinds of qualities of pleasure, is using "pleasure" to mean something complex, something that is actually pleasure as well as the source of pleasure: "If one pleasure can differ from another in quality, that means, that *a* pleasure is something complex, something composed, in fact, of pleasure in addition to that which produces pleasure."[6]

This accusation misses the point. Pleasurable experiences are complex and have causal relational properties, but Mill does not include the source of a pleasurable experience as part of the meaning of pleasurable experience. My previous discussion of the role of association shows that Mill maintains that pleasures can take on relational properties through association. The pleasurable experience of a person who is knowledgeable about classical music, for example, may have a causal relational property such as "being a pleasurable experience caused by listening to Mozart." This does not show that the pleasurable experience is something complex in Moore's sense. The pleasurable experience in this case is a single entity that has, among other properties, one that is relational. Mill takes these sorts of relational property to be relevant to the value of a pleasurable experience, but he does not add the source of the pleasurable experience.

With these weak objections out of the way, we can now look at objections that cannot be as lightly dismissed. Perhaps the most fundamental of these maintains that qualitative differences must refer to degrees of something, that is, that they must be differences in the relative presence of some characteristic. As Bradley puts it,

[6]G. E. Moore, *Principia Ethica*, 79.

"'higher' and 'lower', as comparative terms, refer to degree. What is higher has a greater degree (or it has a greater number of degrees) of something definite; what is lower has a less degree or number of degrees" (118).[7] Mill must explain what this property or "something" is that pleasures that are more valuable qualitatively have to a greater degree.

A second standard criticism claims that quantity and quality are incommensurable, or cannot be reduced to the same terms, or cannot be measured by a common standard. Bradley gives a standard formulation: "Given a certain small quantity of higher pleasure in collision with a certain large quantity of lower, how can you decide between them? To work the sum you must reduce the data to the same denomination" (119). But if such quantities cannot be measured by a common standard, then an overall measure of value cannot be obtained.

It is also often argued that, if an overall measure of value cannot be obtained by examining properties of the pleasures themselves (which assumes the soundness of the second criticism), then the only choice left is the rather loose requirement that pleasures that are more valuable qualitatively are those in fact preferred by those acquainted with all the relevant pleasures. And when differences of opinion arise, as they invariably do, serious difficulties for the theory result.

Mill's theory must meet these three questions: what is the "something" that pleasures that are more valuable qualitatively have to a greater degree? are quantity and quality incommensurable in a problematic way? and does the measurement of value reduce to the loose requirement that pleasures that are more valuable qualitatively are those preferred by those acquainted with all the relevant pleasures? I deal with the first two criticisms in the discussions of measurement and objectivity and the third in the light of Mill's doctrine of development and self-development. Mill's measurement procedure uses the informed preferences of competent and developed moral agents, but there is much more theoretical heftiness built into this procedure than its critics allow. Mill's competent judges are like the rational moral agents at the core of many modern moral theories.

[7]G. E. Moore echoes this point: "'Pleasant' must, if words are to have any meaning at all, denote some one quality common to all things that are pleasant; and, if so, then one thing can only be more pleasant than another, according as it has more or less of this one quality" (ibid. 78).

False Friends

False friends of Mill are concerned that his inclusion of quality may make him vulnerable to objections that his theory is not objective and that it leaves utilitarianism behind. Concurring with critics' claims that Mill is stepping into philosophical quicksand, these friends go to great interpretive lengths to put him back on solid ground. I argue that two such attempts misinterpret Mill and that the apparent *terra firma* of orthodox Benthamism is an illusion.[8]

In discussing the place of quality and quantity in Mill's system, scholars rarely map out categories of possible interpretations clearly and precisely. The first distinction that can be drawn regarding possible positions is that between reductionism and nonreductionism. Reductionists maintain that quality of pleasure is reducible to quantity. Since quality and quantity are properties, not substances, a reductionist position in this case is that the properties of quantity and quality are interdefinable, that there is some true analytic proposition that links the two properties. In contrast, nonreductionists maintain that quality and quantity are not interdefinable, that there is no such analytic connection.

In an example of the reductionist approach Ernest Sosa agrees with the general thrust of objections and concedes that if Mill does hold the position attributed to him he is guilty as charged. Sosa maintains, however, that Mill does not hold this position, or at least that there is a plausible reductionist interpretation of Mill that is not vulnerable to these criticisms.[9] Sosa interprets Mill's position on quality as reductionist and claims that, since quality and quantity are interdefinable, the criticisms of Mill obviously miss the mark. Sosa does not provide a precise formulation of his interpretation, yet it is apparent from his remarks that he does attribute logical reductionism to Mill. His interpretation of Mill is that "qualitative pleasure-differences [are] basically differences in degree," and that "ethically relevant qualitative differences among pleasures [are] merely differences in degree transformed into differences in kind" (162–63). By differences in degree Sosa means differences in degree of quantity. He means to do away with what he

---

[8]For an exception to this approach, see Jan Narveson, *Morality and Utility.*
[9]Ernest Sosa, "Mill's *Utilitarianism*," in *Mill's Utilitarianism*, ed. James M. Smith and Ernest Sosa (Belmont, Calif., 1969), 154–72.

sees as the problem of quality by wholly reducing quality to quantity. But the analytic connection for Sosa is complex, not simple. His interpretation is complicated by his claim that there are different kinds of pleasurable experience. The key to understanding Mill, he claims, is a comment in the last chapter of *Utilitarianism* where "Mill observes that it is 'often the case in psychology' that a 'difference in degree . . . becomes a real difference in kind' " (162). Although there are different kinds of pleasure, such as contentment and ecstasy, these kinds are based wholly on underlying differences in degrees of intensity. Sosa bases his classification on phenomenal differences among the pleasures. Within a kind category, such as contentment, the quality or kind is constant but the intensity can increase, and increases of intensity within a category do not produce qualitative differences. Once this increase in intensity reaches a certain threshold, however, the kind of quality changes—for instance, contentment changes into cheerfulness. So, although there may be differences of intensity within the category of contentment, with some states of contentment being more intense than others, they are all states of contentment until the underlying degree of intensity increases to such an extent that the pleasure becomes one of cheerfulness.

Sosa believes that his interpretation makes sense of Mill, although he admits that certain passages in *Utilitarianism* are bothersome. Sosa's attempt to save Mill from himself does not succeed. His interpretation collides with Mill's own direct statements on the issue, and rather than avoiding Mill's supposed inconsistencies, it leads to implausible conclusions. Because he believes that Mill is inconsistent, Sosa offers an interpretation that, on the face of it, does not fit Mill's own comments. The more constructive approach is to show that Mill's statements are not inconsistent. Given the fruitfulness of qualitative hedonism and the number of avenues it opens which are closed to the quantitive approach, it is worth the effort to see if this approach is consistent and objective. My interpretation suggests that it is. Sosa chooses another route, with unhappy results.

Sosa's interpretation misses the whole spirit of Mill. It is clear from even a first reading that quality is quite consequential to Mill, that he means to make something of it. What reason would Mill have to even mention quality if he were satisfied with quantity alone? So much notice has been taken of Mill's views on quality partly because he makes such a point of including it. If he meant to reduce quality to quantity in the end, why would he go through such elaborate discussions about it? In fact, Mill elaborates for good reason.

The central defect of Sosa's interpretation of Mill is that it makes trivial what Mill says about quality and quantity, whereas in fact what Mill says about them is far from trivial. The interesting kind of case for Mill, the kind of case that is in fact a paradigm of a judgment involving both quantity and quality, is one in which we must choose between an intellectual and highly valuable (qualitatively) pleasurable experience of low intensity and a sensual and less valuable (qualitatively) pleasurable experience of high intensity. Sosa's interpretation rules this kind of case out of court, whereas it is clear that Mill himself regards this case as not only relevant but crucial. Mill introduces quality of pleasures as contributing to value because he believes that intellectual pleasurable experiences are more valuable than sensual ones, even though the intellectual pleasures may be far less intense than the sensual pleasures. And so, if Sosa's interpretation denies this paradigmatic case, his interpretation is not very useful when applied to Mill.

Sosa himself recognizes that sensual pleasures, which Mill thinks of as less valuable, can be of high intensity, and that this fact strikes at the heart of his interpretation. He tries to avoid this difficulty by asking rhetorically whether anyone could seriously suggest that the intensity of the physical pleasures is lower than the intensity of more valuable pleasures, and low enough to produce a difference in kind between these pleasures and the more valuable pleasures. He answers:

> In considering this question, it will be helpful to distinguish between the intensity of an object of enjoyment and the intensity or depth of enjoyment taken in that object. Obviously, some physical pleasures may involve, for most of us, more violent or intense experiences than most emotional or intellectual experience. But it does not follow that for most of us the enjoyment . . . derived from such purely physical experience is greater or deeper than that derived from emotional or intellectual experience. (165)

Sosa's claim that the intensity of sensual pleasurable experiences is not a property of the pleasurable experience, but of some other part of the experience, relies on a purely ad hoc distinction—a distinction completely at odds with Mill's view of the nature of pleasurable experiences and their properties. It is perfectly clear that Mill considers the intensity in the case of sensual pleasures to be a property of the pleasures and not of something else. Sosa ignores the underlying associationist psychological base of Mill's argument. But Mill's moral theory cannot be separated from his views on psychology and human nature.

Sosa's argument illustrates the essential weakness of any reductionist interpretation of Mill. Mill thinks that intellectual pleasures may be judged more valuable than sensual ones, even though they may be lower in intensity. Any interpretation that tries logically to reduce quality to quantity is doomed to failure.

With the essential weakness of a reductionist interpretation revealed, we can now turn to nonreductionism. The category of nonreductionism covers two basic varieties: correlationism and noncorrelationism. Correlationists hold that differences of degree of quantity are correlated in some precise way with differences of degree of quality. They maintain that, although quantity and quality are not interdefinable, quantity is an absolutely reliable indicator of quality.

Richard Bronaugh interprets Mill's theory as correlationist. He uses Sosa's treatment of Mill as a prelude to his own reading and presents some valuable criticisms as well as some illuminating misconstruals of Sosa.[10] Bronaugh too sees that a reductionist account is implausible, agreeing that Sosa's form of reductionism, in which the qualities or kinds are particular types of states of feeling, is problematic, for it "would seem to set highest value on a life of rapture or continuous ecstasy, something Mill specifically repudiated" (320–21). His own interpretation is more elaborate and sophisticated than Sosa's, but it does not fare much better. Like Sosa, Bronaugh thinks that a nonreductionist, noncorrelationist position is problematic. For this reason he does not examine the textual evidence on its own merits, and in his eagerness to avoid the obvious interpretation he runs afoul of Mill's own words. Here is Bronaugh's final formulation of his interpretation:

(1″) In the context of normative decision, something's *quality* is defined by the class of which it is a member in virtue of some standard of excellence.

[10]Richard N. Bronaugh, "The Utility of Quality: An Understanding of Mill," *Canadian Journal of Philosophy* 4 (December 1974): 317–25.

(2″) In that context, a *pleasure's* quality is established by the membership of its source . . . in a class defined as in 1″.

(3) (Pleasures not only differ in source and amount but are heterogeneous, having distinct phenomenal natures.)

(4′) Some *sources* of pleasure can cause greater quantities of pleasure than others.

Now (5′) Man's *higher faculties* are a source of pleasure to human beings which cause quantities of pleasure greater than are caused by any source which human beings share with animals or which animals possess alone.

Thus, (6′) Preferring only what yields greatest quantity, i.e., true to the Historic Principle as the only standard of excellence, human beings ought to forbear interfering with the exercise of those higher faculties. (325)

Bronaugh is a correlationist in that he claims that differences of degree of quantity of pleasure are correlated precisely in some way with differences of degree of quality. Since people's higher faculties are a source of pleasure which cause greater quantities of pleasure than are caused by the lower faculties, it follows that the higher faculties cause pleasures of higher quality than are caused by the lower faculties. Bronaugh's theory is not reductionist, for he does not claim that quantity and quality are interdefinable.

Bronaugh believes that Sosa's interpretation establishes a pleasure's quality by its being a kind of state of feeling, whereas his own interpretation establishes a pleasure's quality by its having a particular source in the human faculties. Thus the connections between quantity and quality are bound to be different; Sosa claims that certain states of feelings have more degrees of quantity, whereas Bronaugh claims that certain human faculties cause pleasures of greater quantity than others.

Bronaugh's interpretation is more sophisticated than Sosa's, but ironically it leaves wide open a central problem, one that Sosa does try to resolve: how is one to weigh quantity against quality in particular cases? One pleasurable experience may be more valuable qualitatively than another (by having its source in a higher faculty), and yet it may have fewer degrees of quantity (intensity and duration unrelated to source). Far from dealing with this problem, Bronaugh does not even mention it, and this is a serious deficiency. Any successful interpretation must provide some method for handling this problem. .

The heart of Bronaugh's misconstrual of Mill occurs in his propositions (4') and (5'): this just is not what Mill says or means. What Mill does say is that some sources (both source as cause of the pleasurable experience and source as originating faculty such as the intellect) *tend* to cause pleasurable experiences that are more valuable *qualitatively*. He does not say that they always do so. There is danger in tying the quality of pleasurable experiences to source as strictly as Bronaugh does. No doubt Mill regards the source of a pleasurable experience, in both senses, as part of the basis of its quality. He does not, however, regard it as the entire basis, and for good reason. If he did, numerous counterexamples could be constructed against his position, counterexamples to which Bronaugh's interpretation is vulnerable. Suppose, for example, that one person would derive a great deal of aesthetic pleasure from owning a particular art masterpiece. Suppose that under the circumstances there is only enough money available either to buy the work of art for this person or to buy extra food for several people. If the money were to go for the art work, these latter people would have only enough food to subsist. If quality of pleasures are tied strictly to source, it may well be the case that the pleasurable experience derived by the art lover would outweigh the lower (and therefore less) pain of these other people. Bronaugh would be hard pressed to accommodate cases like this, which are easy to provide but which are not consistent with Mill's position. Yet if we qualify our classification of quality of pleasures so that quality does not depend strictly on source, then Bronaugh's interpretation falls apart at its center.

There is a second problem with Bronaugh's interpretation. Mill says that some sources, including originating faculties, produce pleasures that are more valuable qualitatively; he does not say that they produce pleasures of greater quantity. Bronaugh, like Sosa, resorts to an ad hoc move to rescue his interpretation. It is just not plausible to maintain that the intellect causes pleasures of greater quantity than physical and sensual pleasures. Mill does not say this, and Bronaugh would not say it if he were not already committed to steering clear of a nonreductionist, noncorrelationist position.

Bronaugh attributes to Mill a view of the relation between quantity and quality that is in some ways even stronger than Sosa's. For Sosa, the pleasures Mill takes to be more valuable qualitatively must have more degrees of quantity. Bronaugh says something stronger: that *all* the pleasures produced by the higher faculties must be greater in intensity than those produced by the lower ones—that, of necessity, the pleasures produced by the body are less intense than those produced by the mind. Mill does not even maintain this kind of correlation between source and quality, much less between source and quantity. This view is implausible. It suggests that even the faintest pleasurable experience derived from listening to music is greater in quantity than the most intense physical pleasure. A view that underestimates physical pleasures to this extent simply is not credible.

Sosa and Bronaugh have made two of the best attempts at providing reductionist and correlationist accounts of Mill. Both reductionism and correlationism fail for the same reason, because they make the same mistake. Mill treats quality as an independent variable; any attempt to interpret him as tying quality and quantity, whether by reduction or correlation, is bound to prove fruitless.

A FALSE START

Rem Edwards has attempted to define and defend qualitative hedonism using Mill's theory as a model.[11] His is a false start in the right direction. He correctly characterizes Mill's theory as both nonreductionist and noncorrelationist, but he interprets it as being less empirical than it is and exposes Mill to several standard criticisms. Even more serious, he does not provide the theoretical underpinnings to make his interpretation workable.

Edwards sharply contrasts qualitative hedonism with the quantitative variety. He claims that quantitative hedonists such as Bentham are committed to the psychological assumption that all pleasures must be the same single quality (kind) of feeling, with no qualitative phenomenal differences among them, although they may differ quantitatively in intensity and duration and "in temporal proximity or remoteness" and "extrinsically in their causal connections" (31). Since this psychological assumption is "exceedingly naive" (35), this commitment threatens to undermine the entire position. Qualitative hedonists such as Mill have a much more plausible conception of the nature of pleasures and pains, seeing them as a "wide range of agreeable or disagreeable feelings that are qualitatively distinct" (34). Qualitative hedonists hold that plea-

<hr>

[11]Rem Edwards, *Pleasures and Pains*, especially 30–48.

sures and pains are distinguishable not only according to intensity, duration, and causal connections but "psychologically, as qualities of feeling, and also normatively, in desirability" (32). Some pleasures are superior or higher than others.

Qualitative hedonists also have a plausible method for determining amount of value. According to them, the amount of pleasantness depends on intensity and duration. But qualitative hedonists also add two further considerations: "'More pleasant' also means (a) containing a *greater variety* of those agreeable qualities of feeling which we call 'pleasures'. . . (b) that when two distinct qualities of agreeable feeling are compared, we prefer one to the other" (69–70).

According to Edwards, "qualitatively distinct pleasures may be preferentially ranked on grounds of *qualitative* superiority or inferiority, and their ranking need not vary directly with changes in duration and intensity" (70). This ranking is ordinal, rather than cardinal. "*Cardinal* comparisons of intensities and durations properly take place when we are comparing two instances of *the same quality* of pleasure. . . . Cardinal comparisons of intensity and duration have no use, however, when we are dealing with two entirely distinct qualities of pleasure, and we must resort to ordinal rankings" (70).

It is not entirely clear what Edwards is suggesting with his measurement method, even after his attempted clarification in response to Jan Narveson's criticism.[12] Although quantity and quality are both variables that can admit of degree, they cannot be fully integrated in Edwards's scheme. Intensity and duration come into play only when we compare two pleasures of the same quality (kind). Thus quantity is admitted into the scheme, but only in this limited sense. When we must choose between two pleasures of different quality, we can only rank them ordinally according to their quality, leaving quantity out of the consideration. Qualitatively superior pleasures are to be chosen over inferior ones when we cannot choose both. Taken to the extreme, this position certainly seems to lead to absurdity, but Edwards qualifies the position and holds that inferior pleasures are to be avoided only "when their pursuit interferes with or is incompatible with the actualization of some higher pleasure" (118). This stance could still be problematic, but in his rejoinder

[12]The criticism is given in Jan Narveson's review of Edwards's book in *Mill News Letter* 15 (Winter 1980): 28–31. Edwards's rejoinder, "Narveson on Qualitative Hedonism," is in *Mill News Letter* 16 (Winter 1981): 6–10.

Edwards explains that he intends that inferior pleasures should be avoided only when choosing them blocks the successive actualization of superior pleasures over a long period of time and not merely their simultaneous actualization.[13] After all, they are still valuable, although less valuable than superior pleasures. As well, inferior pleasures can often be enjoyed in combination with superior ones, and these gestalts can be more valuable than their components by themselves. Thus Edwards avoids the worst absurdity—that at any given moment we are obliged to choose the pleasures of, for example, the opera over the pleasures of eating.[14] He makes clear that there is room for both superior and inferior pleasures in his system, but that superior ones have pride of place.

Still, Edwards's scheme is unclear and unsatisfactory. He makes too much of his construal of the discrepant psychologies underlying quantitative and qualitative hedonism; in criticizing quantitative hedonism because of its supposedly inadequate assumptions, he is following a false scent. He fails to keep separate claims about the nature of pleasures and pains and claims about what generates their value and how their value is to be measured. His conclusion that quantitative hedonism is undermined by weak psychology is thus too hastily drawn.

We have seen that Bentham, James Mill, and John Stuart Mill all largely share the same associationist psychology. For Bentham there are many kinds of pleasures and pains, which he classifies according to source rather than to phenomenal difference. He does hold that pleasures and pains remain distinct sensations even when they become attached to other mental entities through association, but he also holds that pleasures can acquire the same kinds of relational properties that Mill uses as much of the basis of their differing qualities. The crucial difference is that Bentham does not take these relational properties to have anything to do with creating the value of pleasures and does not consider them relevant to the measurement of this value. Bentham could, quite consistently with quantitative hedonism, recognize the same range of phenomenal differences as Mill does, while choosing to ignore these differences in estimating their value. A quantitative hedonist can allow any number of phenomenal properties to pleasures and pains and is com-

---

[13]Edwards, "Narveson on Qualitative Hedonism," 9.
[14]This point is raised in Narveson's *Mill News Letter* review of Edwards, 30.

mitted only to the position that the only *good-making* properties are intensity and duration. Thus, no matter how complex these psychological states may be, the quantitative hedonist only "picks out" quantity in evaluating their worth. On the other hand, Mill and other qualitative hedonists could consistently hold that all pleasures are the same quality of feeling. They could base quality (kind) classifications solely on source or faculty affected. For them, the important point is that kinds of pleasures, however categorized, are taken into account in estimating their value. Edwards does separate two questions (32): what is the nature of pleasure, and how are we to measure value of pleasures? But he overlooks the question of what constitutes the value of pleasure, conflating it with his first question. Having given an account of the nature of pleasurable experiences, he leaves open the question of what constitutes their value.

Because of the infirmities of his own theory, Edwards does not defend Mill as strongly as he deserves. Although Edwards makes the right move in presenting quality as a distinct and independent dimension, he falls into the old trap of depicting it as more normative than is quantity. We have seen that in Mill's system quality is no more or less empirical than quantity. Quality, or kind, is an empirical property that is also normative, or productive of value, in exactly the same way as is quantity. Because he vacillates between treating quality as simply kind of pleasurable experience and as a special, mysterious normative characteristic, Edwards creates confusion and whittles away at the objectivity of the theory. The point of a defense of Mill's theory is to answer the objections and preserve the objectivity of the theory. This point is not served but rather sabotaged by inserting a normative property at such a basic theoretical level. Pleasures are not appropriately depicted as higher and lower when we speak of different qualities; rather, there are just different kinds of pleasures, some of which are preferred or ranked more highly by agents who are competent to adjudicate. We can make sense of Mill while protecting the objectivity of his theory, but only if we treat quality strictly as empirical kind.

Edwards's faulty notion of the special normative nature of quality infects his method of comparing and measuring the value of pleasures, which seems to raise as many problems as it solves. He avoids the worst problems by prohibiting the pursuit of presumably lower pleasures only when this blocks the successive realization of some higher pleasures. But the problem arises because his theory does not provide a mechanism for choosing lower pleasures. Edwards wants to allow us to choose the pleasurable experience of eating at some point, even though the choice of reading is always available.[15] How can we do this? On his account, quantitative considerations cannot be used when we are dealing with pleasures of different qualities, like reading and eating. On a correct interpretation, quantitative considerations would be included and thus eating would sometimes be the optimal choice. But Edwards insists that different kinds of pleasures can be compared only in terms of their quality by an ordinal ranking. Thus, when we sometimes choose eating over reading, we are choosing the alternative that affords us a less pleasurable experience. Yet we are supposed to be maximizing the good.

Such examples point to a deeper problem in the theory. It is simply a mistake to make quality a special property and to erect two different standards for judging quantity and quality. Mill says that they are judged by the same standard. Edwards is mistaken in assuming that strictly cardinal comparisons of quantity are viable. I argue in the following critique of Bentham that strict cardinalization does not work because there are no definite units of intensity. But even if these cardinal rankings were workable, the postulation of cardinal rankings for quantity and ordinal rankings for quality would make the integration of these two properties for the purpose of value estimation exceptionally difficult. If the problem posed by the above example is to be overcome, quantity and quality must be combinable on the same scale. But on Edwards's scheme this cannot be done; we need a common standard and the same ranking scheme.

Edwards's approach also misses the spirit of Mill. Although Mill stresses that the quality of pleasurable experiences is an important independent consideration in the judgment of their value, he does not intend that quality should dominate. Mill wants to allow cases in which we would choose a faint intellectual pleasurable experience over an intense physical one, but he also wants to allow the choice of a larger quantity of a less valuable kind over a small quantity of a highly valuable kind. Both choices must be equally possible, and the correct interpretation of Mill must show how they are. On the interpretation I offer, both quantity and quality are preferentially ranked by competent agents. Their rankings of pleasurable experiences are the outcomes of processes of judgment in which all good-making properties are taken into account.

[15]This example is Narveson's; see *Mill News Letter*, 30.

CRITIQUE OF BENTHAM'S DOMINANT ACCOUNT

Given the fruitfulness of the qualitative hedonist approach, it is worth the effort to see if it is consistent and objective. As a first step, I argue that Benthamite measurement is not as unproblematic as is assumed by Mill's critics and false friends. From this argument we can gain a clear and realistic perspective of what may be expected of utility measurement.

There are two standard criticisms of Mill's position. According to one, for the value of pleasures to be measured it must be susceptible of division into definite units. Only quantity is so divisible, so if quality cannot be reduced to quantity no units are available and measurement is not possible. According to the second criticism, for measurement to work these units must be commensurable. Quantity and quality are incommensurable, and thus a measurement cannot be obtained.

Bentham's dominant account is also vulnerable to these two criticisms, and for this reason later theorists have abandoned this account in favor of his secondary one. The dominant account uses the felicific calculus and provides for measurement of value of pleasure by means of introspective reports on their intensity and duration. The first criticism applies because of the difficulty with demarcating units of intensity. Pleasures and pains are assumed to be private mental entities. Given Bentham's view of the ontological status of pleasures and pains, there is agreement among subsequent theorists that the kind of strict measurement of intensity required by this account presents problems that have yet to be solved. People can make rough and ready calculations of intensity, but the definite, clear-cut, public units that Bentham needs are not forthcoming. Bentham himself wavers on this point. As Wesley Mitchell points out, in some of his writings Bentham claims that units can be identified and intensity measured: "The degree of intensity possessed by that pleasure which is the faintest of any that can be distinguished to be pleasure, may be represented by unity. Such a degree of intensity is in every day's experience: according as any pleasures are perceived to be more and more intense, they may be represented by higher and higher numbers."[16] But in another place Bentham thinks

---

[16]Bentham quoted in Eli Halevy, *La Formation du radicalisme philosophique.* 3 vols. (Paris, 1901), 1:398; also quoted in Mitchell, "Bentham's Felicific Calculus," 172.

differently, saying that intensity is not "susceptible of measurement."[17]

Bentham is not alone in his doubts. Later thinkers agree that, even if it were possible to develop units of intensity that could be applied consistently to a person's own private states (a dubious possibility), there would be no way to check publicly whether this person's units were the same as other people's. If two people disagree about the length of a building, they need only refer to a measuring rod, a public object that can be used to settle the dispute decisively. Nothing similar can be done in the case of pleasures, for there is no public object against which internal states can be measured. Bentham is quite clear that a person's private states are inaccessible to other people, ruling out the possibility of a public check. If Bentham held a different view of the ontological status of pleasures and pains, this problem would not be as serious. But since he does hold them to be private and inaccessible, the development of this unit of intensity of pleasures remains a fundamental difficulty for his theory. The difficulty presented by the privacy of pleasures and pains has also been noticed by other theorists.[18]

Even the private demarcation of units is problematic. Bentham says that the first unit of intensity is the degree possessed by the faintest distinguishable pleasure. But can it be claimed that a person can be certain enough about the size of this unit to tell whether a slightly more intense pleasure is two units or merely one and a half? People can become quite sophisticated judges of the intensity of their own pleasures, of course, and can make acceptable rough estimates, but the definite measurement required by Bentham is not realistic. I am not claiming that people's introspective judgments are inherently unreliable and imprecise, but I am claiming that the kind of rigid units envisioned by the dominant account are illusory. Rough estimates are all that can be obtained. Bentham does not recognize that people's raw introspective reports are relatively unreliable, and that, if their reports are to be reasonably accurate, they must be prepared by training for the exercise of introspective reporting. This point, central to Mill's view but overlooked by Bentham, is also emphasized by later writers: Thomas Lewis, for example, says that "descriptions of pain taken from the inexperienced are neces-

[17]Bowring, *Works of Bentham,* 4:542.
[18]See, e.g., J. L. Cowan, *Pleasure and Pain* (London, 1968); Thomas Lewis, *Pain* (New York, 1942).

sarily inaccurate, just as descriptions of colour by a child are inaccurate. To acquire accuracy, experience must be obtained."[19]

The difficulties noted by Lewis concern occurrent physical pains that are the *easiest* to measure. His pessimism regarding these pains makes one wonder how much more difficult it would be to measure pains that are not so occurrent. How, for example, are we to measure sadness over the loss of a lover or happiness over the good fortune of a friend? The problems of such measurement seem overwhelming. Moreover, all these difficulties concern the case in which only one person's experiences are involved. When we attempt to compare different people's pleasures and pains, the problems are compounded. No one with an introspective account has completely solved the problem of interpersonal comparisons of such precision. Bentham's theoretical troubles stem from his attempt to combine full comparability and a mental-state account of utility. Mental-state accounts can incorporate interpersonal comparisons of utility, but these are less than fully comparable. Thus definite public units of intensity are not available and pleasures and pains cannot be added or compared interpersonally as fully as Bentham's dominant account assumes and requires.

The second standard criticism, that an overall measurement cannot be obtained because quantity and quality are incommensurable, affects Bentham's dominant account as well, for intensity and duration are also incommensurable. They are different dimensions of pleasures and pains with no common denominator. Of course, Bentham and his followers do not see it this way. They assume that we can construct scales of intensity and duration with definite units and in each particular case simply multiply the intensity and duration of a particular pleasure to get a precise and objective total. This assumption overlooks the infinite number of ways intensity and

---

[19]Lewis, *Pain,* 178. Cowan stresses the same point, using the example of different discriminations of certain sounds by speakers of different languages: "The three *Ks* will sound the same to the English speaker because his language does not require him to differentiate them—and thus, in a sense, requires him *not* to. It is just so with the Arab and "key" and "sky" and the Indian and "key" and "cow." But Arabic and Hindu respectively do require a distinction of frontal from backed *k* sounds in the one case and aspirated from unaspirated ones in the other. The speakers of these languages will have learned to make a distinction, to hear a difference. The philosopher who thinks he can make fundamental discoveries of general significance by introspection . . . without taking such factors into consideration is oversimplifying to say the least" (Cowan, *Pleasure and Pain,* 88).

duration can be weighed against each other; the choice of weighting is arbitrary. It is hard to see how any one weighting could be defended as the correct one. Such is not the case, for example, with area. We know that area is the product of length and width, because independent measures of area are available. We do not have such precise and independent measure in the case of pleasure and pain. And so, in the case of pleasure and pain, intensity and duration could be weighted in a number of ways. Why not add them? Why not keep the unit of duration constant and multiply it by the square root of intensity? Since intensity and duration are incommunsurable, any choice of weighting is arbitrary.

The most important point is that Bentham's quantity is already a composite measure. His dominant account provides an illusion of monism that on closer scrutiny vanishes. Thus, although Mill has more dimensions to integrate in his rankings, he does not break with Bentham, as is assumed by critics and false friends, by taking the crucial step from a unidimensional to a multidimensional measure. This step has already been taken by Bentham himself.

Bentham's dominant account is susceptible to exactly the same criticisms as those leveled at Mill. Clearly it is a mistake to think that the assumed precision is to be found in Bentham. Using the felicific calculus, one cannot calculate pleasure and pain precisely— first, because no definite intensity units are available, and second, because intensity and duration are incommensurable. This does not mean that Bentham's position is hopelessly imprecise, but it does mean that the kind of precision called for by his theory is unrealistic. That degree of precision is not to be found in this area of inquiry.

CRITIQUE OF BENTHAM'S SECONDARY ACCOUNT

Bentham's secondary account does not fare any better than his primary. This approach is one that Bentham only began to explore, but it has been developed in this century in utility and social-choice theory. This approach measures utility not by introspective reports on pleasure and pain but by behavioral substitutes that are not assumed to be correlated with internal states.

In the secondary account, Bentham substitutes the external criterion of amount of money for the felicific calculus:

> If then between two pleasures the one produced by the possession of money, the other not, a man had as lief enjoy the one as the other, such pleasures are to be reputed equal. But the pleasure produced by the possession of money, is *as* the quantity of money that produces it: money is therefore the measure of this pleasure. But the other pleasure is equal to this; the other pleasure therefore is as the money that produces this: therefore money is also the measure of that other pleasure. It is the same between pain and pain; as also between pain and pleasure.[20]

The problems with this approach have already been pointed out. The assumption that amount of money is an accurate gauge of pleasure is crude and unworkable. The value placed on money varies greatly from person to person. In the case Bentham has in mind here, which is personal, the fact that the value of money can vary among persons is not a problem. But it becomes one if we try to generate an interpersonal measure. A second obstacle is that it is not possible to measure all things that people take pleasure in against money; some goods are priceless.

Diminishing marginal utility is also troubling, as Bentham recognizes:

> Money being the current instrument of pleasure, it is plain by incontrovertible experience that the quantity of actual pleasure follows in every instance in some proportion or other the quantity of money. As to the law of that proportion nothing can be more indeterminate. . . . For all this it is true enough for practice with respect to such proportions as ordinarily occur . . . that *caeteris paribus* the proportion between pleasure and pleasure is the same as that between sum and sum. So much is strictly true that the ratios between the two pairs of quantities are nearer to that of equality than to any other ratio that can be assigned.[21]

Bentham does not work out this method rigorously, for he realizes its problems. His basic claim that there is some proportion between

[20]Bentham, quoted by Halevy, *Radicalisme philosphique*, 1:410; also quoted in Mitchell, "Felicific Calculus," 174.

[21]Bentham quoted by Halevy, *Radicalisme philosophique*, 1: 406, 408; also quoted in Mitchell, "Felicific Calculus," 175.

quantity of money and quantity of pleasure is not and cannot be substantiated satisfactorily. The difficulty is deeper than that the law of this proportion is indeterminate. There are so many clear counterexamples that the evidence for this law is very weak. Someone can value an increase in amount of money a great deal or not at all, depending on a variety of internal and external circumstances.[22]

Bentham does not succeed in overcoming these problems in his own writings on the secondary account, and there are difficulties, for classical utilitarian aspirations, with the philosophical underpinnings of later theories in this tradition. We can take the theory of R. Duncan Luce and Howard Raiffa as an example.

Luce and Raffia break with Bentham's dominant account in two respects: they do not claim that their theory is based on data about mental states, or even that what constitutes data within their theory correlates with mental states; and they recognize only ordinal, not cardinal scales. Luce and Raiffa emphasize that they do not assume a correlation between behavioral substitutes and internal mental states. If a subject ranks all the alternatives and assigns a numerical index, they say, care must be taken not to assume that a more highly ranked alternative was preferred because of greater underlying "satisfaction" or "utility": "In this theory it is extremely important to accept the fact that the subject's preferences among alternatives and lotteries came prior to our numerical characterization of them. We do not want to slip into saying that he preferred A to B because A has the higher utility; rather, because A is preferred to B, we assign A the higher utility" (22).

Luce and Raiffa also stress that utility theory uses only ordinal scales—it is too easy to assume mistakenly that the numbers of an index can be added to that the magnitudes of differences between them can be compared. However, other thinkers argue that intermediate scales between cardinal and ordinal can be constructed.

Thus Luce and Raiffa's theory of individual decision making abandons a major part of Bentham's original theory, much more than Mill abandons. Despite this sacrifice of much of the theory, two problems remain. First, a decision is inevitably influenced by the subject's attitude toward gambling. Since a utility function reflects

[22]R. Duncan Luce and Howard Raiffa dismiss money as an external criterion: "The utility association to money is completely *ad hoc*. There are an infinity of functions which increase at a decreasing rate, and, certainly, the association may vary from person to person—but how?" *Games and Decisions* (New York, 1957), 20.

preferences in the particular situation, in this situation we cannot abstract out the subject's attitude toward gambling (21). More serious, the best that can be expected is a personal scale, not an interpersonal one. The problem with interpersonal comparison has always plagued Bentham and his theoretical descendants. As long as the scales in the theory are individualistic and there are no interpersonal standards, this problem with the objectivity of the theory remains. Luce and Raiffa maintain that utilities between two people cannot be compared because the relationship between the units of utility of the two is not known. There is no procedure for publicly measuring the units of each of the subjects to ascertain this relationship, and no public object is available against which subjects can each measure their unit. Proposals for a public standard which have been suggested do not satisfy our intuitive sense of accurate interpersonal comparison. We are continually trying to decide what an alternative means to another person. Luce and Raiffa conclude that interpersonal comparison is a real problem: "Since it is not solved, one can either assume that such comparisons are possible, knowing that this creates (at least at present) an Achilles' heel in the theory, or one can attempt to devise theories in which comparisons are not made" (34).

Luce and Raiffa's theory is objective in the sense that it provides a thoroughly empirical procedure for measuring utility. It is weak, however, in that it works only with ordinal scales.

Amartya K. Sen points out the problems of attempting to go beyond an ordinal scale to something strong enough for social choice.[23] He also abandons the attempt to correlate behavioral substitutes with mental states. Much of his discussion concerns the question of cardinalization, and his attempt to work out a theory with stronger than ordinal scales faces serious difficulties. He admits that individual utilities do not occur naturally in cardinal units and that these cardinal units are the result of experiments, not the underpinning of them (90). "The utility scales have arbitrary 'units', writes Sen. He elaborates "they also have arbitrary 'origins' " (92). The problem of arbitrary units and the zero point still faces modern heirs of Bentham.

Sen discusses several attempts at setting up cardinal scales of individual utility, among them those of Goodman and Markowitz

---

[23]Amartya K. Sen, *Collective Choice and Social Welfare* (San Francisco, 1970), 94.

and of von Neumann and Morgenstern, and concludes that their problems are certainly significant but not overwhelming.[24] These conclusions support my argument. Sen claims that units and the zero point are arbitrary; thus the strong, precise theory envisioned by Bentham is unrealistic, but weaker, less precise theories can be made to work. The important point is that, for these other theories to work, much of Bentham's dominant account is sacrificed.

Even with such weaker theories, the problems pointed out by Luce and Raiffa remain. Neither the problem of the influence of the subject's attitude toward gambling nor the objectivity problem of interpersonal comparison has been fully eliminated. How seriously we take this latter problem depends partly on how seriously we take the need for full comparability. Sen maintains that the situation is serious but not hopeless. His solution is to opt for partial comparability, that is, rough interpersonal comparisons, or a "case intermediate between noncomparability and full comparability of units" (99). The choice of this weaker theory accords with my argument about what can be realistically expected with regard to theories measuring utility. The strong account put forth by Bentham's dominant view is not workable.

The situation for Bentham's dominant and secondary approaches and their theoretical descendants is far from hopeless, but it does not constitute a firm citadel from which to attack Mill. His dominant account faces the critical measurement problem of a lack of nonarbitrary units of intensity and, therefore, the problems of aggregation and interpersonal comparison. His own secondary account, with money as an external measure, was never developed because it is so problematic. The twentieth-century theories developed along the lines of this secondary approach have given up critical parts of Bentham's theory. Besides abandoning cardinality (or having difficulty developing satisfactory cardinal accounts) and correlation with internal states, there remain two major problems: the effect of the individual's attitude toward gambling, and seemingly subjective, personal scales.

From this critique of Bentham a clearer picture of measurement

[24]See, e.g., L. A. Goodman and H. Markowitz, "Social Welfare Functions Based on Individual Rankings," *American Journal of Sociology* 58(1952): 257–62; J. von Neumann and O. Morgenstern, *Theory of Games and Economic Behavior* (Princeton, 1947).

and objectivity has emerged. We see that Bentham's original goal of a strong, precise, and empirical measurement is unrealistic, but this need not lead us to abandon the goal of objectivity as a counter to intuitionism's much more radical subjectivity.

Mill's method of measurement of value of pleasurable experience and pain is not, as commonly assumed, hopelessly inadequate in comparison with Bentham's. In some ways it is more problematic than Bentham's, in others, less so, and the latter may turn out to be more significant than the former. Mill does not take the key step from unidimensional to multidimensional measure, but he does have more dimensions to contend with and this creates some measurement problems. The integration of quantity and quality is somewhat more complicated than the integration of intensity and duration. Mill deals with the measurement of value by providing a procedure for determining how much value something has: preferential rankings by rational moral agents. The agents rank pleasurable experiences on scales that measure their value. Their preferences represent a judgment of the value of the experiences resting on the good-making properties of quantity and quality. Their rankings do not determine value, and this is why they can be mistaken. Human nature and potential is the determinant of value in the long run. Mill's procedure is not as precise as Bentham's. On the other hand, it is not hampered by individualistic judgments as is Bentham's. Central to Mill's procedure is the development of interpersonal standards, which opens the possibility of judgments that are much more objective in one sense than those allowed in Bentham's procedure. Mill's development of interpersonal standards allows for an interpersonal dimension—an estimation of utility that can be applied to different people.

3

Models of Utility

Bentham's conception of utility as set out in his dominant account seems dated to twentieth-century readers, but his secondary account is a precursor of modern desire-satisfaction trends. Mill anticipates some current trends better, and his conception of utility acquits itself well in current views. In this chapter, I situate Mill's account in the twentieth-century context and evaluate his views on utility in this arena.

In contemporary thought there are two general approaches to the nature of utility. Of these two divergent viewpoints, James Griffin says that "one sees [utility] as a state of mind, the other as a state of the world." Richard Brandt calls them the "happiness theory" and the "desire theory." L. W. Sumner discusses the "experience model" and the "desire model." Jonathan Glover uses the terms "mental state version" and "desire version."[1] The simplest or purest of the mental-state theories holds utility to consist of pleasures as simple sensations, while more sophisticated forms take it to consist of more complex states such as satisfactions, happiness, or enjoyments. The second general approach maintains that utility lies in

[1]James Griffin, *Well-Being* (Oxford, 1986), 7; Richard Brandt, *A Theory of the Good and the Right* (Oxford, 1979), 246; L. W. Sumner, *Abortion and Moral Theory* (Princeton; 1981), 179; Jonathan Glover, *Causing Death and Saving Lives* (Harmondsworth, Middlesex, 1977), 64.

satisfaction or fulfillment of desires. As Brandt sums it up, the difference between the two approaches is "whether fully rational persons will support a moral system which promises to *maximize happiness* in a society, or to provide the collection of events which sentient creatures in some sense *most want.*"[2]

The mental-state or experience model is the classical theory that fell into disrepute in the earlier part of this century; the desire-satisfaction version emerged to fill the gap and has become somewhat of an orthodoxy until recently. Lately the tables have been turned; some of the strongest defenses of utilitarian theory have been mental-state accounts, and desire accounts have been receiving a larger share of criticism. As I survey this field, it becomes apparent that each of these approaches faces lively objections and that no alternative has yet emerged as the undisputed winner.

MENTAL-STATE ACCOUNTS

Much fault has been found with the simplest form of mental-state approach, according to which utility is found in homogeneous simple mental states of sensations of pleasure. Proponents of this view claim that all mental states we find valuable have these simple pleasures in common as discernible elements of the experience, and it is exactly this element of the experience we pick out as desirable and no other. Griffin says of this view, "Pleasure or happiness is presented as a 'state of feeling', and pain or unhappiness as a feeling on the same scale as, and the opposite of, pleasure or happiness. And the utilities of all our experiences are supposed to be determinable by measuring the amount of this homogeneous mental state that they contain."[3]

This view, it should hardly bear repeating, is not Mill's, who turns to a more complex version of hedonism. In fact, Mill's theory is a hybrid of these two general approaches, for although he clearly sees that utility is found in certain inner experiences, his procedure for measuring utility uses preference scales that are usually associated with the desire approach. It is because Mill moves beyond claiming that the things that have value are just these simple pleasures that

[2]Brandt, *Good and Right*, 246.
[3]Griffin, *Well-Being*, 8.

some have argued that he is not a hedonist. His theory is a complex hybrid, but I have argued that the label "hedonist" has a certain attractiveness because of the role of pleasures in the formation of the complex mental states.

Again, the root of the matter for classical utilitarians is that utility lies in internal mental states. James Mill puts it this way: "Some sensations, probably the greater number, are what we call indifferent. . . . There are sensations, however, and of frequent recurrence, some of which are painful, some pleasurable. The difference is, that which is felt. A man knows it, by feeling it; and this is the whole account of the phenomenon."[4] This puts it bluntly; utility lies in mental states. We cannot give a further definition of pleasure and pain, because these are basic, felt experiences. We can, however, give criteria or marks of these to distinguish them, and here the account broadens even on James Mill's theory: "The first is of such a kind, that I care not whether it is long or short; the second is of such a kind that I would put an end to it instantly if I could; the third is of such a kind, that I like it prolonged. To distinguish those feelings, I give them names. I call the first Indifferent; the second Painful; the third, Pleasurable."[5]

From this distinguishing test it was a short step even for Bentham and James Mill to construe these experiences more widely than simple sensations. As Sumner puts it, "pleasure had to be interpreted broadly as any feeling that the individual enjoys and wishes to have prolonged."[6] So even James Mill is already moving toward a broader account than the view that only simple sensations have utility. But John Stuart Mill has other reasons for holding a broader account; both his qualitative hedonism and his views on the workings of association lead him even farther from the simple sensation account, and I explained earlier how complex experiences that competent agents evaluate are formed.

Griffin puts an objection to this simplest mental-state account:

> The trouble with thinking of utility as *one* kind of mental state is that we cannot find any one state in all that we regard as having utility—eating, reading, working, creating, helping. What one mental state runs through them all in virtue of which we rank them as we do? . . . The truth seems, rather, that often we just rank options, *peri-*

[4]James Mill, *Analysis*, 2:184.
[5]Ibid.
[6]Sumner, *Abortion*, 181.

od. Some preferences . . . are basic. That is, preferences do not always rest upon other judgments about the quantity of some homogeneous mental state found in, or produced by, each option. When, in these cases, one speaks of one thing's yielding greater satisfaction than another, this seems best understood as saying that having the first is the fulfillment of a greater desire than having the second would be. One wants the first more than the second. But these desires are not ranked by independent quantities of satisfaction.[7]

Griffin is correct in pointing out that value does not reside in simple mental states whose quantity we compute to measure value. The mental states are complex, and the procedure to measure value does not consider quantity only. But Griffin is not presenting a defensible thesis when he argues for an actual-preference or -desire account, as he admits. Actual-desire accounts are those that base utility purely on people's expressed desires, without in any way evaluating those desires. It is strange indeed that he argues against a mental-state account from the position of an actual-desire account that he himself admits is indefensible. People may, in fact, "just rank options, period," but there is no reason to accept these actual preferences as indicating value when no reasons are offered in their support. Griffin himself says that "what must matter for utility will have to be, not persons' actual desires, but their desires in some way improved. The objection to the actual-desire account is overwhelming"(10), and thus he goes to a version of the informed-desire account in which people can give reasons for their preferences.

Griffin's objection to the simple hedonist theory does not touch Mill's version. The states of experience that are the bearers of value on his account are not simple pleasures but complex states in which the pleasurable component is merged with other elements and cannot be completely distinguished. But another objection, one given by Griffin and Robert Nozick, hits more broadly at mental-state accounts. This objection generally is that not all desirable things are mental states. States of the world, in Griffin's terminology, must enter in: "We do seem to desire things other than states of mind, even independently of the states of mind they produce"(9). Nozick makes this objection in *Anarchy, State and Utopia:*

> There are also substantial puzzles when we ask what matters other than how *people's* experiences feel "from the inside." Suppose there were an experience machine that would give you any experience you

[7]Griffin, *Well-Being,* 8.

desired. Superduper neuropsychologists could stimulate your brain so that you would think and feel you were writing a great novel, or making a friend, or reading an interesting book. All the time you would be floating in a tank, with electrodes attached to your brain. . . . Would you plug in? *What else can matter to us, other than how our lives feel from the inside? . . .*

What does matter to us in addition to our experiences? First, we want to *do* certain things, and not just have the experience of doing them. In the case of certain experiences, it is only because first we want to do the actions that we want the experiences of doing them or thinking we've done them. (But *why* do we want to do the activities rather than merely to experience them?) A second reason for not plugging in is that we want to *be* a certain way, to be a certain sort of person. Someone floating in a tank is an indeterminate blob.[8]

What Nozick is attacking is, in Griffin's terms, the mental-state advocate's "Experience Requirement," which holds that utility must "enter our experience"(13). Griffin, too, argues against this requirement:

The mental states involved in believing something that really is true and believing a successful deception are the same. Or if a father wants his children to be happy, what he wants, what is valuable to him, is a state of the world, not a state of his mind; merely to delude him into thinking that his children flourish, therefore, does not give him what he values.(13)

In *Philosophical Explanations*, Nozick develops a theory of intrinsic value and make a similar point from this vantage.

For a life to have meaning, it must connect with other things, with some things or values beyond itself. Meaning, and not merely of lives, seems to lie in such connections. To ask something's meaning is to ask how it is connected, perhaps in specified ways, to other things. Tracking, either of facts or of value, is a mode of being so connected, as is fitting an external purpose. The experience machine, though it may give you the experience of transcending limits, encloses you within the circle of just your own experiences. The phrase "the meaning you give to your life" refers to the ways you choose to transcend your limits, the particular package and pattern of external connections you successfully choose to exhibit.[9]

That this objection comes dressed in such a bizarre example is a hint that something is astray. It is easy to respond that, since in the

[8]Robert Nozick, *Anarchy, State and Utopia* (New York, 1974), 42–43.
[9]Robert Nozick, *Philosophical Explanation* (Cambridge, 1981), 594–95.

actual world people are not floating in tanks (Nozick's "experience machine") their entire lives, we need not worry about this objection. In fact, I argue that Nozick's example is inconsequential for just this reason, among others. Richard Hare argues that defenders of utilitarianism need not take as seriously as their opponents demand the sort of desert island examples that are thrown at them.[10] And tank-floater examples are much more improbable than desert island ones. Russell Hardin also complains about critics of utilitarianism who use peculiar hypothetical examples in attempts at refutation.[11] Although the tank-floater example is a logical possibility, it is not a practical possibility and thus need not concern a moral theory that is constructed for the actual world. There is, however, an interesting kernel in this objection which hits at simple quantitative hedonism though not at Mill's complex qualitative variety.

Nozick and Griffin deny that value resides only in human experience. We value not just satisfying experiences but doing or being certain things. Our experiences must track facts or values. Value is tied into an external reality, to certain states of the world. What matters is not just how things feel from the inside, but how they tie into or track reality. Very well, but as a bizarre counterexample to Nozick shows, what counts first and foremost is that value be rooted in internal experience and consciousness. If we need an outside world as well as an inside feel, we are absolutely nowhere without the inside feel, the grounding of value in consciousness. It is a weakness of desire-satisfaction versions that they cannot adequately account for the significance of value rooted in consciousness.

We can imagine a person living the most ideally valuable life in Nozick's terms. She seems to have it all, being a Harvard professor of neuropsychology as well as an accomplished cellist and winner of the Boston marathon. She has the most lovingly supportive husband and an (adopted) teenage daughter. Her life is filled with deep, loving, meaningful relationships. It is a tragedy when she dies unexpectedly. To everyone's astonishment, an autopsy reveals that she is not human at all but a robot. Her accomplishments are not the result of human agency but of an elaborate computer program. How

[10]R. M. Hare, *Moral Thinking: Its Levels, Method, and Point* (Oxford, 1981), 47–51; 131–42.

[11]Hardin says, "If we get a moral theory that is compelling for our own world, we should be delighted at the success and not worry whether it would be compelling in some fanciful alternative world;" *Morality within the Limits of Reason* (Chicago, 1988), 25.

does this affect our estimation of the value and meaning of her life? For some it is not at all obvious that robots lack consciousness, and they are quick to impute a charge of "robotism" (similar to racism, sexism, and speciesism) to those who value robots less than humans. They would not be perturbed by the example as it stands. But we can build in the assumption that robots do not have consciousness, for the salient point here is that the "accomplishments" have no base in agency and consciousness. Thus elaborated (and I think even without the elaboration), it is plausible to put the value of my character's life at zero, its meaning and authenticity at nothing. Without feeling and consciousness, there is no value, nothing desirable. We need the inside. Here we run into a parallel with criteria for moral personhood.

This example does not affirm that any inside, any experiences, will do as candidates for value. Qualitative hedonists insist that we make value discriminations among experiences. The experiences must be authentic, real ones, not hallucinations. Nozick's unsettling example is not based on an accurate description. It is not accurate to say that someone floating in a tank with electrodes stimulating her brain is experiencing writing a book or engaging in friendship. She is having a hallucinatory experience that she is writing a book. She is not having authentic experiences that accurately represent the external world. It is quite permissible for qualitative hedonists to take into account authenticity of experience when classifying kind, indeed it would make no sense not to, and to discount inauthentic or hallucinatory experiences as having little or no value. What is valuable about running the four-minute mile may be the satisfaction of running the four-minute mile. But we cannot have the authentic experience of running the four-minute mile unless we do in fact run the four-minute mile. If we are in fact floating in a tank, we may believe that we are running the four-minute mile and thus may place a high value on our experience—wrongly. We would be mistaken both about our experience (we are hallucinating running the four-minute mile) and about its value. A person observing us from the outside, knowing both the content of our hallucination and our actual situation, would know that we were deceived about both our experience and its value. In the real world, experience is not severed from external reality, and our experiences represent the interaction of human consciousness and agency with the external world.

Nozick's ingenious example may point out a theoretical vulnerability in simple quantitative hedonism, since such a theory does not have a means of distinguishing experiences on any basis other than quantity of satisfaction and thus is more pressed to explain why hallucinatory experiences are less valuable than the real thing. The cause of an experience does not enter into its evaluation. But complex qualitative hedonism does have the theoretical tools to single out and discount hallucinatory experiences. Satisfactions can be classified into kinds according to several principles, but at the very least we may systematize kinds of satisfaction according to the cause of the satisfactions (or their causal properties), faculty affected, and phenomenal features of the experience itself, including its intentional properties. Qualitative hedonists care about intentional and causal properties, and since Nozick's experiences are caused by electrode brain stimulation rather than by normal events in the external world we need look no farther for a reason to discount such hallucinatory satisfactions.

Nozick's example is striking, but it need not worry the complex qualitative hedonist. It should be emphasized, however, that even it if were not legitimate to classify kinds of experiences by causal properties and to isolate such hallucinatory experiences as having the peculiar cause of electrical stimulation this example would not pose a serious practical objection. It may in this case be unsettling theoretically, but even so the example is so far removed from reality that the complex qualitative hedonist need not be concerned. Since we must construct and defend moral theories for the world as we know it, the fact that our theory has uncomfortable consequences for tank floaters' worlds is insignificant.

Nozick's example is, to be sure, designed to do more than just point out the vulnerability of mental-state accounts for tank floaters. It is to show that we value things other than experiences. The argument can be transferred to the world as we know it and used to generate examples that are more familiar. Normally our experiences intersect with external reality and reflect the real world, so that if we experience writing a novel we are accomplishing this in reality. We may be assured that our experiences represent states of the world and our agency and actions in the world. Since action and experience of action occur in tandem, we need to question whether the ground of value is a state of the world, a fact about the world, or human experience interacting with states of the world; we need to know which is theoretically more basic.

Griffin gives some examples which he claims show that some

values are not consistent with the experience requirement; that is, he argues that value can be completely severed from experience, that it can reside entirely in states of the world:

> Suppose that someone is duped into thinking that those close to him are behaving authentically. What enters his experience is the same whether he has the real thing or a successful deceit. But it is only the real thing, he thinks, that makes his life better. According to the enjoyment account, what affects well-being can only be what enters experience, and the trouble is that some of the things that persons value greatly do not. My truly having close and authentic personal relations is not the kind of thing that can enter my experience; all that can enter is what is common to both my truly having such relations and my merely believing that I do. . . . And if I want to accomplish something, it is not necessary that I want my accomplishment to enter my experience—say that I know about it. . . . If either I could accomplish something with my life but not know it, or believe that I had but not really have, I should prefer the first.(19)

Griffin is arguing that welfare resides only in states of the world when he claims that accomplishment is valuable even if it does not enter experience. His two examples are from the everyday world, but they present somewhat different issues. We should look separately at cases of hallucination and deception, which present different challenges to the qualitative version of the mental-state account.

Griffin maintains that there is value in accomplishing something even if the agent does not know of the accomplishment. The mere accomplishment in itself, even though it does not enter experience, is worthwhile. This is a difficult claim to evaluate in the abstract, but Griffin is not particularly specific and detailed. The plausibility of this claim may well fade rapidly in the light of day and detail. It is not unknown to value accomplishment even though the achiever does not have knowledge of the feat, as when someone designs an experiment that leads to a new treatment for a disease but dies before realizing the value of the work. But in these cases, I maintain, it is the benefit to other people, the effect on their experience and welfare, that gives value to the accomplishment. It is more difficult to imagine a case of an accomplishment that impinges on no one's consciousness, that benefits no one in this way, and yet has value. It is possible to go the limit here and maintain that accomplishment in itself, even if no one's experience is affected, is of value, but I think this strains credibility. I would think that these examples are like examples of people striving mightily over trivial and inconsequential feats just to enter the *Guinness Book of World Records*. If the reply is that Griffin does not have in mind trivia but genuine accomplishment, then the rejoinder is that genuine accomplishments benefit somebody, that this benefit enters their experience, and that in this way their value is grounded. This benefit must reside in mental states, and thus must enter their experience, although knowledge of who is their benefactor need not also enter.

The qualitative hedonist can also downgrade or discount the value of feelings of satisfaction based on self-deception. It is difficult to generate a set of principles to govern value assignment, because the range of cases and relevant considerations is wide. But it is surely important whether a sense of satisfaction is based on deception or self-deception, and many cases of successful deception also involve self-deception to some degree. At one end of the range of examples is the drug abuser who convinces herself that she is writing the world's great novel when in fact her pen produces trash. Her satisfaction actually springs from an impairment of valuable human faculties which must be detrimental to many of her other life pursuits. Quite different is the case of one who genuinely strives to to write poetry but deceives himself into believing that it is brilliant when it is just good or even mediocre. This person is exercising and developing natural talents to their fullest potential, and the sense of achievement is in some measure deserved. What these sketchy examples show is that our principles of evaluation discredit self-deception but credit effort as well as genuine merit. The list of reasons competent agents can give for their value choices is open ended, but many if not most refer to effects on human abilities and talents.

Being taken in by others' deception is a different case again. I believe that Griffin's examples again show power by hiding detail. It is difficult to imagine cases of feeling deeply loved when one in fact is not loved at all, when this occurs over a long period of time with no self-deception whatsoever. If a realistic and detailed example were to be provided, it would become clear that self-deception was involved to some extent, that it was a case of not wanting to face the facts and reality of not being loved. The fact that one is not loved does not enter experience because the agent uses denial and blocks the fact from entering, and this surely affects our evaluation. A qualitative hedonist has the resources to take into account that a satisfaction is grounded in deception and self-deception and hence

to value it less. Although the agent may put a falsely high value on
the experience, such an evaluation would be defective, distorted, and
incorrect. One with fuller knowledge would be in a position to correct and downgrade it.

I have argued that the plausibility of Mill's mental-state version
meets the counterexamples and objections of Griffin and Nozick.
The examples discussed have been designed to reveal the methodology of giving reasons for our value choices, reasons that refer to
causal, intentional, and phenomenal properties of the experiences
and the relation and effect of such experiences on human faculties
and abilities.

The superiority of qualitative hedonism over the quantitative alternative lies partly in its ability to discriminate among numerous
experiences and rank them on the basis of their differences, even as
it is recognized that it is only experiences that can be candidates for
value. Although Mill was concerned centrally to answer the objection that hedonism is "a doctrine worthy only of swine" and thus
rule out degrading satisfactions, the theory equally can downgrade
or rule out entirely inauthentic, hallucinatory, or self-deceptive experiences. I have argued that causal properties provide reasons for
these discriminations, but intentional and phenomenal properties
can also play a role. It can be such a reason that an experience is one
of creating a work of art rather than eating a doughnut. Intentional
properties may provide extra tools for discrimination, and thus a
response to Nozick's tank-floater examples, as I next suggest.

Rem Edwards gives a fine analysis of the role of intentional and
causal properties in a theory of qualitative hedonism. Intentional
pleasures and pains have objects, that is, "those nonaffective properties of experience from which they are inseparable."[12] Edwards explains that we need to keep separate causes and intentional objects
of mental experiences: "The source of a pleasure is its cause. . . .
Usually there is a close relation between source and intentional
object, but they are logically distinct and often actually separated. In
speaking causal language we are talking about the actualities of the
real world, whereas intentional objects involve phenomenology
alone" (91–92). Edwards elucidates the role of intentional properties
of pleasurable experiences in characterizing qualitative hedonism,
but he lets an important opportunity slip by. According to Edwards,

[12]Edwards, *Pleasures and Pains*, 87–88.

it would have been a poor defense of qualitative hedonism to have argued that the real world is to be preferred to an electronically stimulated universe of experience because intentional pleasures are not available to us except through their normal *sources*, for the most that can be claimed for intentional pleasures is that they are not available to us except through their intentional *objects*, that is, those nonaffective properties of phenomenal experience from which they are experientially and conceptually inseparable. But intentional objects of pleasure don't have to *exist* in the real world, though often they do. If by electronic brain stimulation, the phenomenal taste of peppermint ice cream could be richly reproduced, then we would not need to eat real peppermint ice cream to experience just that form of enjoyment. The same thing is true in principle of all other intentional pleasures (or pains). Normally, however, the most efficient way to experience these forms of enjoyment is to stay in touch with the real world. (92)

Edwards gives up this point too easily, for he too offhandedly assumes that intentional properties of mental experiences must be entirely internal to the experience; that is, he assumes a position of individualism in the current debate in the philosophy of mind (a different sense of "individualism" than that used in ethical theory and political philosophy). The intricacies of this debate range far beyond the confines of the questions I pursue, but I suggest that it may well be the case that intentional properties of mental experiences could provide yet another defense against Nozick's example.[13]

Tyler Burge also argues against individualism in philosophy of mind and theory of reference.[14] The way that mental contents—beliefs, desires, intentions, hopes—are individuated also provides the basis for their classification into kinds. This general procedure for kind classification can be used in the case of pleasurable mental experiences as one of the bases of value measurement. This principle applies to the intentional elements of a thought as well as to the thought as a whole. The view Burge squares off against is internalist, according to which

the specifically mental features of the propositional attitude can . . . be understood purely in *individualistic* terms—in terms of the subject's internal acts and skills, his internal causal and functional relations, his surface stimulations, his behaviour and behavioural dis-

---

[13]In fact, Nozick himself suggests one of the lines of argument, built on this point, that could counteract his example (*Philosophical Explanation*, 168, 168n).
[14]Tyler Burge, "Other Bodies," in *Thought and Object*, ed. Andrew Woodfield (Oxford, 1982), 97–120.

positions, and his qualitative experiences, all non-intentionally characterized and specified without regard to the nature of his social or
physical environment.(98)[15]

Burge thinks, on the contrary, that there is a "complex relation
between a person's mental states and his environment. . . . identifying a person's mental states depends on the nature of his physical
environment—or on specification, by his fellows, of the nature of
that environment" (98). He argues that the content of mental states
crucially depends on the physical and social environment—that
"what attitudes a person has, what mental events and states occur in
him, depends on the character of his physical and social environment (117). Such mental events as beliefs, desires, and intentions are
partly identified and determined by external facts and relations, including social facts and relations.[16] The physical environment,
whether the world as we know it or merely a tank or vat, goes a long
way in determining this content. The content varies as the environment changes, so the content of an authentic experience of writing a
book is different from the content of a hallucinatory experience of
writing a book. This difference in content can be seen as the basis for
differing valuations of the experiences. The two are not equally valuable—far from it.

The debate is complex, far reaching, and controversial. All I can do
here is suggest that, if Burge is correct, another way of countering
Nozick's example emerges. If we accept Burge's approach, then Edwards is wrong in identifying the experience of eating ice cream
with the hallucinatory experience of eating ice cream. The contents
of these experiences cannot be individuated by internal properties
alone; note must be taken of the external environment. These are
differents kinds of experience, in terms of both their contents and
their value. Edwards adopts an individualistic perspective on this
question which may not hold up.

[15]It should be noted that Burge uses "qualitative" in a different (and narrower) sense
than I have been using it. "Qualitative" here has to do with the "feel" of an experience, and nothing more. I have been using "qualitative" to mean kind, where kinds
can be classified by feel but can also be classified in other ways.

[16]See also Donald Davidson, "Knowing One's Own Mind," Presidential Address,
Proceedings and Addresses of the American Philosophical Association 60 (January
1987):441–58.

DESIRE-SATISFACTION ACCOUNTS

The satisfaction of desires in twentieth-century preference accounts is usually not interpreted in terms of internal experiences like intensely felt pulls toward or pushes away from objects of desires. This was the usual interpretation in nineteenth-century accounts, but this way of looking at it has been given up in contemporary forms of this model, because otherwise the contemporary model then reduces to or collapses into an internal-state account. John Stuart Mill, Bentham, and James Mill all reduce desires to mental states of pleasures. It is to avoid the problems thought to be facing mental-state accounts that contemporary desire-satisfaction accounts of utility were developed. Utility is thus defined via preferences, rather than preferences being used as indicators of utility. Want or desire satisfaction is interpreted propositionally, or in terms of behavior. As Sumner puts it, "wanting the inflation rate to decline is wanting the proposition 'The inflation rate declines' to be true. A want is satisfied when the corresponding proposition is true."[17]

Objections to the desire-satisfaction account have been well argued by Sumner, Brandt, and others. One set of objections quarrels with the rather loose fit between the satisfaction of our desires or wants and the enhancement of our welfare, interests, or utility. It seems all too easy to imagine cases in which desires are satisfied and yet the agent is clearly harmed, or at least not better off; we can be mistaken about what promotes our interests. Moreover, these examples are common and realistic, in contrast to the rather exotic examples on which objections to mental-state accounts so often rely. Sumner, a philosopher in the mental-state camp, holds that, "if something enhances my welfare, it must, directly or indirectly, immediately or in the long run, either produce states of mind I find agreeable or prevent states of mind I find disagreeable" (184). He puts the problem with the desire-satisfaction account succinctly: "Although the desire model now furnishes the orthodox view, it is hopeless as an analysis of interest or welfare. Having a want satisfied is neither necessary nor sufficient for having one's interest furthered" (182).

[17]Sumner, *Abortion*, 180.

That having a want satisfied is not a necessary condition of having interest furthered is illustrated by accidental or unanticipated enjoyments. We can find many things agreeable quite unexpectedly; there are pleasant surprises. I have already indicated why it is argued that having a want satisfied is not a sufficient condition. Brandt also advances this line of argument:

> . . . what we seem to care about securing for other persons . . . is their happiness; and we seem to care about getting them what they want . . . only to the extent we think that so doing will bring them happiness or avoid distress and depression. . . . what we are sympathetically motivated to secure for others is happiness and freedom from distress (although we may want desire-satisfaction because we believe it a means to these).[18]

The problem with the desire-satisfaction account is that the satisfaction of any particular desire is no guarantee that our welfare will be enhanced. Furthermore, we are concerned about satisfying desires because we believe that in fact this is the way to enhance happiness. The conditions for satisfying a desire are often met and yet the desirer is frustrated, unsatisfied, or unhappy. In this unfortunately common situation, the desire-satisfaction account forces us to say that the desirer's welfare is increased, yet this is clearly wrong. This is the fatal flaw in the desire-satisfaction account. It is ironic indeed that economic theories of consumer choice use the desire-satisfaction model of utility and the principle of consumer sovereignty, and yet the satisfaction of consumer desires leads not to happiness but to a continuous cycle of frustration in which new desires are created, only to lead to more frustration.

This problem with desire-satisfaction accounts is easily recognized and has resulted in a move away from actual-desire accounts among adherents of state-of-the-world perspectives. A more sophisticated model is advanced. As Griffin says, "notoriously, we mistake our own interests. It is depressingly common that when even some of our strongest and most central desires are fulfilled, we are no better, even worse, off. . . . what must matter for utility will have to be, not persons' actual desires, but their desires in some way improved."[19] We must opt for the informed-desire account, according

[18]Brandt, *Good and Right,* 248–49.
[19]Griffin, *Well-Being,* 10.

to Griffin. But he also points to what seem to be powerful objections to such refined accounts. The desires that these theories are to count must be informed, but they must be actual as well, and equilibrating these two elements can be as frustrating and elusive as trying to fit actual desire satisfaction to enhancement of utility. It seems that the only way to ensure a perfect fit between desire satisfaction, actual or informed, and enhancement of welfare is purely ad hoc. We must specify that agents have enough information to ensure that satisfaction of their desires in fact makes them happy. As Sumner points out, "disappointment or harm is possible even under ideal conditions, where all that remains concealed from me is the fact that I will detest the object of my pursuit once I have attained it. To require *that* information to be included is simply to trim the desire model so that it coincides with the experience model."[20] It is difficult to see how this ruinous objection can be met convincingly by desire-satisfaction accounts, and this too highlights the superior plausibility of Mill's experience account.

Brandt's chief reason for rejecting the desire account leads us in a somewhat different direction. Brandt's problem is with understanding how we are to maximize satisfaction of desires over the course of a life, in view of the fact that desires change. He does not think that a workable plan to maximize want satisfaction is plausible on this model:

> Nevertheless we shall see that the desire theory of welfare becomes elusive when we raise the question which programme of action would maximize the desire-satisfactions of an individual (or collection of individuals) over a lifetime. . . .
>
> . . . What, then, is the programme of desire-satisfaction maximization to be, if different from happiness-maximization? As far as I know, no proposal has been put forward by advocates of the desire theory which tells us in principle, and generally, how to decide which of two possible courses of action would produce more desire-satisfaction, even if we can predict the impact of the events on the individual, and how long and how intensely each of the several outcomes has been or will be desired. I have the temerity to suggest that the whole concept is unintelligible.[21]

The desire-satisfaction model thus is up against two objections that cut deep. One is the loose fit between desire satisfaction and

[20]Sumner, *Abortion*, 182–83.
[21]Brandt, *Good and Right*, 247, 250–51.

promotion of welfare, a fit that can be adjusted only by ad hoc stipulations of amount of information. The second is the difficulty of setting out a program for promoting someone's welfare over an entire lifetime, given that desires change over a lifetime. This problem does not bear on Mill's mental-state theory, since even if the things we get happiness from change over our lives there is still in principle a method for comparing the happiness we would derive from pursuing different paths in life. Mill's complex qualitative hedonism thus acquits itself well when pitted against the other contenders.

4

The Sensory Evaluation
of Wines

Mill's inclusion of quality as a good-making characteristic of pleasurable experiences and his procedure for measuring the value of pleasurable experiences make his theory more complex than Bentham's. Bentham is interested only in the quantity (intensity and duration) of pleasures in this context. Not only does he regard intensity and duration as simple properties of pleasurable experiences, but in his dominant account the method of measurement is relatively simple and straightforward (though not without serious weaknesses). Although the use of the preferences of competent agents is implicit in many of Mill's writings, he does not set out his measurement procedure precisely in one place, as does Bentham. So we need some help in explicating Mill. A fruitful way to go about doing this is to set out an analogy between Mill's views on the good-making characteristics of pleasurable experiences and the measurement of their value, and the sensory evaluation of wines. These two procedures are structurally similar, and a thorough and perceptive account of the aesthetic evaluation of wines is available in the work of enologists Maynard A. Amerine and Edward B. Roessler.[1]

Amerine and Roessler discuss what they call the sensory evaluation of wines, but their discussion provides both an account of the

---

[1]Maynard A. Amerine and Edward B. Roessler, *Wines: Their Sensory Evaluation* (San Francisco, 1976).

aesthetic value of wines and a procedure for evaluating it. As might be expected, they regard fine wines as works of art with great aesthetic value. They do not maintain that the aesthetic value of wine is identified with any of its phenomenal characteristics. Often they speak about the chemical composition of the wine, which has some relation to its phenomenal characteristics. Such a way of speaking can be troublesome because the relationship between the chemical composition and the phenomenal characteristics is difficult to specify. Chemical properties and phenomenal characteristics are not interchangeable, and talk about chemical composition is unnecessary. Thus it is best to disregard it, because the explication of value measurement is put forth in terms of phenomenal characteristics. If Amerine and Roessler were to claim that the aesthetic value of wine was identical with any of its phenomenal characteristics, they would be maintaining naturalism. They are not. What they do say is that the value of wine is dependent on its possession of certain specifiable phenomenal properties. Their view is similar to C. D. Broad's argument that goodness is related to the possession of good-making characteristics by the object being evaluated.[2]

The first element in the account of the value of wines is their possession of certain phenomenal characteristics that are like Broad's good-making characteristics. Amerine and Roessler classify the relevant phenomenal characteristics under the headings of the senses that perceive them—sight, smell, taste, touch, pain, and temperature. The relevant visual attributes of wine are color and appearance. The appropriate color varies with the type of wine. In appearance, clarity or freedom from suspended material is judged. The most important sense in wine appreciation is smell, and over one thousand different odors can be identified by wine experts. Three types of odors are important: aroma, bouquet, and foreign and undesirable. Aroma is the "gamut of wine odors derived from the grape itself." Bouquet consists of "those [odors] derived from fermentation, processing, or aging." The presence of foreign or undesirable odors clearly diminishes the value of a wine (19–31).

Taste is considered to be less important than odor, and the only pertinent tastes are sweetness, sourness, and bitterness. Sweetness is due primarily to the reducing sugars, glucose and fructose, and to

[2]C. D. Broad, "Certain Features in Moore's Ethical Doctrines," in *The Philosophy of G. E. Moore*, ed. Paul Arthur Schlipp (Lasalle, Ill., 1968), 60.

a lesser extent to glycerol and ethanol. Sourness is "the tart taste of wines. . . . the acid taste in the mouth." Bitterness is difficult for inexperienced judges to identify and evaluate and is often confused with astringency, which is a tactile sensation. Under the heading of touch the authors discuss astringency, thinness, and fullness. Astringency is a puckery feel in the mouth; viscosity is due primarily to ethanol. The sensation of pain also enters into judgments of wine; it results from overstimulation of sensory receptors, usually because of acidity. Finally, temperature is important both for the sensations of warmth and coldness themselves and for their effects on the other senses (40–45).

These different types of phenomenal properties must be present if a wine is to be judged a fine wine, a wine possessing great aesthetic value. But clearly not just any color, or degree of sweetness, or type of bouquet suffices to produce a wine of great value. To pick out the phenomenal characteristics possessed by wines of great value and not possessed, or possessed in a different degree or in a different balance with other phenomenal characteristics, by ordinary or inferior wines, we require a set of interpersonal standards of taste. In particular, we require a different set of standards for good wines of different types; wines from different districts, or of different kinds, may differ significantly in their good-making characteristics. As well, we can develop an overall standard that picks out good wines of all different types, although comparisons and rankings among these are difficult.

The crucial point is that, although wine's aesthetic value has a basis in phenomenal properties, which form an objective empirical foundation for the measure of value, these properties do not themselves constitute and are not identical with the value. This is clear in the case of color. Amerine and Roessler claim that the appreciation of color is a learned response. The fact that a wine from a particular area in France has a particular color does not in itself enhance the value. We must first know whether that color is appropriate for that type of wine. And so a set of standards, learned through a process of training and cultivation, is also necessary:

> Our first reaction to an aesthetic object such as wine is apt to be purely subjective: we like it or dislike it. For a more lasting judgment however, we apply certain objective criteria, consciously or unconsciously. These may enhance our enjoyment of the wine or confirm

our aversion to it. As we gain experience with a certain type of wine
we may reverse our original judgment. . . . This is a part of the learning process that everyone undergoes in arriving at personal standards
for evaluating the quality of any aesthetic object.(5)

Amerine and Roessler are especially firm in their view of the role
of the professional wine judge. The task of wine judges is to

> evaluate the sensory quality of wines *according to some agreed-
> upon standards*. Generally their personal preferences in wines do not
> come into play or are consciously ignored. This is why it is vital for
> the judges to have common, fixed standards for each type of wine. To
> achieve such standards a great deal of experience with the types of
> wines they are called upon to judge is absolutely essential. A profes-
> sional judge may not like sweet table wines but can still be a good,
> dispassionate judge of their quality if he has sufficient experience with
> them. (10)[3]

Thus there are two elements in the explication of the value of
wines: the phenomenal, good-making characteristics, and a set of
standards applied by trained judges to pick out these characteristics.
The relation between these two elements merits further consideration, for the role of the standards can be conceptualized in very
different ways. It is possible, for example, to conceive of the standards as playing a very weak or trivial role, as merely indicating or
pointing out all the good-making characteristics of the wine. The
strength of the standards can vary from this, through intermediate
stages, to a stage at which they are so strong that they are actually
used to *decide* which properties of the wine are its good-making
ones. Neither the phenomenal characteristics of the wine nor the
standards used to judge them can rest on their own merits, for,
though the phenomenal properties can affect the standards, the standards themselves can change and by this change can affect which
properties of the wine are considered good-making. The relationship

[3]The general emphasis on the necessity of standards is repeated throughout the
book. Here is one example: "Our enjoyment of wine is thus essentially a learned
response and is a complex mixture of intellectual and sensory pleasures. In addition,
it has overtones of sensual pleasure and is obviously related to social customs. Our
appreciation of wine is to a major extent subject to sensory skills and aesthetic
principles that depend on experience. Individual preferences are, of course, important; to the individual they are all-important. All we can do is postulate that they
have some rational basis and hope that some general principles may eventually
emerge for each individual" (5).

between the two elements is dynamic. Amerine and Roessler seem to believe that the standards are "out there" waiting to be discovered, which explains why they do not believe that the standards should change very much.

Standards do, however, change to some extent, and even in some cases where they do not there is room to ask whether they should. In the nineteenth century, for example, standards of wine evaluation tolerated "high volatile acidity, . . . cloudiness, darkening of the color of white wines, brownish-red colors in red wines, or relatively low ethanol content" (8). These properties are not tolerated in contemporary standards. Besides the fact that standards change, in some cases wine experts disagree about standards:

> How much woody odor . . . can be tolerated in a white table wine? Almost all enologists would agree that a conspicuously woody odor in a white table wine is undesirable, even intolerable. Most enologists would also agree that at very low concentrations . . . a non-recognizable woody odor may contribute to the complexity of the wine and thus be a positive quality factor. In between, enologists disagree. (31)

In still other cases, there is room to question the basis of the standards. In the case of temperature, for instance, the standard for optimum taste and odor is not unchallengeable. It may well be that our preferences for chilled white wines and warmer red wines are conditioned responses; on the other hand, there may be reasons for these preferences. But we do not know why these standards have been developed (45–46).

The general picture is clear enough. The standards do not have unchallengeable authority; not only have they changed over time, but in some cases experts disagree about specific characteristics. There is a dynamic relationship between the good-making phenomenal properties of wine and the standards used to pick them out. The standards are based on actual phenomenal characteristics, but they also have a life of their own and can and do change over time, effectively changing those good-making characteristics. Consequently, wines with the new characteristics are produced, while wines with undesirable characteristics are not. Presumably, to a certain extent these new desirable properties in turn reinforce the new standards that produced them. Although actual properties of the wines are the basis of the standards, these standards selectively pick out those properties that are deemed desirable. These interpersonal standards for evaluating wines are central to the process of measurement of their value.

Thus an understanding of the training judges undergo is crucial. Training judges consists of providing them with a set of interpersonal standards for evaluating wines. The training influences what the judge finds in the wine. The properties in virtue of which the wine is deemed a fine wine were always there, but an untrained judge either did not recognize them or did not acknowledge them as contributing to value, that is, did not appreciate them. Training teaches discernment, appreciation, and critical awareness. A judge learns to discern the difference between aroma and bouquet, but also the differences among many aromas and bouquets. And the judge learns to appreciate certain aromas more than others, or to appreciate the balance between a certain aroma and a certain level of sweetness and the appropriateness of these to a particular type of wine. All these discernments and appreciations emerge with training. Amerine and Roessler describe what is involved in this training process:

> The overwhelming majority [of people] have all the physical equipment we need to become excellent judges of wine quality. . . .
>
> The serious amateur wine judge usually wishes to improve his judging ability, but how does he go about it? Obviously, he practices. His main problem is finding a fixed frame of reference for each of the major odor and taste components of wines. What, for example, is low or high sourness?
>
> . . . For each specific sensory characteristic, one must also know the level of intensity that is appropriate in the wine in question, and one must be able to recognize the proper balance among the various sensory characteristics. Experience is what really counts. (12, 170–71)

This recognition of the centrality of interpersonal standards and of a training process designed to teach those standards leaves open the question whether judges are trained to accept standards uncritically or merely to accept them as a starting point for expertise. With the latter position, judges are trained not only to be discerning and appreciative but also to be critical. This critical capacity can then be used to change and improve the standards and thus to expand the limits of the art of wine evaluation. It is clear that Amerine and Roessler do not accept this latter position. Although they note that standards do change, their conception of training militates against developing critical judges. Their training procedure is designed to produce judges who accept the standards as they are. They suggest that wine-judging sessions be preceded by qualifying trials to eliminate judges who are "off," and that judges whose evaluations are found to deviate from those of others be eliminated from future trials. They suggest eliminating both judges who are not competent at discerning properties of wines, for example, different levels of sweetness, and judges whose evaluations are anomalous with regard to the application of accepted standards, for example those who judge that a certain level of sweetness is appropriate for a certain kind of wine when that level is not the accepted level. With this view of training and with these procedures for wine-evaluation sessions, the wonder is that Amerine and Roessler expect standards to change at all. Their emphasis is clearly on training to accept the status quo, the prevailing standards. Deviation and innovation are discouraged.

Finally, Amerine and Roessler recognize an overall value judgment that is separate from all the other judgments: "Apparently the sensory reactions together mediate a combined response, which we call general quality. This requires experience. . . . General quality is a separate and distinctive factor. . . . it is the memorableness of the character of the wine" (71).[4]

Let us summarize the salient points of Amerine and Roessler's account. They claim that the value of wine is dependent on its possession of certain specifiable good-making characteristics. But also central to their account is the notion of a set of interpersonal standards that pick out these phenomenal characteristics. There is a

[4]One point should be noted. Throughout the book the authors maintain that their goal is to reduce the quality of wines to quantitative terms. How, then, can I argue that their theory is analogous to Mill's, which is not reductionist? The answer is that the authors are talking about a different kind of procedure; in fact, what they mean by quality (of wines) is different from what I mean by quality. It is clear from their discussion that in talking about quality they are actually referring to what Mill means by value (see, e.g., 6). Their theory does not conform to the quantity/quality classification I have set out for Mill. Instead, when they speak of quality, they mean any one of these good-making characteristics. According to them, quantity plays a small role in terms of Mill's schema, whereas quality has many subcomponents. They also want to be able to quantify all the different phenomenal properties that they set out. Although in light of my discussion of Bentham's attempts at quantification this seems like an unrealistic goal, still Mill might want to do the same thing with quality of pleasures, namely, to quantify it, if that were realistic. The important point is that Amerine and Roessler are not talking about reducing quality in the strong (Sosa/Bronaugh) sense.

dynamic relation between these two elements: the standards pick out the good-making characteristics, but they can also change, thus changing the good-making characteristics. It is also possible that those characteristics considered as desirable can change, in turn changing the standards. The training of expert wine judges consists of providing these potential experts with this set of standards and training them to apply the standards to discern and appreciate the appropriate phenomenal characteristics. Finally, this training is designed to preserve the status quo; students are trained to be uncritical of prevailing standards and to adopt them as is.

The analogy with Mill's view is strong, with some notable exceptions. Mill maintains that pleasurable experiences are valuable in virtue of their possession of certain good-making characteristics, quantity (intensity and duration) and quality (kind). He does not claim that the value of such experiences is identical with these characteristics, nor that the possession of these characteristics logically entails possession of value. The connection is contingent. A close statement of Mill's position is that advanced by Broad in his discussion of G. E. Moore; Broad interprets Moore as holding that goodness is dependent on the possession by the object in question of good-making characteristics.[5]

Mill also maintains that there must be a set of interpersonal standards that are developed through a training process and allow the judge to discover and appreciate the good-making characteristics of pleasurable experience. These standards teach discrimination among different pleasurable experiences and different aspects of pleasurable experiences as well as appreciation of certain experiences above others. As with wine, development influences what the judge finds in the experience, for the properties were always there but the judge did not recognize them or did not acknowledge them

---

[5]Broad is here discussing Moore's theory of intrinsic value. Although I assume that Bentham and Mill have a theory of intrinsic value, I do not enter into the controversy over the question of whether they do. Despite the fact that Broad's discussion is in this context, it is still useful for my purposes. He says: "If an experience is good (or if it is bad), this is never an ultimate fact. It is always reasonable to ask: 'What *makes* it good?' or 'What *makes* it bad?' as the case may be. And the sort of answer we should expect to get is that it is made good by its pleasantness, or by the fact that it is a sorrowfully toned awareness of another's distress, or by some other such non-ethical characteristic of it;" "Moore's Ethical Doctrines," 60. Broad also holds that the connection between the possession of good-making characteristics by the object and its being good is contingent, although for different reasons.

as contributing to value. In Mill's view, the standards play a stronger role than in that of Amerine and Roessler; Mill's standards are to be applied by people who are the linchpins of the theory. According to Mill, the standards are not "out there" in the universe but rather depend ultimately on the potential of human nature. Qualified judges may be mistaken about human potential; in turn, their value choices may be mistaken. Qualified judges are the best judges of what has value—they have the best chance of getting it right—but the final arbiter is human nature and the judges' choices indicate rather than determine value. The sense in which these judges are linchpins and the process by which they become so are matters dealt with in Mill's doctrine of development and self-development— Mill's doctrine that holds that agents are trained to be critical and progressive in a way not allowed by Amerine and Roessler.

This brief sketch prepares the ground for a full account of the process by which agents are trained to be judges of the value of pleasurable experiences—a process that preserves the objectivity of the theory. The situation of an educated wine judge faced with a choice between a small quantity of a truly fine wine and a large quantity of ordinary wine is strongly analogous to the situation posed by Mill in *Utilitarianism:*

> Of two pleasures . . . if one of the two is, by those who are competently acquainted with both, placed so far above the other that they prefer it, even though knowing it to be attended with a greater amount of discontent, and would not resign it for any quantity of the other pleasure which their nature is capable of, we are justified in ascribing to the preferred enjoyment a superiority in quality, so far outweighing quantity as to render it, in comparison, of small account. (10:211)

5

The Doctrine of Development

Mill's doctrine of development is a key to many of the complexities arising from his inclusion of quality in the measurement of value of states of happiness or pleasure. We have seen that Bentham provides a method of measurement of such value in his felicific calculus; Mill also provides a procedure for determining value, albeit a radically different one. This procedure consists of eliciting the preferences of a certain kind of judge. If judges who are competently acquainted with two enjoyments decidedly prefer one or judge it to be more valuable, then that enjoyment, in Mill's view, should be taken to be more valuable. The notion of competent acquaintance is, however, intricate; a competent judge is developed in certain ways, ways that are discussed at great length throughout a wide range of Mill's writings. I devote this chapter to an investigation of Mill's doctrine of development—his views on the first stage of the education of competent agents. In the normal course of the process, development transforms into self-development at the threshold of adulthood, and in Chapter 6 I take up this subsequent stage. Mill's method of measurement specifies the kind of preferential ranking to be used and the kind of good-making characteristics to be taken into consideration. But, more fundamentally, it also specifies the kind of competent agents who are to do these rankings. These agents are developed intellectually, affectively, and morally. They resemble the rational agents at the core of many contemporary moral theories, with one notable difference: Mill's rational agents make their judgments and rankings from an impersonal, social vantage point rather than from an egoistic one. Here Mill's theory relies on conceptions of rationality as well as objectivity.

Mill stresses throughout his work the importance of education—the process by which individuals become developed and become competent judges of experiences. Thus my discussion of the doctrine of development must be selective. For my purposes here, development partly consists of the development of interpersonal standards for judging the value of happiness, standards analogous to those learned by potential wine experts. There is an analogy between the processes involved in learning to appreciate wine and happiness (see Chapter 4). As in the case of wine, these standards teach discrimination among different experiences, and among different aspects of pleasurable experiences, as well as appreciation of certain forms of happiness above others. Standards allow individuals to discover and appreciate certain good-making characteristics of happiness, among them their quality. As in the case of wine, development influences what the judge finds in the experience, for the properties were always there but the judge did not recognize them or acknowledge them as contributing to value. There are also differences from the case of wine evaluation; Mill's standards are much stronger than Amerine and Roessler's. The latter maintain that standards are "out there" in the world, waiting to be grasped by the initiates; Mill asserts that the question of what form of happiness is more valuable depends on human nature and on what educated agents judge. Thus people are crucial to Mill's system. Another difference is that Mill's judges are cultivated to be critical and thus have the ability to change and improve current standards. Mill claims that more valuable forms of happiness are those that would be sought by persons developed or cultivated in this manner.

The doctrine of development is about a process of education that is basic to all kinds of education, and an agent who undergoes it becomes the kind of highly developed being who is at the heart of Mill's concerns. Development not only brings about the goals of the art of education by nurturing maximally happy people, it also ensures that there are agents in a position to judge which experiences are worth pursuing and thus capable of formulating social goals and changing standards to promote societal well-being. Since they are in the best position to judge which pleasurable experiences have more value and so which will produce the most happiness, this development takes on added significance. It is not surprising, then, that Mill attaches a great deal of importance to the art of education.

In the *Logic* Mill brings forth the distinction between science and art, sketching the connection between the two and showing how the fruits of the moral scientific enterprise work with the practice of art. The province of science is the "course of nature." Science takes the facts of nature and, using inductive and deductive methods, discovers the laws that explain them and can be used to make predictions about them. Art comprises rules and precepts for practice, and its function is to define ends that are desirable and ought to be aimed at (8:949).

Every art has a corresponding science, and the two spheres are coupled via the linkages between the precepts of the art and the theorems of the science (8:943–44). Rules of art demand reasons or justifications—as compared with the rival intuitionist claim that at least some such rules are self-evident—and these reasons are the theorems of the science. Art has jurisdiction over decisions about what ought to be done, and it alone has the authority to articulate goals or purposes. Mill describes this affiliation:

> The art proposes to itself an end to be attained, defines the end, and hands it over to the science. The science receives it, considers it as a phenomenon or effect to be studied, and having investigated its causes and conditions, sends it back to art with a theorem of the combinations of circumstances by which it could be produced. Art then examines these combinations of circumstances, and according as any of them are or are not in human power, pronounces the end attainable or not. (8:944)

If art is satisfied that the means are feasible, the scientific theorem becomes a rule of practice. But although science has this significant role to play in ensuring that the chosen goals are realized, it must not in any way intrude on the selection of these goals, an activity that remains entirely in the realm of art. Each of the arts has a first principle, and grouped together these constitute the "art of life," which underlies all particular arts. In this teleological domain, the goals of all specific arts are ranked according to value. These goals can conflict with each other, and when they do "there must be some standard by which to determine the goodness or badness, absolute and comparative, of ends, or objects of desire." There must be a single standard to resolve those disputes among ends, for a multiplicity of ultimate standards would simply reduplicate the problem on a more basic level. The only alternative is intuitionism, which postulates a moral sense to decide not only the desirability of particular ends but also their order of precedence—an alternative Mill cannot accept. Mill's ultimate standard is the principle of utility, which underlies the whole structure of our practical reasoning and from which all subsidiary precepts of art must be deduced (949–51).

Education fits into this framework as one of the more important of the particular arts, with certain special bonds to morality; it corresponds to the pivotal science of ethology. Mill has a broad notion of education; by it he means the art of character formation. He thinks of education as a process of cultivation or development rather than simple schooling. Much of what he has in mind would today be called socialization. The related study of ethology is the science of character formation (869). Although he never got around to the comprehensive study of ethology he hoped to accomplish, many of the questions that interested Mill are examined by contemporary social psychologists and socialization theorists.

In Chapter 6 I discuss in more detail the structure and relations among the various moral arts and sciences and the shape of Mill's political philosophy of liberalism. Here it is sufficient to point out that in education art and science are brought together, for if we have done our scientific homework we understand at least the tendencies of the laws of association to have a certain effect in a given situation. The resulting scientific truths can be marshalled in the order useful for the practice of art. The laws of association explain how the elements of our mental life develop on the basis of the data we get through our senses, and how these elements are united to form our inner life. If our educational goal is to create specified qualities in people, and ultimately certain types of character, or to socialize people in particular ways, then we can apply these laws to character formation. Education and development essentially consist in creating the right associations, first to build the right mental states and then the right character. Understanding how the laws of association work, we can use their operation to accomplish goals we have previously formulated. Thus we must determine the traits of character that would produce the most utility if they were manifested by the members of a society. Mill says, "When the circumstances of an individual or of a nation are in any considerable degree under our control, we may, by our knowledge of tendencies, be enabled to shape those circumstances in a manner much more favourable to the ends we desire, than the shape which they would of themselves assume" (869–70).

Here again Mill's differences with intuitionism are highlighted. Mill thinks that many character differences can be explained by differences in life circumstances. Progressive reform is thus appropriate; humans are malleable and can be cultivated in many ways to be improved and happier. Intuitionists, on the other hand, assume that what are fixed are not the laws of psychology and character formation, as Mill holds, but certain features of human nature itself. Certain individual psychological differences are also firmly fixed, so there is little point in trying to change or eliminate these, or to eradicate the differences in social condition that are usually their result, if not their cause. If we believe that some aspects of mental life are innate and completely beyond the reach of development, then the degree of improvement to which reformists can aspire is reduced to that extent.[1] Mill does think that each individual has a natural endowment that must be discovered and developed, but this endowment is not fixed to the degree maintained by intuitionism. I take up this issue later in my discussion.

Since development is partly the development of interpersonal standards, it is natural to divide the discussion into the different kinds of development that produce these standards—affective, intellectual, and moral. Each kind of development has two distinct elements—what may be called the element of experience and the element of judgment. The element of experience is analogous to the process of gaining experience with wines by tasting a great many of them. This element in the evaluation of pleasures consists of gaining experience by developing our feelings, by becoming people who feel deeply, and in particular by becoming experienced in the kinds of pleasure in question. For this reason, affective development, the process through which we learn to feel, is deeper and more basic to development than the other kinds. Development of the feelings underlies the broadening of experience in all three kinds of development because the objects involved in these evaluations are mental states containing feeling. Therefore, the more of a feeling person we

[1] See F. W. Garforth, *John Stuart Mill's Theory of Education* (Oxford, 1979), 46–54.

are, the more feelings we have at our disposal, the larger is our stock of pleasures to enjoy, and the broader is our experience with these pleasures. But we also need specific experience with the particular type of pleasure involved in our evaluations.

In the element of judgment, standards are presented and the student learns to apply them to the objects in question. This part of the process is different in all three kinds of development.[2]

Affective Development

Mill makes it clear in the *Autobiography* that he regards affective development as the foundation of all types of development. He explains there that, even though he had intellectual training, he could not enjoy it because he was not taught to take deep pleasure in it. He realized that he would have to cultivate his feelings in order to enjoy the intellectual pursuits at which he was so skillful. At the height of his well-known mental crisis, he felt that "there seemed no power in nature sufficient to begin the formation of [his] character anew, and create in a mind now irretrievably analytic, fresh associations of pleasure with any of the objects of human desire" (1:143). His recovery was aided by nourishment of his feelings through poetry, so that he could again take pleasure in the things that had left him numb during his crisis.

Affective development enlarges the feelings and generally teaches students to respond emotionally to appropriate objects. Mill's own autobiographical experiences were that aesthetic experiences, and in particular encounters with the writings of the romantics, helped him to recover from his depression and revitalize his feelings; as a consequence he often uses responses to poetry to illustrate this form of development. But it does not have to be so, for many pursuits can train and enlarge the feelings. We must keep separate the form of affective development from particular examples for nurturing it that

[2]F. Parvin Sharpless says, "To Mill . . . culture suggests a broadening and expansion and development of human character along two lines. On the one hand, culture means intellectual culture, the expansion of the rational and analytic powers of the mind. . . . On the other hand, the term suggests a broadening and opening out of the feelings, an extension of the capacity for sympathy, and an ability to 'feel' and imagine the emotions of others;" *The Literary Criticism of John Stuart Mill* (The Hague; 1967), 183.

are often drawn from poetic and aesthetic cultivation in Mill's theory. But Mill does view affective development as also functioning to teach agents in particular to respond to that which is truly beautiful and so to evaluate aesthetic enjoyments competently.

Mill believes that there is an objective basis for the great value of aesthetic enjoyments, since the objects really are beautiful, and that taste must be built up in students through a development process that teaches them to appreciate these enjoyments. They gain experience or develop their feelings by reading poetry, and their judgment is trained by presenting appropriate standards in the form of good poetry. This poetry contains models of beauty that are the right ones to respond to, and in learning to respond to them the student assimilates the right standards. Besides being trained to enjoy aesthetic pleasures, the practical result of development is that the students identify with these models and are encouraged to produce beautiful objects of their own.

In the period preceding his mental crisis in 1826, Mill tells us, it would not have been untrue to describe him as "a mere reasoning machine" (1:111). The Benthamite radicals deprecated the cultivation of feeling and the value of poetry; they looked for improvement solely through the alteration of people's opinions. In spite of this doctrine, Mill personally was not immune to poetry's effect on development of feeling and was "very susceptible to some kinds of it" (1:115). He looks on this time as a period before he "enlarged in any considerable degree, the basis of [his] intellectual creed" (1:115). He fell into a depression when he realized that he would not be happy even if the main goal of his life, the improvements hoped for by the radicals, was accomplished. There have been various interpretations of this crisis, but the salient point is that Mill found himself unable to feel anything. He quotes Coleridge's lines from "Dejection, an Ode" as a description of his condition:

> A grief without a pang, void, dark and drear,
> A drowsy, stifled, unimpassioned grief,
> Which finds no natural outlet or relief
> In word, or sigh, or tear. (1:139)

Mill felt that the basis of his difficulty was that his education, designed and supervised by his father, had been very narrow, concentrating almost exclusively on forming intellectual associations and ignoring the use of the laws of association to cultivate feelings, except for the feeling of sympathy:

> My teachers had occupied themselves but superficially with the means of forming and keeping up these salutary associations. They seemed to have trusted altogether to the old familiar instruments, praise and blame, reward and punishment. . . . But there must always be something artificial and casual in associations thus produced. The pains and pleasures thus forcibly associated with things, are not connected with them by any natural tie. (1:141)

The result of this education, he believed, was that the emphasis on intellectual analysis wore away his feelings, leading him to a crisis from which he saw no escape.

He was rescued by poetry. The first sign of relief came while he was reading a passage of Marmontel's *Memoirs;* "A vivid conception of the scene and its feelings came over me, and I was moved to tears" (1:145). He realized that he was still capable of feeling, and with this awareness he was able gradually to pull himself out of his depression. Now, "for the first time, [he] gave its proper place, among the prime necessities of human well-being, to the internal culture of the individual. . . . [He] ceased to attach almost exclusive importance to the ordering of outward circumstances, and the training of the human being for speculation and for action" (1:147). The development of feeling as well as thought became central to his philosophy, and he searched out means of furthering this development. He soon observed the power of poetry for nurturing feeling. His reading of Wordsworth in 1828 supplied just what he needed at that time, "a source of inward joy, of sympathetic and imaginative pleasure, which could be shared in by all human beings" (1:151). His impression that poetic cultivation could always be relied on to counterbalance intellectual analysis was reaffirmed. Mill found Wordsworth's use of natural rural scenery ideal for his needs, since he derived great pleasure from this kind of beauty. It was not the use of scenes of nature in themselves that was most valuable, but the fact that "they expressed, not mere outward beauty, but states of feeling, and of thought coloured by feeling, under the excitement of beauty" (1:151).

Mill never relinquished his belief in the power of poetry to develop feeling. In the 1820s, as later, he recognized three distinct purposes of poetic development. Emphasized in the *Autobiography* is its power of correcting overintellectualization, of nurturing a balanced or whole person who can function harmoniously. Also mentioned is the value of poetry in the development of feeling, which is the basis of all three kinds of cultivation. Poetry develops feeling, and without feeling we cannot take deep pleasure in anything. Finally, it provides the individual with a set of standards for judging the value of poetry and acquaints the individual with the pleasures of poetry.

In the *Autobiography* Mill gives us a picture of the actual workings of the process of poetic development in himself; in other places he gives us a more general description. In his description of the effect of Wordsworth's use of natural scenery, we see how imaginative representations of the beautiful can serve to evoke reverberative emotions in the reader, at the same time allowing her to perceive and appreciate these more valuable pleasures. By presenting good examples of poetry, we provide the student with a set of standards.[3]

Mill's first systematic treatment of the theory of poetry is his article "Thoughts on Poetry and Its Varieties" (1:341–65), which places him squarely in the middle of the romantic movement in

---

[3]An early aberration from Mill's typical views should be noted. This trend is found in his early letters to Carlyle, in which he presents an overly exalted view of the powers of the poet, a view he soon abandons for a more moderate vision of the poet's capacity. In this early tendency, Mill regards the poet as a prophet or seer, one who sees the highest truths intuitively, truths that are not recognized at all by many and only faintly by others. In a letter to Carlyle in 1833, Mill states, "I conceive that most of the highest truths are, to persons endowed by nature, in certain ways . . . intuitive; that is, they need neither explanation nor proof, but if not known before, are assented to as soon as stated. Now it appears to me that the poet or artist is conversant chiefly with *such* truths and that his office in respect to truth is to declare *them*, and to make them *impressive*" (12:163). This is a common theme in letters of this period; see Mill to Carlyle, 12:113; Mill to Carlyle, 12:173; Mill to Robert Barclay Fox, 13:469. This tendency is deviant in two ways. The later Mill does not regard the poet as the wise person, but rather simply as one who can convey certain truths and feelings convincingly and impressively. See Mill's 1854 diary entry in Mill, *Mill's Essays on Literature and Society*, ed. J. B. Schneewind, (New York, 1965), 351–52. John Robson says of this transition in Mill's views, "As expressed in the early 1830's, it involved the belief that the poet is one who speaks *truth*, who deals in *realities*; later Mill was to be more chary of such Carlyleanisms, but the poet remained for him the one who represents a scene and characters so representative of valid human feelings as to be morally didactive to all his readers. He teaches men to share the feelings of others, and only on such empathy can genuine and enduring morality rest"; *The Improvement of Mankind*, (Toronto, 1968), 119–20. As well, the early Mill has a different view of the process of poetic cultivation, one in which only those readers who are also poets are affected directly by the poet's words; the majority of people need a translator (called the scientist or logician) to put the poetry in such language as allows them to understand and appreciate it. This opinion is far removed from the view Mill was to maintain later, that poetry acts on the emotions directly.

aesthetics.[4] This movement is well known for the widely differing theories it embraces, but similarities on various points connect Mill's views and those of other romantics such as Shelley, Coleridge, and Wordsworth.[5] The first question Mill asks himself is, what is

[4]This article first appeared as two separate articles in the *Monthly Repository,* January and October, 1833. It was edited into its later form for *Dissertations and Discussions,* first published in 1859.

[5]See, e.g., M. H. Abrams, *The Mirror and the Lamp: Romantic Theory and the Critical Tradition* (London, 1981), 57–68. Mill's alliance with romantic theorists in his recognition of the centrality of emotion should not be allowed to obscure his very real differences with them, some fundamental. Mill describes Coleridge as a prime representative of the transcendental metaphysical school of philosophy, which is the polar opposite of Mill's own British empiricism (10:31). Their differences clearly emerge in their thoughts on the process of poetic creation. Coleridge unsparingly criticizes associationism, which he disparages for reducing poetic creation to a blind and mechanistic process; see Samuel Taylor Coleridge, *Biographia Literaria,* ed. J. Shawcross, (London, 1962), vol. 1, especially chaps. 5–7. Coleridge assails the associationist explanation of the role of the mind in perception. Since empiricism allows no place for innate principles of organization in the mind, Coleridge claims that associationists do not see the mind as shaping and adding to sensory experience, only as statically absorbing it; ibid., 1:82. This view leads to what he calls "the despotism of outward impressions, and that of senseless and passive memory" (1:77), making our minds the witness rather than the creator of our inner life. Coleridge asserts, on the contrary, that the will and reason control our mental workings, and that our minds to some extent create the world we perceive by contributing structure to the given of experience; see Abrams, chap. 7, and Basil Willey, *Nineteenth Century Studies* (New York, 1966), 14. Coleridge emphasizes and indeed makes central the power of mental faculties in the act of poetic composition, faculties that often are not even admitted into the empiricist worldview (1:193, 202; 2:106, 123).

Coleridge's criticisms of Mill's associationism are more interesting for their revelation of the connections and contrasts between the two thinkers than for their argumentative strength. For one thing, it is a mistake to say that empiricist and associationist theories must be blind and mechanistic. Empiricists may maintain that our minds have no innate organizing structures, and that all our knowledge must derive from experience, but they also say that once we come to experience the world we develop mental structures to give purpose and order to our mental life. The question of whether we are onlookers or controllers of our mental life does not depend on whether our mental structures are innate or born with experience. The will, or reason, or emotion, can be equally in command on either account. James Mill's *Analysis* and John Stuart Mill's editorial notes provide one account of how our mental organization is built up through association.

The interesting difference between Mill and Coleridge resides in their explanations of the faculties at work in the genesis of poetry. Just as Mill admits no special faculty of intuition in making moral judgments, he equally rejects a special faculty of imagination as being responsible for the conception of poetry. Coleridge's creative imagination has generated much discussion but little acceptance, in large part because of the obscurity of his comments. And although he makes strong claims about the superiority of poetry that is a dynamic fusion of elements and not a simple repatterning of parts, he describes this generative process in terms strikingly similar to Mill's process of chemical combination of elements in association. We can recall that Mill

poetry? A basic tenet of romanticism is the importance of internal cultivation, or cultivation of feeling. Although Mill ultimately changes his views on the relative importance of feeling and thought, he does not waver in his beliefs that poetry is a powerful tool for development of feeling, and that the processes of development of feeling and of thought are different:

> The object of poetry is confessedly to act upon the emotions; and therein is poetry sufficiently distinguished from . . . its logical opposite . . . matter of fact or science. The one addresses itself to the belief, the other to the feelings. The one does its work by convincing or persuading, the other by moving. The one acts by presenting a proposition to the understanding, the other by offering interesting objects of contemplation to the sensibilities. (1:344)[6]

Mill distinguishes poetry not only from matter of fact, but also from fiction and eloquence; in all these distinctions he emphasizes the basic core of poetry and its relation to affective and aesthetic development. His point is that individuals are trained aesthetically by being moved emotionally, and that this is done by presenting stirring objects that work on their feelings. This stirring effect is accomplished by presenting states of human feeling, and poetry's truth is "to paint the human soul truly" (1:346). Poets may understand little of the workings of the world, but they understand their own internal states well, and these states are expressed in their poetry in ways that produce an echo in their readers: "Poetry is

---

likens the associative process in these instances to a chemical reaction in which the original simple mental particles are fused and blended into a totality of new character. Mill and Coleridge have no quarrel over the nature of the product in the best poetry, or even over the dynamism of the process that brings it about. The dispute is just over the faculties that give rise to the best poetry. Mill sees no need to postulate extra faculties of mind and thinks that the special character of this poetry can be fully accounted for by thought and emotion and chemical association. Mill's higher synthesis must be capable of being analyzed into its simple elements, but this does not mean that the product is a mechanical combination of these elements (see 8:853–54).

[6]See also Robson, *Improvement of Mankind*, 26. This is a common theme of romantic theories. Wordsworth, for example, stresses the value of poetry as a spur to the feelings when he says that "all good poetry is the spontaneous overflow of powerful feelings"; W. J. B. Owen, ed., *Wordsworth and Coleridge: Lyrical Ballads, 1798* (London, 1967), 157. Shelley concurs, claiming that "the pleasure resulting from the manner in which [poets] express the influence of society or nature upon their own minds, communicates itself to others, and gathers a sort of reduplication from that community"; Percy Bysshe Shelley, *The Prose Works of Percy Bysshe Shelley*, 4 vols., ed. Harry Buxton Forman (London, 1880) 3:103.

feeling, confessing itself to itself in moments of solitude, and embodying itself in symbols, which are the nearest possible representations of the feeling in the exact shape in which it exists in the poet's mind" (1:348).

Mill assumes that the training process is accomplished by presenting the novice with, not just any poetry, but the best poetry, so that emotions are stirred and standards of the best poetry are presented simultaneously. He believes, with other romantic theorists, that the poet's task is to enlarge this capacity of feeling and to instill standards of taste.[7]

When he turns to the question, what is a poet? Mill distinguishes between the poet by nature and the poet by culture. The poet by nature is one whose associations are habitually linked by emotions rather than by thoughts; the poet by culture, like the majority of people, has associations linked by thoughts. In the poet by nature, therefore, emotion is the central controlling element, whereas in the poet by culture it is thought. Mill points to Wordsworth as a poet by culture and to Shelley as a poet by nature. He makes it clear that he regards poetry of the poet by nature as better: "Such poetry . . . is much more poetry, is poetry in a far higher sense, than any other; since the common element of all poetry, that which constitutes poetry, human feeling, enters far more largely into this than into the poetry of culture. . . . the natures which we have called poetical, really feel more, and consequently have more feeling to express" (1:361).

Mill's next statement on poetry, "Tennyson's Poems," was written only two years after "Thoughts on Poetry and Its Varieties," yet his views underwent one important change. He still thinks that poetry does its cultivating work by offering representations of valid human feelings which evoke similar states in the audience and provide a set of standards. He emphasizes the moral effect of this process, claiming that the noblest end of poetry is that of "acting upon the desires and characters of mankind through their emotions, to raise them towards the perfection of their nature" (1:414). He is more specific

---

[7]Wordsworth, for instance, says, "The human mind is capable of excitement without the application of gross and violent stimulants; and . . . one being is elevated above another in proportion as he possesses this capability. It has therefore appeared to me that to endeavour to produce or to enlarge this capability is one of the best services in which, at any period, a Writer can be engaged" (Owen, *Wordsworth and Coleridge,* 159.

here about the actual mechanism of this process. He points out what he will be even more explicit about later—the fact that poetry presents ideal models for the reader to sympathize with and to emulate: "The faculty of thus bringing home to us a coherent conception of beings unknown to our experience, not by logically *characterizing* them, but by a living *representation* of them, such as they would, in fact, *be*, if the hypothesis of their possibility could be realized—is what is meant, when anything is meant, by the words creative imagination" (1:415n). This much has remained the same. What changes is the relative influence of thought and emotion. Now Mill claims that the best poetry must have thought as the dominant influence and changes his estimations of Wordsworth and Shelley accordingly. A poet receives fine sensitivity from nature, he says, but the poet who is to produce anything of value must cultivate reason (1:414).[8] Mill's views here are in harmony with those of Wordsworth, the romantic theorist who best exemplifies the poet of culture.[9]

In line with this new evaluation appears a much less laudatory view of Shelley's poetry, as likely to please readers with poetic minds, but as not likely to reach others, who will not understand it. The production of the best poetry is "the work of cultivated reason" (1:414). This new approach is in keeping with Mill's general move to soften some of the more extreme reactions to his earlier Benthamite views. Hereafter he clarifies and develops his views, but he does not change them significantly. Thus in the later essays on literature we find some of his typical views reiterated. In "Carlyle's *French Revo-*

[8]Mill also says, "Every great poet . . . has been a great thinker;—has had a philosophy . . . has had his mind full of thoughts, derived not merely from passive sensibility, but from trains of reflection, from observation, analysis, and generalization" (1:413). See F. Parvin Sharpless, *Literary Criticism*, for a good account of the transition in Mill's views on the question of the relative influence of thought and emotion. For another interesting discussion, see Robson, *Improvement of Mankind*, especially 27, 31–32.

[9]Wordsworth says that "poems to which any value can be attached, were never produced on any variety of subjects but by a man who being possessed of more than usual organic sensibility had also thought long and deeply. For our continued influxes of feeling are modified and directed by our thoughts, which are indeed the representatives of all our past feelings." He continues, "I have said that Poetry is the spontaneous overflow of powerful feelings: it takes its origin from emotion recollected in tranquility: the emotion is contemplated till by a species of reaction the tranquility gradually disappears, and an emotion, similar to that which was before the subject of contemplation, is gradually produced, and does itself actually exist in the mind (*Lyrical Ballads, 1798*, 157, 173).

lution," for instance, he states again that poetry presents the deepest and truest human feeling.[10] And in "Writings of Alfred de Vigny," he says that the standards of taste are developed by those who are competent judges, for the greatest poets "must themselves create the tastes or the habits of thought by means of which they will afterwards be appreciated" (1:496).[11]

Mill's editorial notes to his father's *Analysis of the Phenomena of the Human Mind* provide further insight into his doctrine of development. Here Mill more explicitly connects development and the theory of association. He says that our perceptions of beauty and sublimity are more imposing than others because "the associations which form those impressions are themselves of a peculiarly imposing nature" and points with approval to Ruskin's method of showing that emotions of beauty are associated with lofty ideas.[12] Once again he indicates that these lofty ideas provide the audience with models to sympathize with and emulate. The ideas "represent to us

[10]Mill says, "Not falsification of the reality is wanted . . . only a deeper understanding of what it is; the power to conceive, and to represent, not the mere outside surface and costume of the thing, nor yet the mere logical definition . . . but an image of the thing itself in the concrete, with all that is lovable or hateable or admirable or pitiable or sad or solemn or pathetic, in it, and in the things which are implied in it. That is, the thing must be presented as it can exist only in the mind of a great poet"; J. B. Schneewind, ed., *Mill's Essays on Literature and Society* (New York, 1965), 190–91.

[11]Despite their differences, all the romantic theorists agree that the purpose of this process of development, accomplished through exhibiting models that elicit a sympathetic response in the audience, is to develop taste in this audience by inculcating in them a set of standards. Wordsworth claims that "an *accurate* taste in Poetry and in all the other arts . . . is an *acquired* talent, which can only be produced by thought and a long continued intercourse with the best models of composition"; Wordsworth, *Lyrical Ballads, 1798,* 177. Shelley speaks more in terms of the moralizing effect of aesthetic development than in terms of the effect of aesthetic development in producing competent judges of aesthetic pleasures. He gives the example of Homer, who provided ideal models of human character in Achilles, Hector, and Ulysses so that "the sentiments of the auditors must have been refined and enlarged by a sympathy with such great and lovely impersonations, until from admiring they imitated, and from imitation they identified themselves with the objects of their admiration"; Shelley, *Prose Works,* 110. And finally, Coleridge, on this point, agrees with the others. He claims that "good taste must be *acquired,* and . . . is the result of thought, and the submissive study of the best models. If it be asked, 'But what shall I deem such?' the answer is; *presume* these to be the best, the *reputation* of which has been matured into *fame* by the consent of ages. For wisdom always has a final majority, if not by conviction, yet by acquiescence"; Coleridge, *Biographia Literaria* 2:26.

[12]James Mill, *Analysis,* 2:252n.

some valuable or delightful attribute, in a completeness and perfection of which our experience presents us with no example, and which therefore stimulates the active power of the imagination to rise above known reality, into a more attractive or a more majestic world."[13]

Mill's last major statement on aesthetic theory is in his *Inaugural Address Delivered to the University of St. Andrew's*. In this work Mill does not specifically address the use of affective development for producing competent judges; instead, his attention is concentrated on the moralizing effects of affective development. Here affective and moral development overlap more completely than in other places. He introduces a distinction, in line with his tripartite division of the art of life, between the effects of poetic development on conscience and on virtue or nobility. Poetry can be used not only to prevent people from breaking moral rules but also to inspire them to have noble aims. Poetic cultivation is achieved by the representation of elevated and noble characters with which the audience can sympathize. Mill suggests that Plato, Demosthenes, and Tacitus, for example, insofar as they are poets and not philosophers, provide these models for their readers. He also suggests that people can uplift themselves by observing the image of "ideal perfection embodied in a Divine Being."[14] Poetry as well as all other arts can be used for this purpose, for "all the arts of expression tend to keep alive and in activity the feelings they express" (45). Contemplating beauty of great value naturally has this uplifting effect on character. Mill goes as far as to say that there is a close connection between goodness and cultivation of the beautiful: "He who has learnt what Beauty is, if he be of a virtuous character, will desire to realize it in his own life—will keep before himself a type of perfect beauty in human character, to light his attempts at self-culture" (46). Thus, although in this final work Mill somewhat confusingly conflates the different purposes of affective development, the process of this development is clear enough. Sympathy and identification have a dual function of inculcating a set of aesthetic standards of taste and of moralizing the audience.

[13]Ibid., 2:255n.
[14]Mill, *Inaugural Address*, 44.

INTELLECTUAL OR COGNITIVE
DEVELOPMENT

The training process for intellectual development is more complicated than that for affective development. The latter involves only
feelings, and the same overall procedure develops both experience
and judgment. With intellectual development, thoughts as well as
feelings are centrally involved. Intellectual development teaches the
student to take pleasure in intellectual activity and the discovery of
truth, and to this end both thoughts and feelings must be affected.
We must forge an associative link between our enjoyments and our
intellectual activities. We can be highly trained intellectually, but if
we have no deep feelings then the pleasure we get from our intellectual endeavors is limited. To broaden the foundation of our enjoyment, we expand our feelings in the same way that we develop feeling in the case of affective development: we read poetry and become
people who feel deeply. Thus affective development underlies intellectual development. But gaining experience is only one facet of
development. The other, judgment, is brought about by work with
our thoughts. Standards must be provided in this case too, by training the intellectual powers through intellectual activity. We expand
ourselves intellectually and thus have more to take pleasure in than
if we were not so developed. Mill offers various pedagogical suggestions for providing standards. In contrast with his views on the
process for affective development, he does not believe that only the
best models of truth should be provided to the student. He thinks
that truth is discovered by exercising the intellectual powers in different ways, and that we learn, not simply by emulating the best
models, but by contrasting them with other models, some of them
poor ones. In this process, the poor models are used as a counter-
point to the right models, those high on the scale of truth. Thus the
student learns to pick out the good models, and the process produces
its own enjoyments.

The first element of development, that of gaining experience, is
accomplished in the same manner as in the case of affective development. Mill differs in his approach with respect to the second element, that of training judgment through presentation of standards.
In several writings he offers us various methods for training the
intellect. Intellectual pleasures, in Mill's view, are the paradigm of

valuable pleasures—despite his strong reaction to excessively ana-
lytical habits of mind and his insistence on a balance with internal
affective development.

Once again, the best place to start the discussion of training intellectual judgment is the *Autobiography*, where Mill talks about his
own unusual and remarkable education. Intellectual judgment is
developed by means other than those used for affective development.
In the case of affective development, moving models are presented to
stir the emotions and provide standards of beauty. The presentation
of models is sometimes useful, but such models are not the only
means to develop the intellectual powers. In the present case there is
not just one basic means of training judgment. Mill offers various
methods for developing the intellect, but they all have a common
basis: active exercise of the intellect. Learning by rote, drilling, or
memorization of facts and opinions does not help the process of
training judgment (1:33, 35). Mill illustrates his point with examples
from his own intellectual training. He learned Greek at three years
of age. He began by learning lists of Greek words, and then before
learning very much grammar he began to translate *Aesop's Fables*.
Thus, instead of learning Greek mechanically, he was immediately
encouraged to think about the problems presented by translation.
His father was demanding and insisted on more achievement from
him than it was possible to accomplish, but this kept him actively
working on the problems. He was expected to read a wide variety of
books and discuss them with his father on their daily walks. When
he was himself studying Latin, he was expected at the same time to
teach it to his younger siblings. Later Mill developed his powers
further by writing his own versions of the subjects he was studying.
After reading a great variety of histories, for example, Mill wrote his
own version of a piece of Roman history (1:9, 17).

When he was twelve years old he began studying logic, and for this
subject he always maintained a high regard. Of logic he says, "I
know of nothing, in my education, to which I think myself more
indebted for whatever capacity of thinking I have attained" (1:23).
He claims that it is the best tool for training exact thinkers, and he
extends this high regard to the Socratic method exhibited in the
Platonic dialogues:

> The close, searching *elenchus* by which the man of vague gener-
> alities is constrained either to express his meaning to himself in defi-

nite terms, or to confess that he does not know what he is talking about; the perpetual testing of all general statements by particular instances; the siege in form which is laid to the meaning of large abstract terms, by fixing upon some still larger class-name which includes that and more, and dividing down to the thing sought. . . . all this, as an education for precise thinking, is inestimable. (1:25)

Mill's father designed these exercises to develop his son's critical intellectual powers. Mill learned to recognize truth by observing models. His father did not explain anything to him until he had made every possible attempt to explain it to himself. On the other hand, his father always explained why he was asking him to do something, and he always explained it after he had reached the boundary of his understanding. Mill summarizes the principle underlying the method: "My father never permitted anything which I learnt, to degenerate into a mere exercise of memory. He strove to make the understanding not only go along with every step of the teaching, but if possible, precede it" (1:35).

Mill's letters reveal that his crisis and recovery period affected his views on intellectual development. He first reacted harshly to his early training and later retreated somewhat to a middle ground. The reaction took the form of repudiating a sectarian defense of a particular point of view. He at first rejected Benthamite radicalism as the only true cause and correct worldview and went on a campaign against one-sidedness. He carried on discussion and correspondence with a wide variety of thinkers, including the Saint-Simonians, Carlyle, Coleridge, and Wordsworth, to such an extent that he convinced some of them that he was a potential convert to their point of view, even though he himself knew better. Mill states in a letter to Carlyle: "I saw . . . so much of good and of truth in the positive part of the most opposite opinions and practices, could they but be divested of their exclusive pretensions, that I scarcely felt myself called upon to *deny* anything but Denial itself" (12:204). He was interested in gleaning whatever was true and valuable from each of these divergent streams of thought, and at the time this was a canon of his doctrine of development. In one of his early letters he says, "I am averse to any mode of eradicating error, but by establishing and inculcating . . . the opposite truth; a truth of some kind inconsistent with that moral or intellectual state of mind from which the errors arise. It is only thus that we can at once maintain the good that already exists, and produce more" (12:45). He would not, then,

be an advocate for any cause, but he would read and consider different points of view and then make up his own mind. If he thought
that someone's opinion was mistaken, he would suggest the opposite truth to that person. He wanted to combine the various truths
he was encountering into one new perspective.

This remained Mill's position throughout his recovery period,
even while he recognized that his early education had allowed him
to undergo this transformation because it developed his critical
powers of thought (12:128). After this period of growth, Mill consoli-
dated his new beliefs. Later he was to become much more fixed in
his opinions, but even the later Mill maintains that there is value in
seeing the truth contained in positions different from his own.[15]
One of Mill's later letters reveals that his practical views on education did not change. He still believes that development of the intellect requires active training and not passive memorizing:

> What the poor as well as the rich require is not to be indoctrinated,
> is not to be taught other people's opinions, but to be induced and
> enabled to think for themselves. . . . after reading, writing, and arith-
> metic . . . the desirable thing for them seems to be the most mis-
> cellaneous information, and the most varied exercise of their faculties.
> They cannot read too much. . . . By such reading they would become,
> to a certain extent, cultivated beings.[16]

In two essays written during the 1830s, Mill reiterates his early
position that education by rote is unprofitable. In "On Genius,"
written in 1832, he decries the lack of genius in society and blames
the education of the day. He maintains that the purpose of education
should be, not to teach opinions, but to equip students to learn for
themselves.[17] All men and women, in their own areas of work and in
areas of concern common to all, must be capable of judging things
for themselves. Society must promote independent thinkers. Mill

[15]For example, in a letter of 1861, Mill says the following about a book with which
he disagrees: "Dupont-White takes decidedly the governmental side . . . and as the
things he says in favour of centralization are about the best that can be said for it,
there would be some use in a review which would concede the portion of truth
contained in them and at the same time bring forward the still more important truths
which as stated by him they contradict" (Mill to Henry Reeve, 15:726).

[16]Mill to Rev. Henry William Carr, 15:780–81.

[17]"Let the education of the mind consist in calling out and exercising these faculties; never trouble yourself about giving knowledge—train the *mind*. . . . Let all
cram be ruthlessly discarded" (1:338).

points to logic and metaphysics as subjects well suited to his goal. Similarly, in "Civilization," published in 1836, Mill claims that the cause of the problem of lack of progress is sectarian education, an education that attempts to produce students who accept teachers' opinions. Education, he says, must be reformed so that students are developed in the proper way, so that they are trained for themselves.[18] Once again Mill points to the value of logic and philosophy of mind in achieving this objective.

Mill also displays the importance of mental development and some of the methods for ensuring its achievement in *On Liberty*. Mental development is important for all members of society, so that all people can reach their full capacity. To this end, discussion and debate of all issues must be encouraged, or society will not achieve a "generally high scale of mental activity" (18:243). Full and frequent discussion of opinions is the only way to ensure that opinions are held as living truths, or, in other words, that people do maintain a certain level of mental development (18:243). Moreover, mental development requires that people know, not only the grounds and the content of their own opinions, but also the opinions on the other side of the question. "He who knows only his own side of the case, knows little of that" (18:245). If there are not genuine intellectual opponents, then devil's advocates are needed, for without such opponents and frequent debate the very meaning of the opinions is lost. Often the accepted opinion is only half the truth, says Mill, and the conflicting opinion may be the other half. He concludes that mental development requires liberty of discussion. This discussion in *On Liberty* is also relevant to Mill's views on the higher-level capacities of individuality and autonomy.

In his inaugural address at St. Andrew's, Mill discusses the best form of formal education for intellectual development—scientific instruction. He again stresses the importance of training people to evaluate conflicting opinions competently and to discriminate truth.[19] There are two basic methods of arriving at truth—observa-

---

[18] "The very cornerstone of an education intended to form great minds, must be the recognition of the principle, that the object is to call forth the greatest possible quantity of intellectual *power*, and to inspire the intensest *love of truth:* and this without a particle of regard to the results to which the exercise of that power may lead, even though it should conduct the pupil to opinions diametrically opposite to those of his teachers" (18:144).

[19] Mill, *Inaugural Address*, 22.

tion and reasoning—which can both be taught by means of physical science. Mathematics is the best example of the method of discovery of truths by reasoning, and experimental science is that of truths of direct observation (22). Mill also stresses the importance of logic, which complements mathematics and the experimental sciences by providing the theory for their practice: "It declares the principles, rules, and precepts, of which they exemplify the observance" (26). He argues that all people should know generally the issues covered by metaphysics but should not be expected to devote much time to them. Still, metaphysics is valuable for those who devote themselves to it, and its study invariably results in "increased vigour of understanding" (32). Other subjects which, though not strictly sciences, are valuable for intellectual training include ethics, political economy, and jurisprudence.

From this examination of Mill's statements it becomes clear that the two elements of cognitive development interact. Affective development of feelings provides us with a reservoir of feeling with which to enjoy our intellectual endeavors, and the training of intellect through provision of standards of truth and other means deepens and expands the intellectual activities to which our enjoyments are linked.

MORAL DEVELOPMENT

The same pattern of development applies to moral development. As in the case of affective development, moral development is primarily a matter of feelings. But unlike affective and intellectual development, which each involve only one basic object of pleasure, the process of moral development teaches students to enjoy two separate things: it teaches students to take pleasure in both the good of others and in nobility. Models of both sympathetic and noble characters are presented to impart standards to students. The element of experience is inculcated in the same manner as in the other cases, and once again affective development underlies the whole process. Moral experience is used particularly to deepen feelings in order to promote sympathy with our fellows and pleasure in their good. But this element is separate from the judgment process by which standards of sympathy and nobility are inculcated.

In the *Autobiography* Mill discusses his own moral education.

His father directed him to read the *Memorabilia* of Xenophon, and he "imbibed from that work . . . a deep respect for the character of Socrates; who stood in [his] mind as a model of ideal excellence (1:49). Mill often mentions the use of ideal or noble models to develop moral character in this work. He notes that the writings of Plato had a profound effect on him (1:49). He was also cultivated to enjoy the good of others. Moral feelings, he tells us, are produced by the operation of the laws of association; we take pleasure in certain things because these have acquired associated pleasurable ideas through development. He is "convinced, that the object of education should be to form the strongest possible associations of the salutary class; associations of pleasure with all things beneficial to the great whole, and of pain with all things hurtful to it" (1:141).

Mill emphasizes the importance of experience for deepening the feelings. The laws of association can create links between our enjoyments and the good of others. But feelings are necessary for motivation, are the very material of motivation, and if our feelings are not strong and extensive we may not have the desire to put our theory into practice. Part of Mill's problem during his crisis, he believed, was that he was "without any real desire for the ends which [he] had been so carefully fitted out to work for: no delight in virtue or the general good, but also just as little in anything else" (1:143). The development of feeling would remedy this, would give him desire for these ends. So the two distinct processes of experience and judgment work together.

Mill's essays on ethics express his ideas on moral development. In "Remarks on Bentham's Philosophy," Mill maintains that feelings such as benevolence, conscience, and moral obligation could be dominant in all people, and that until this is the case people will be much less happy than they could be:

> . . . there is nothing in the constitution of human nature to forbid its being so in all mankind. Until it is so, the race will never enjoy one-tenth part of the happiness which our nature is susceptible of. I regard any considerable increase of human happiness, through mere changes in outward circumstances, unaccompanied by changes in the state of the desires, as hopeless. (10:15)

In one of his most open public critiques of the narrower utilitarian theory of his intellectual predecessor, Mill castigates Bentham for holding to a belief in "the predominance of the selfish principle in human nature":

> By the promulgation of such views of human nature . . . I conceive Mr. Bentham's writings to have done . . . very serious evil. . . . It is difficult to form the conception of a tendency more inconsistent with all rational hope of good for the human species, than that which must be impressed by such doctrines, upon any mind in which they find acceptance. (10:14–15)

In a comment that foreshadows his own concentration on the powers of the state to promote self-development of its citizens, Mill continues the critique: "It never seems to have occurred to him to regard political institutions in a higher light, as the principal means of the social education of a people" (10:16).

In "Sedgwick's Discourse" Mill explains again the importance of development of feeling for morality. Reason can indicate the proper ends and the means to these ends, but it cannot provide the desire to attain them. This desire depends on feeling, which determines the will (10:50).

To counter intuitionist claims that moral feelings are innate, Mill explains their origins. Because feelings are not innate, but developed, our views on education and culture must be worked out first; these become the groundwork of a philosophy of morals (10:56). What work has been done in this area has been done by utilitarian philosophers. Since moral feelings are artificial and developed, children must be trained to be moral agents. The first step is "a child's knowledge of the simple fact . . . that some acts produce pain and others pleasure" (10:58–59). A child originally applies this knowledge to a particular person and later expands this to include a group of people and then society as a whole. These ideas of pain and pleasure caused to others are the original basis of moral feelings:

> The idea of the pain of another is naturally painful; the idea of the pleasure of another is naturally pleasurable. From this fact in our natural constitution, all our affections both of love and aversion towards human beings . . . originate. In this, the unselfish part of our nature, lies a foundation, even independently of inculcation from without, for the generation of moral feelings. (10:60)

These unselfish feelings provide the basis for the development of moral feelings. Mill regards these fellow feelings as a basic part of human nature and the basis of the tendency of sociality. Thus our moral or social side is an element of our nature that needs development along with our critical and intellectual side, and Mill's refusal to elevate the intellectual above the moral and social has important consequences for his conception of self-development and, more broadly, for his liberal political philosophy. But these feelings are only the basis of moral feelings and not themselves moral feelings. A long process of education is required to produce the latter. Mill considers his position progressive, one that allows for constant improvement and change in moral standards.

In "Whewell on Moral Philosophy," also written to counter intuitionism, Mill continues this last point. He points out that intuitionism has popular force because many people find it difficult to accept that their strong feelings of right and wrong could be thought mistaken by others. On the contrary, Mill argues, these feelings that seem so natural are actually artificial, and development can produce "senseless and pernicious" feelings as well as beneficial ones (10:179). Utilitarianism, which recognizes this fact and tries to produce beneficial association, is progressive, whereas intuitionism is static. Once again Mill looks at the genesis of moral feeling: ". . . what we desire unselfishly must first, by a mental process, become an actual part of what we seek as our own happiness . . . the good of others becomes our pleasure because we have learnt to find pleasure in it" (10:184). This is the goal of moral development: to train individuals to take enjoyment in the good of others, using association on our natural feelings of sympathy to produce moral feelings from the fellow feelings that gave rise to them.

Mill argues in *Utilitarianism* that unless we have developed moral feelings and an interest in the good of others our chances for satisfaction in life are seriously limited (10:215). There is no reason for any person to be so lacking in moral culture as to be a selfish egotist, since society could so arrange things that everyone would be properly developed morally. Laws and social forces could promote harmony between individual and social interests, which education and public opinion could reinforce by promoting a close association in people's thoughts between the happiness of the individual and the happiness of others (10:218). The current moral norms are not the only possible ones, but the same forces currently operating could be improved and used so that "the feeling of unity with our fellow creatures shall be . . . as deeply rooted in our character, and to our own consciousness as completely a part of our nature, as the horror of crime is in an ordinarily well-brought up young person" (10:227).

Moral development depends on the use of both external and internal sanctions. External sanctions are rewards and punishments such as hope of praise from our friends or fear of God's anger, which prevent us from transgressing moral laws. Internal sanctions are our conscience and other moral feelings, built up by our moral training. These feelings are

> in general, all encrusted over with collateral associations, derived from sympathy, from love, and still more from fear; from all the forms of religious feeling; from the recollections of childhood and of all our past life; from self-esteem, desire of the esteem of others. . . . Its [moral obligation] binding force . . . consists in the existence of a mass of feeling which must be broken through in order to do what violates our standard of right. (10:228–29)

The natural basis of these moral feelings is our fellow feeling or social feelings, which need direction and encouragement. We feel ourselves part of society and recognize the need to take account of others' interests, and so our own feelings become more and more identified with the feelings of others. Thus, from the basis of fellow feelings that are part of human nature are built moral feelings and sociality:

> But there *is* this basis of powerful natural sentiment. . . . This firm foundation is that of the social feelings of mankind; the desire to be in unity with our fellow creatures, which is already a powerful principle in human nature, and happily one of those which tend to become stronger, even without express inculcation, from the influences of advancing civilization. The social state is at once so natural, so necessary, and so habitual to man, that, except in some unusual circumstances or by an effort of voluntary abstraction, he never conceives himself otherwise than as a member of a body. . . . In this way people grow up unable to conceive as possible to them a state of total disregard of other people's interests. . . . They are also familiar with the fact of co-operating with others, and proposing to themselves a collective, not an individual, interest, as the aim . . . of their actions. . . . Not only does all strengthening of social ties, and all healthy growth of society, give to each individual a stronger personal interest in practically consulting the welfare of others; it also leads him to identify his *feelings* more and more with their good. (10:231)

Thus "the smallest germs of the feeling are laid hold of and nourished by the contagion of sympathy and the influences of education;

and a complete web of corroborative association is woven round it, by the powerful agency of the external sanctions" (10:232). These come to seem more and more natural. This growth would be particularly vigorous if the same social forces that now operate to teach religion, such as education and public opinion, were directed to this end.

Mill illustrates how virtue becomes connected to our happiness through association. Originally virtue is desired, not for itself, but only as a means to pleasure and prevention of pain. Through development, however, an association is formed in our minds between virtue and pleasure, and we come to desire it for itself: "Those who desire virtue for its own sake, desire it either because the consciousness of it is a pleasure, or because the consciousness of being without it is a pain, or for both reasons united" (10:237). To produce a desire for virtue in someone, we have only to arrange things so that that person comes to think of it as pleasurable because it has been associated with pleasure.

Mill explains in his notes to James Mill's *Analysis* how the moral feelings are produced by a quasi-chemical process through the operation of the laws of association on our natural feelings.[20] The ideas of acts beneficial to others become pleasurable, while the ideas of hurtful acts become painful.[21] The feeling of sympathy is the basis of moral feeling, but is not identical with it: "To constitute the moral feeling, not only must the good of others have become in itself a pleasure to us, and their suffering a pain, but this pleasure or pain must be associated with our own acts as producing it, and must in this manner have become a motive, prompting us to the one sort of acts, and restraining us from the other sort.[22]

In the inaugural address at St. Andrew's, Mill says little about moral education beyond that which overlaps affective development. He does not consider it part of a university education. Moral education consists of training of the will and development of the feelings, which are concerns of the family and society at large. He does see some value, however, in having the universities teach moral philosophy, as long as this is not done dogmatically.

[20]James Mill, *Analysis*, 2:233n.
[21]Ibid., 2:297n.
[22]Ibid., 2:309n.

6

From Development
to Self-Development

Alan Ryan has commented that "Mill's concern with self-development and moral progress is a strand in his philosophy to which almost everything else is subordinate."[1] When adulthood is achieved, the individual takes full control of the process of development, which then transmutes into self-development. Mill marks this transition in his own life in the *Autobiography* as the "Last Stage of Education, and First of Self-Education" (1:65). This later stage of self-development erects on the generic capacities higher-level capacities of individuality, autonomy, and sociality. I take up a more detailed treatment of Mill's views on individuality, autonomy, and sociality shortly within the framework of an interpretation and defense of his brand of liberalism. But some preliminary background explanation is needed. Mill offers his conception of the good in terms of the happiness appropriate for humans, and this view of happiness, with self-development at its core, shapes his political theory.

MILL'S CONCEPTION OF HAPPINESS

Mill's qualitative hedonism emphasizes the happiness of humans who have undergone a process of development and then self-devel-

[1]Ryan, *Philosophy of John Stuart Mill*, 255.

opment. His conception of happiness is sophisticated. It is rooted in his views on human nature and its capacities, faculties, and potential and shaped by the idea that humans are the sort of beings who can experience and appreciate many varied and complex forms of happiness and enjoyment. As I have noted, Mill regards human nature as being in some significant respects quite malleable, adaptable, and able to be expanded or channeled in various directions, but there are some grounding elements that shape the forms of happiness of such creatures. For all of its malleability and adaptibility, human nature also has certain generic capacities or faculties, the capacities I have discussed under the doctrine of development. These are our intellectual and affective faculties and our fellow-feeling.

My discussion of development lays the groundwork for outlining the process of self-development and the conception of happiness within Mill's theory. Since humans have certain capacities and faculties, certain enjoyments involving the use and fulfillment of those faculties are essential components of their happiness. Thus the development of these generic faculties of human nature is a requisite for an appreciation of the more valuable forms of happiness open to and appropriate to beings of our nature, and enjoyment involving the use and further development and flourishing of the human capacities is an essential element of Mill's conception of happiness.[2] To be self-developed, to have undergone the process of development transformed into self-development, is both an indispensable condition for and an essential element of happiness. Without at least a threshold level of self-development normally reached at adulthood, we cannot engage in these valuable forms of happiness and cannot competently measure the value of alternative kinds of happiness.

As Fred Berger puts this, according to Mill "the ultimate criterion of the value of all actions . . . is what is requisite for the happiness of man *as a creature of elevated faculties*"; "*human* well-being—given human capacities—requires some particular elements."[3] As well, in the concluding passages of the *Logic*, Mill reflects on the conditions it would take to make "human life happy; both in the

---

[2]The use of this terminology of human nature and human capacities creates some problems for those who believe, as I do, that many nonhuman animals also have capacities that are the basis of moral standing. Nothing in my discussion is intended to deny this position or to deny the important implications for the moral status of animals and for the moral obligations of humans toward nonhuman animals.

[3]Berger, *Happiness, Justice and Freedom*, 43, 40.

comparatively humble sense, of pleasure and freedom from pain, and in the higher meaning, of rendering life . . . such as human beings with highly developed faculties can care to have" (8:952). These generic capacities are part of human nature and they can be stifled or nurtured. The selfish tendency of human nature exists along with the social side, and the complacent and apathetic along with the active and intellectual. Educators and agents themselves who have reached the age of self-development can make choices to emphasize and nurture or stifle these faculties, but Mill claims, arguing from experience and observation, that competent judges would choose to emphasize the social and intellectual side over the selfish and passive (10:211–22, 230–33). As Berger says, "Mill held that it is a part of human nature that we sympathize with others— take pleasure in their pleasure and feel pain at the thought of their pain."[4] These social feelings, as I have already noted in my discussion of the doctrine of development, form the foundation for the development of full moral feeling. Berger notes in following up on the effects of development on social feelings that "Mill recognized no limit to the extent to which people could come to take on the well-being of others as their own, through the influences of education, political authority, religion, and public opinion."[5]

It is an essential component of Mill's conception of happiness that the most valuable forms of happiness are states involving the use and enjoyment of our distinctively human faculties and that humans cannot experience the greatest well-being unless these capacities are developed and used. But we must distinguish between two aspects of development, and this distinction has important implications for Mill's political philosophy. Self-development is essentially bound up with the development of the generic human faculties, but it also essentially involves the development of autonomy and individuality. In broad brush strokes, individuality centers on the process by which each person discovers his or her own unique mix of generic capacities, talents, and abilities. Autonomy is concerned with the critical reflection, choice, and endorsement of character, projects and pursuits in harmony with one's nature. Mill does not believe that we have one fixed and unchangeable essence; that is the position of his intuitionist opponents. But he does hold that, whether due to genetic endowment, physiological makeup, or early

---

[4]Berger, *Happiness, Justice and Freedom*, 19; see also Mill, 10:231.
[5]Berger, *Happiness, Justice and Freedom*, 23.

environmental influences, each person has a range of potential and consequently a range of lifestyles, projects, and pursuits in harmony with this nature, a nature Mill conceives of more broadly than an Aristotelian essence. Our greatest happiness comes from seeking out and discovering this range and then choosing and creating lifestyles, projects, pursuits, and traits of character on its foundation. There are a range of options within our potentials, and our futures are to some extent open, but if we move outside the range we deny or repress our nature and suffer the consequence that our greatest well-being is not achieved.

John Gray has some interesting insights on the idea of individuality of nature. He explains that "one part of [a person's] happiness, a necessary part, in Mill's view, will be that he has fulfilled the peculiar demands of his own nature."[6] This "suggest[s] the thesis that each man has a unique range of potentialities, expressible in a relatively small range of possible lives, and that the actualisation of these potentialities is indispensable for any man's greatest well-being" (80). Gray adds that "Mill's theory of individuality, then, combines the claim that man is his own maker with the claim that, for each man, a nature exists which awaits discovery" (86).

Mill's claim that each person has an endowment or nature consisting of a particular mix of generic human capacities has some resonance with Aristotelian views. This similarity has led some to ask whether Mill's stance on this point undermines or is in conflict with his empiricism.[7] Two considerations meet this concern. The first is that, as I have already mentioned, a human nature is not unitary and fixed but rather consists of a range of possibilities on the basis of which the agent constructs and creates an actual life, emphasizing appropriate traits, talents, and pursuits. The second point is that empiricist methods of experiment and observation are used to buttress Mill's claims about human nature in general, and empiricist methods are used by agents in the process of discovering and creating their own natures. On this latter point Gray says:

> As an empiricist, Mill is compelled to build his theory of men on the evidences of observation and experiment. Mill absorbed the Romantic belief that each man possessed a peculiar and in-born endowment which might or might not be realised in the course of his life. This belief does not overthrow Mill's empiricism, so long as the iden-

[6]John Gray, *Mill on Liberty: A Defence* (London, 1983), 81.
[7]Wesley Cooper has raised this problem in discussion.

tification of any man's essence or nature remains a matter of observation and experiment . . .

So long as we allow Mill the notion of an individual endowment open to discovery by observation and experiments in living, the rationalist or essentialist idiom of individual essences or natures can be given an empiricist translation. (83–84)

Recall Mill's eloquent plea in *On Liberty* for the need to conduct experiments in living in order to discover the mode of life best suited to the individual. This is empiricist methodology writ large. It is useful, Mill says, "that there should be different experiments of living; that free scope should be given to varieties of character . . . and that the worth of different modes of life should be proved practically, when any one thinks fit to try them" (18:260–61). Humans must both discover and create their selves and characters by discovering the range of mix of talents and creating a distinctive self on this groundwork: "A person whose desires and impulses are his own—are the expression of his own nature, as it has been developed and modified by his own culture—is said to have a character" (18:264).

As well, Mill consistently applies empiricist methodology to establish claims covering the whole gamut of issues within the moral arts and sciences. One famous example is an argument for hedonism in *Utilitarianism:*

> And now to decide . . . whether mankind do desire nothing for itself but that which is a pleasure to them. . . . we have evidently arrived at a question of fact and experience, dependent, like all similar questions, upon evidence. It can only be determined by practised self-consciousness and self-observation, assisted by observation of others. (10:237)

Mill also uses arguments from experience to claim that pleasures involving the use of the human faculties are preferable and more valuable.[8] He claims that "the test of quality, and the rule for measuring it against quantity, being the preference felt by those who, in their opportunities of experience, to which must be added their habits of self-consciousness and self-observation, are best furnished

---

[8] "Now it is an unquestionable fact that those who are equally acquainted with, and equally capable of appreciating and enjoying, both, do give a most marked preference to the manner of existence which employs their higher faculties" (10:211).

with the means of comparison" (10:214). In a more general example, Book 6 of the *Logic* outlines an empiricist methodology for gaining knowledge about the moral arts and sciences. Mill's philosophy of social science is methodological individualism, according to which the driving forces of historical progress are the mental powers of individual thinkers. Mill claims to establish the importance of intellectual development for progress by sociological and historical observation—by an empirical study of history.[9]

Mill embeds value in forms of happiness that are appropriate for humans as creatures with a certain nature, with capacities and faculties that can be developed and exercised. He grounds his views on value in his conception of and facts about human nature. And although his conception of human nature thus plays a fundamental role in his theory, he does not try to prove that this conception is the correct one; instead he provides the same kind of appeal to evidence that he turns to in his "proof" of the principle of utility. To this degree Mill's theory could have limitations; some critics consider his view of human nature controversial. Mill is sometimes criticized for holding an overly optimistic view of human nature as evolutionary and progressive, ignoring the human potential for evil. As well, it is claimed, Mill does not do justice to the human capacities for apathy and passivity, except to claim that competent agents would eschew such capacities and seek to transform them.

A more general difficulty is that, while on the one hand Mill maintains that human nature is extremely pliable and can be developed in many directions, on the other hand he maintains that human happiness requires development of certain capacities. He bases this requirement on the claim that these faculties are essential elements of human nature, but the test for this claim, as for other values choices, consists in eliciting the preferences of competent agents. Mill claims that competent agents who have experienced both sides choose the life of activity over passivity, the life of love over hate, and so on. But there are well-known logical difficulties

[9]Mill outlines his inverse deductive or historical method for social science and argues that this knowledge cannot be obtained a priori: "While it is an imperative rule never to introduce any generalization from history into the social science unless sufficient grounds can be pointed out for it in human nature, I do not think any one will contend that it would have been possible, setting out from the principles of human nature and from the general circumstances of the position of our species, to determine *a priori* the order in which human development must take place" (8:915).

surrounding a situation of choice in which agents compare lives or pursuits actually chosen with those that could have been chosen (it is claimed) but in fact were not chosen. The agent who has chosen the life of love and service to humanity of course rejects the alternative life of the hate-filled bigot. The husband who has chosen a marriage based on equality and love similarly rejects the rage and need to dominate of the wife-battering husband. But how can such agents make such choices and comparisons in Mill's terms? Although some agents may experience a transformative process in which they begin as rage-filled abusers and evolve into loving spouses, many loving husbands begin and end that way and cannot imagine, much less actually experience, the rage-filled alternative that they have rejected in their actual choice of life. The general problem that lurks here is that of meaningful comparisons among alternative lives, some actually chosen but many rejected. Fred Berger puts this problem well:

> What gives Mill grounds for his view that one sort of life which is *not* desired by such persons is more satisfactory, is his view that persons who can experience both prefer the one; but *these* people *cannot* fully experience both, and can have no grounds for rating the life they do not want over the life-style they lead. Moreover, it is claimed, if you *are* the sort of person who requires dignity, freedom, and so on, to be happy, then you do *not* appreciate the satisfyingness of the alternative life-style. Given different capacities, there can be no real comparability.[10]

Mill appeals to general historical, psychological, and sociological evidence. His claim is that, given an effective or meaningful choice, one in which people's life circumstances do not effectively block certain options, people do tend to choose the development and exercise of their distinctive human capacities. Mill's appeal here is to the evidence of history, and although the evidence is not conclusive there is much that supports his view of the choices that people actually make if certain options are not blocked. This is some empirical evidence in support of his claims about the strengths of certain tendencies of human nature. And, as Berger points out, these criticisms often underestimate the degree to which people are able

[10]Berger, *Happiness, Justice and Freedom*, 284.

to understand other lifestyles. So these criticisms are not as compelling as they first appear.[11]

The free play of individuality has a multifaceted and multilayered place in Mill's theory. As with other noted related elements, it is both a central element of well-being and a prerequisite for other elements of human happiness:

> If it were felt that the free development of individuality is one of the leading essentials of well-being; that it is not only a co-ordinate element with all that is designated by the terms civilization, instruction, education, culture, but is itself a necessary part and condition of all those things; there would be no danger that liberty should be undervalued, and the adjustment of the boundaries between it and social control would present no extraordinary difficulty. (18:261)

This is one illustration of the multiple roles played by central notions such as individuality and self-development. This tendency of Mill's to see things in complex and interwoven ways contributes greatly to the richness of his theory. As Berger notes in commenting on the above quote, "Mill began his account and defense of individuality with his claim that it is both an *ingredient* of the good life and a *necessary condition* for the achievement of the other components of well-being."[12]

The process of discovering and developing our individuality is also necessarily interwoven with autonomy, the rational and critical reflection on and endorsement of the search. I have more to say about both crucial notions shortly, but first I take up some of the important implications of human self-development.

The Role of the State and Neutralism

When we separate the two aspects of development—the development of generic human capacities and the autonomous search for the individual mix of these capacities—we can clarify and keep in proper focus Mill's stance on the appropriate role of the state vis-à-vis different conceptions of the good. Some contemporary theorists,

---

[11]Ibid., 285.
[12]Ibid., 233.

most notably Ronald Dworkin and John Rawls, argue that a liberal state is neutral regarding different conceptions of the good. Mill, in strong contrast, is not a neutralist on this issue, but his position can be misunderstood if we do not distinguish these aspects of development. Mill maintains that the state has a central role to play in the development of its citizens, and indeed that this role is one of the main functions of the state. His argument on this point in *Representative Government* and other political writings is unmistakeable and unequivocal. But the proper role of the state in this regard is to see that all citizens have an opportunity to develop their generic human capacities. The relevant contrast here is between development and lack of development of these human faculties. Our human faculties of critical awareness, feeling, and sociality can, however, develop in many different ways and take many different forms. The state must not overstep its jurisdiction in dictating the form of development; it must leave it to individuals to direct and pursue diverse forms of development and must provide support for different developmental experiments. Government is the "agency of national education" (*Considerations on Representative Government*, 19:393).

> The first element of good government, therefore, being the virtue and intelligence of the human beings composing the community, the most important point of excellence which any form of government can possess is to promote the virtue and intelligence of the people themselves. The first question in respect to any political institutions is, how far they tend to foster in the members of the community the various desirable qualities . . . moral, intellectual, and active. The government which does this the best, has every likelihood of being the best in all other respects, since it is on these qualities, so far as they exist in the people, that all possibility of goodness in the practical operations of the government depends. (19:390)
>
> We may consider, then, as one criterion of the goodness of a government, the degree in which it tends to increase the sum of good qualities in the governed, collectively and individually; since . . . their well-being is the sole object of government. (19:390)
>
> We have now, therefore, obtained a foundation for . . . the merit which any set of political institutions can possess. It consists partly of the degree in which they promote the general mental advancement of the community, including under that phrase advancement in intellect, in virtue, and in practical activity and efficiency. . . . A government is to be judged by its action upon men . . . by what it makes of the citizens, and what it does with them; its tendency to improve or deteriorate the people themselves. (19:392)

> Such a philosophy [Bentham's] will be most apt to fail in the consideration of the greater social questions—the theory of organic institutions and general forms of polity; for those (unlike the details of legislation) to be duly estimated, must be viewed as the great instruments of forming the national character; of carrying forward the members of the community towards perfection, or preserving them from degeneracy. (10:9)

It is indisputable that these passages do not lend weight to a neutralist interpretation of Mill. Mill's eloquent arguments for individuality in *On Liberty* are equally unmistakable in insisting that government not impose the *form* of development. In Chapter 5 he argues that the state has a duty to educate and develop its citizens. But he goes on:

> If the government would make up its mind to *require* for every child a good education, it might save itself the trouble of *providing* one. . . . The objections which are urged with reason against State education, do not apply to the enforcement of education by the State, but to the State's taking upon itself to direct that education: which is a totally different thing. That the whole or any large part of the education of the people should be in State hands, I go as far as any one in deprecating. All that has been said of the importance of individuality of character, and diversity in opinions and modes of conduct, involves, as of the same unspeakable importance, diversity of education. A general State education is a mere contrivance for moulding people to be exactly like one another. . . . it establishes a despotism over the mind. . . . An education established and controlled by the State should only exist, if it exist at all, as one among many competing experiments, carried on for the purpose of example and stimulus, to keep the others up to a certain standard of excellence. (18:302)

Because the conception of human good and happiness essentially involves the development and exercise of autonomous intellectual and social capacities, governments promote these ends nonneutrally by both allowing and providing genuine opportunities for human development. But self-development is short-circuited by a paternalistic imposition by "authorities" of "the right values," so this promotion of human interests must be done carefully. As I argue in my examination of the applications of Mill's theory, much must be decentralized and left to the resources of local control and to those most affected by the outcomes. Government should appropriately encourage cooperative organizations and promote conditions that allow their development, for example, while not interfering in the operations of the members ("Claims of Labour," 4:385–86).

Mill's arguments for the importance of individuality in *On Liberty* also highlight the fact that the form of development must be self-selected and cannot be imposed or fixed by other members of society, including members of the developed elite, or the state. His arguments on this point are also relevant to the related issue of elitist versus egalitarian currents in his thought.

> Nobody denies that people should be so taught and trained in youth, as to know and benefit by the ascertained results of human experience. But it is the privilege and proper condition of a human being, arrived at the maturity of his faculties, to use and interpret experience in his own way. It is for him to find out what part of recorded experience is properly applicable to his own circumstances and character.[13] (18:262)

> . . . nor is it only persons of decided mental superiority who have a just claim to carry on their lives in their own way. . . . If a person possesses any tolerable amount of common sense and experience, his own mode of laying out his existence is the best, not because it is the best in itself, but because it is his own mode. (18:270)

> But neither one person, nor any number of persons, is warranted in saying to another human creature of ripe years, that he shall not do with his life for his own benefit what he chooses to do with it. He is the person most interested in his own well-being. . . . In this department, therefore, of human affairs, Individuality has its proper field of action. (18:277)

Mill raises many of the same points in arguing that individuals have priority and authority in choosing the mix of life pursuits most appropriate to their natures and are quite justified in warding off interference by either the state or more developed agents. This individualist theme thus counters elitist interpretations of his theory.

A common but incorrect superficial interpretation of Mill as elitist begins with the claim, obviously central to many aspects of his

---

[13]Mill also says, "To conform to custom, merely *as* custom, does not educate or develope in him any of the qualities which are the distinctive endowment of a human being. The human faculties of perception, judgment, discriminative feeling, mental activity, and even moral preference, are exercised only in making a choice. He who does anything because it is the custom, makes no choice. He gains no practice either in discerning or in desiring what is best. The mental and moral, like the muscular powers, are improved only by being used" (18:262).

argument, that there are varying degrees of competence, with some agents highly developed, others just at the threshold, and most somewhere on the continuum in between. It is then claimed, mistakenly, that a large or majority share of social resources would justifiably be spent on the developed elite, giving them everything they need to fully satisfy their developed desires, while the majority of less developed could be ignored or given a proportionally smaller share of resources. A related elitist view mistakenly attributed to Mill is that the value choices of the elite could justifiably be imposed on the less developed members of society, since the elite are the ones who make the correct value choices; we would not want to give a voice to the less developed members of society.

To pinpoint why this elitist view of Mill does not hold up under scrutiny, it is wise to sort out questions of the private and the social realm. I take up questions of social choice when I examine representative government and economic democracy (see Chapter 10). In the private realm, the elitist view would seem, on a superficial reading, to lead to policies allocating more social resources to the more highly developed to satisfy their tastes. But this view overlooks the basic structure of Mill's moral theory, which is not a simple maximizing act utilitarian theory. Mill's theory is rights-based, and a basic right is the right to liberty of self-development, as I argue shortly. If the elite are allocated a large share of resources to satisfy their desires and happiness, the rights of the majority are violated by the denial of resources to satisfy their developmental efforts. The misery resulting from this policy far outweighs any marginal gains to the happiness of the more developed. Mill's rights-based theory would not, however, decide such questions on a case-by-case weighing of misery over happiness, but on the basis of respect for rights.

This elitist interpretation also overlooks the developmental continuum embedded in Mill's theory. Mill makes clear that there is a threshold beyond which a normal adult member of society is entitled to self-control and a voice in public choices. He makes it equally clear that the more developed are not entitled to impose their choices on others. The role of the more developed is set out on quite a different model. Mill repudiates the "strong man" view of the role of the elite and visualizes it instead as that of a guide to those who voluntarily choose to learn from the guide, and as an example for those who choose to follow an example. This position is in keeping with his fundamental view, a view that sets him off from some other liberal political theorists, that power over or domination of others is always and fundamentally corrupting and depraving:

> There is always need of persons not only to discover new truths . . . but also to commence new practices, and set the example of more enlightened conduct, and better taste and sense in human life. (18:267)
>
> I am not countenancing the sort of "hero-worship" which applauds the strong man of genius for forcibly seizing on the government of the world and making it do his bidding in spite of itself. All he can claim is, freedom to point out the way. The power of compelling others into it, is not only inconsistent with the freedom and development of all the rest, but corrupting to the strong man himself. (18:269)
>
> . . . the love of power and the love of liberty are in eternal antagonism. . . . The desire of power over others can only cease to be a depraving agency among mankind, when each of them individually is able to do without it.[14]

Mill's view here is in marked contrast to a liberalism that is fundamentally wedded to possessive individualism. Possessive individualism, unlike Mill's individualism, sees humans as ever seeking control over more and more resources—including other people—to satisfy their desires for property. Mill's individualism, in contrast, sees individualism as flowing from the development and use of the higher human powers, which is antagonistic to a desire to control others. The view that the more developed are justified in fixing the value choices for society and imposing them on the less developed is thus self-defeating on Mill's principles. An agent who argues for this view or acts on it is clearly corrupted and depraved rather than highly developed. The elitist position also contradicts radically Mill's view of how development is achieved. Once we pass from development to self-development at adulthood we take over control of our own developmental process. At this stage we are in the best position to know what will advance or impede our development and which activities and pursuits are in harmony with our nature. Any attempt to impose values or pursuits on us, even in the name of better values, only serves to short-circuit our self-development, which must unfold from within.

Mill's arguments in *Representative Government* in favor of the

[14]Mill, "Subjection of Women," in *Essays on Sex Equality,* ed. Alice S. Rossi (Chicago, 1970), 238.

weighted ballot are sometimes used to buttress an elitist interpretation. But Mill later abandons this position, which has merely strategic significance for him. His arguments in *Representative Government* are not designed to give to the developed elite influence out of proportion to their numbers. On the contrary, Mill supports proportional representation because he is concerned that in a representative democracy the developed elite would be entirely ignored; he wants to ensure that they have at least a voice in proportion to their numbers: "But if the *élite* of these classes formed part of the Parliament, by the same title as any other of its members—by representing the same number of citizens, the same numerical fraction of the national will" (19:459–60).

THE MORAL ARTS AND SCIENCES

Mill's views on the good essentially involve views on development. Competent agents need to be developed in order to judge the good or value that underlies the practical arts, including ethics. Mill's ethics and social and political philosophy all presuppose this view of the good and so all essentially depend on this conception of development. The structure of the moral arts and sciences helps to illuminate how development underlies and is essential to the conception of the good in ethics and social and political philosophy. Thus self-development bridges ethics and social and political philosophy, shaping Mill's views on qualitative hedonism in ethics and liberalism in social and political philosophy.

Mill's theory of the moral arts and sciences is hierarchical; its architecture, as assumed in the ethics and social and political philosophy, is elaborated in other writings, most notably for our purposes in Book 6 of the *Logic* (8:831–952) and in "On the Definition of Political Economy" (4:309–39). This structure illuminates the connections between the different levels of the moral arts, for our interests in particular the connections among the moral arts of ethics and politics and economics. A conception of self-development as essential to human well-being connects ethics and political philosophy, and the shape of Mill's liberalism depends on the conception of the good for humans which underlies it. One set of interpretive problems arises because, although this structure is the backbone of his other writings on ethics and political philosophy and is there in the background, it is rather complex and not always explicitly discussed. Some of the fine points of Mill's analysis which depend on this implicit structure are thus obscure and must be made explicit.

The moral arts and sciences, in Mill's theory, include not only ethics and social and political philosophy but also what in contemporary terms are classified as the social sciences. Every moral art is coupled with a corresponding moral science. In addition to this coupling structure, the sets of both the moral sciences and the moral arts are hierarchical; the more particular moral sciences presuppose the more basic moral sciences, and the more particular moral arts presuppose the more basic arts. Since in a different way each art presupposes its corresponding science, while at the same time this corresponding science presupposes the more basic sciences, the scheme is intricate.

I have previously examined Mill's understanding of the provinces of art and science. Now I need to survey the rest of the structure. In the *Logic* Mill works out in great detail the structure and methodology of the moral sciences, so it is best to focus our examination there. He begins with psychology, the most basic moral science, which studies the general laws of mind. Mill's concept of utility presupposes a view of human nature, and one of my tasks is to show what is encompassed in this view. The moral sciences give us knowledge about human nature which is then used by the moral arts to promote the ends or the good of beings with such a nature. Mill holds that there are universal laws of human nature which are the most basic level of the moral sciences. These are the laws of mind. "The phenomena of mind, then, are the various feelings of our nature . . . and by the laws of mind, I mean the laws according to which those feelings generate one another" (8:849).

Psychology is the science of the laws of mind and is thus the foundational moral science on which all the other moral sciences rest. There is a hierarchy of laws of social science which parallels the arrangement of rules of art, and just as the art of life forms the foundation for all other rules of art, so the laws of mind, or of psychology, are the most basic in social science. These laws of human nature filter up to all layers above and shape the laws of all moral sciences that rest on their foundation. The general laws Mill refers to here are the laws of association (8:852), which we encountered in Chapter 1. Mill refers the reader to his father's *Analysis* for a complete treatment of the laws of psychology, but he adds that "the laws of mind . . . compose the universal or abstract portion of the philosophy of human nature" (8:861).

The universal laws of the formation of character fall under the moral science of ethology, the science of character that corresponds to the art of education. This moral science is second only to psychology in the hierarchical structure of the moral sciences.

> There exist universal laws of the Formation of Character. And since it is by these laws, combined with the facts of each particular case, that the whole of the phenomena of human action and feeling are produced, it is on these that every rational attempt to construct the science of human nature in the concrete, and for practical purposes, must proceed. (8:864–65)
>
> The laws of the formation of character are, in short, derivative laws, resulting from the general laws of mind; and are to be obtained by deducing them from those general laws; by supposing any given set of circumstances, and then considering what, according to the laws of mind, will be the influence of those circumstances on the formation of character. . . .
> . . . Ethology is the science which corresponds to the art of education; in the widest sense of the term, including the formation of national or collective character as well as individual. . . . When the circumstances of an individual or of a nation are in any considerable degree under our control, we may, by our knowledge of tendencies, be enabled to shape those circumstances in a manner much more favourable to the ends we desire, than the shape which they would of themselves assume. (8:869–70)

Ethology is the source of the scientific knowledge that enables educators to promote the ends of their moral art, namely, the production of desirable features of human character formed out of the interaction of the laws of mind and the social and physical environment. Ethology is second only to psychology in the hierarchical structure of the moral arts. Its laws are also universal, but they derive from the laws of psychology. Ethological principles describe the effect of the laws of mind, conjoined with different sorts of concrete situations, on the development of character. Sex role differences, for example, may be explained by the different social situations of men and women. Along with ascertaining these laws deductively, social scientists must verify them by testing the correctness of inferences from theory in the situation under study. In this way the laws are linked with everyday commonsense generalizations that previously were only empirical laws of the lowest level. These latter Mill calls approximate generalizations (8:862); they are gathered inductively and are relatively unreliable until connected to the causal laws that explain them and set out the conditions under which they are true and the limits of their applicability. All the more particular moral sciences rest on the edifice of ethological and psychological knowledge and presuppose laws, principles, and understanding of the more basic sciences and levels. Each corresponding art also presupposes all these prior levels of scientific knowledge.

> The subject to be studied is, the origin and sources of all those qualities in human beings which are interesting to us, either as facts to be produced, to be avoided, or merely to be understood: and the object is, to determine, from the general laws of mind, combined with the general position of our species in the universe, what actual or possible combinations of circumstances are capable of promoting or of preventing the production of those qualities. A science which possesses middle principles of this kind, arranged in the order, not of causes, but of the effects which it is desirable to produce or to prevent, is duly prepared to be the foundation of the corresponding Art. And when Ethology shall be thus prepared, practical education will be the mere transformation of those principles into a parallel system of precepts, and the adaptation of these to the sum total of the individual circumstances which exist in each particular case. (8:873–74)

This summary explains the use and relation of the science of character formation to the art of education or cultivation, revealing how ethology presupposes psychology and how the scientific knowledge of both is used to promote the goals of the art. Its relevance here is to emphasize that the scientific understanding of human nature is intimately connected to the promotion of the good of beings of that nature. The end is desirable character traits for beings of a certain nature, namely, beings with a mental and moral nature, or an intellectual and social side. The good of beings with such a nature thus essentially involves development of potential so that these beings can exercise and enjoy their intellectual and moral capacities. The laws of association function at the abstract level of human nature, but there is also the more particular level of human nature, what we may call the developmental aspect of human nature and of the good for humans. This point helps to illustrate the two sides of qualitative hedonism. One side is that, since happiness is of different kinds, competent agents are needed with capacities developed to judge the value of these different kinds. The other side is that, since happiness is of different kinds and these different kinds vary in value, beings must understand their natures to discover the sort of happiness particularly appropriate to them. Mill claims that the forms of happiness rooted in human nature, as opposed to those rooted in the nature shared with other animals, are more valuable. The good of humans with a mental and moral nature, with intellectual, moral, and social capacities, requires the development and exercise of these aspects of their nature. Happiness is intimately connected with the development of generic human capacities and the autonomous search for individual mixes of these abilities.

Now Mill's examination moves to the next level, that of the science of humans in society: "Next after the science of individual man, comes the science of man in society: of the actions of collective masses of mankind" (8:875). Human nature is also at the core of the social sciences. The close linkages among the moral sciences and arts are once again illustrated, for the same laws of human nature form the basis of this grouping of moral sciences:

> The laws of the phenomena of society are, and can be, nothing but the laws of the actions and passions of human beings united together in the social state. Men, however, in a state of society, are still men; their actions and passions are obedient to the laws of individual human nature. Men are not, when brought together, converted into another kind of substance. (8:879)

Neither is it the case that their good or happiness is converted into another kind of thing when they are brought together in the social state: "Human beings in society have no properties but those which are derived from, and may be resolved into, the laws of the nature of individual man" (8:879). Again, "The actions and feelings of human beings in the social state, are, no doubt, entirely governed by psychological and ethological laws: whatever influence any cause exercises upon the social phenomena, it exercises through those laws" (8:896).

Among the central tasks of social science are the discovery of the laws by which societies as well as individuals progress and the provision of the information needed to achieve the particular goals of each art:

> The method now characterized is that by which the derivative laws of social order and of social progress must be sought. By its aid we may

hereafter succeed . . . in determining what artificial means may be
used . . . to accelerate the natural progress in so far as it is beneficial. . . . Such practical instructions, founded on the highest branch
of speculative sociology, will form the noblest and most beneficial
portion of the Political Art. (8:929–30)

Men's actions are the joint result of the general laws and circumstances of human nature, and of their own particular characters; those
characters again being the consequence of the natural and artificial
circumstances that constituted their education, among which circumstances must be reckoned their own conscious efforts. (8:932)

This hierarchical, interwoven structure of Mill's theory is also
elaborated in "On the Definition of Political Economy." This essay
is particularly revealing about the position of one of the particular
moral sciences, political economy, but it also sets out the general
framework of the moral arts and sciences.

Man, who, considered as a being having a moral or mental nature, is
the subject-matter of all the moral sciences, may, with reference to
that part of his nature, form the subject of philosophical inquiry under
several distinct hypotheses. We may inquire what belongs to man
considered individually, and as if no human being existed besides
himself; we may next consider him as coming into contact with other
individuals; and finally, as living in a state of *society,* that is, forming
part of a body or aggregation of human beings, systematically co-
operating for common purposes. . . .
      . . . Those laws or properties of human nature which appertain to
man as a mere individual, and do not presuppose, as a necessary condition, the existence of other individuals (except, perhaps, as mere instruments or means), form a part of the subject of pure mental philosophy. They comprise all the laws of the mere intellect, and those of the
purely self-regarding desires. . . .
      . . . Those laws of human nature which relate to the feelings called
forth in a human being by other individual human or intelligent
beings, as such; namely, the *affections,* the *conscience,* or feeling of
duty, and the love of *approbation;* and to the conduct of man, so far as
it depends upon, or has relation to, these parts of his nature—form the
subject of another portion of pure mental philosophy, namely, that
portion of it on which *morals,* or *ethics,* are founded. For morality
itself is not a science, but an art; not truths, but rules. The truths on
which the rules are founded are drawn (as is the case in all arts) from a
variety of sciences; but the principal of them, and those which are
most nearly peculiar to this particular art, belong to a branch of the
science of mind. . . .

. . . Finally, there are certain principles of human nature which are peculiarly connected with the ideas and feelings generated in man by living in a state of *society*, that is, by forming part of a union or aggregation of human beings for a common purpose or purposes. Few, indeed, of the elementary laws of the human mind are peculiar to this state, almost all being called into action in the two other states. But those simple laws of human nature, operating in that wider field, give rise to results of a sufficiently universal character , . . . to admit of being called, though in a somewhat looser sense, *laws* of society, or laws of human nature in the social state. . . . This science . . . shows by what principles of his nature man is induced to enter into a state of society; how this feature in his position acts upon his interests and feelings, and through them upon his conduct; how the association tends progressively to become closer, and the co-operation extends itself to more and more purposes; what those purposes are, and what the varieties of means most generally adopted for furthering them; what are the various relations which establish themselves among human beings as the ordinary consequence of the social union. . . .

. . . This branch of science, whether we prefer to call it social economy, speculative politics, or the natural history of society, presupposes the whole science of the nature of the individual mind; since all the laws of which the latter science takes cognizance are brought into play in a state of society, and the truths of the social science are but statements of the manner in which those simple laws take effect in complicated circumstances. Pure mental philosophy, therefore, is an essential part, or preliminary, of political philosophy. The science of social economy embraces every part of man's nature, in so far as influencing the conduct or condition of man in society; and therefore may it be termed speculative politics, as being the scientific foundation of practical politics, or the art of government, of which the art of legislation is a part. (4:319–21)

The developmental conception of human nature and the conception of humans as beings with a mental and moral nature with intellectual, affective, and social capacities are fundamental to Mill's utilitarianism; the essential components of human nature must underlie the whole edifice of the moral sciences and inform all the moral arts. The laws, properties, or principles of human nature are the subject of all the moral sciences; they inform and are presupposed by all the moral arts. These principles and laws remain the same, but they take different appearances in different contexts. Mill does not proceed with different conceptions of human nature in different contexts; rather, he holds to one unitary conception that adapts itself in different contexts. And since developmental principles of human nature are the scientific basis of all the moral sciences, their significance filters up to all levels of moral arts, including ethics and political philosophy. It is no wonder, then, that Mill's liberalism, fused around a core value of self-development, differs so profoundly in its concerns, goals, and implications from forms of liberalism built on values of possessive individualism. It is this structure of the moral arts and sciences which gives the unifying basis to the whole, which links Mill's conception of the good and happiness for humans in the realms of ethics and political philosophy and shapes his liberalism. The same layered structure occurs in tandem in the moral arts. The end is the happiness or good of beings of a certain nature—a mental and moral nature and an intellectual and social nature. Mill is a qualitative hedonist because he maintains that the good for such creatures consists not of simple pleasures but of the use of faculties, especially affective, intellectual, and social capacities. Creatures with this nature are not satisfied with passively filling up with happiness; they require an active use of capacities.

The hierarchical structure of the moral sciences is also found in the practical moral arts, which are all geared to the same goal— promoting the ends, enjoyments, and happiness of humans. To this end, these arts must make use of the scientific foundations of the moral sciences, for the ends must be promoted by the appropriate means. Since the end is the happiness and enjoyment of humans, the whole enterprise is futile if we do not have a thorough understanding of what makes such creatures happy, that is, an understanding of their nature. Thus a conception of human nature underlies the entire enterprise. It is natural, then, that a commitment to self-development is something to which all else is subordinate; for the search for self-development is the essential core of human nature, and it is this same conception of human nature which permeates and shapes all the moral sciences and moral arts.

On the most general level, the principles of human nature are simply the laws of psychological association. But there is also no doubt that Mill holds a more substantive developmental view of human nature. Although he believes that environmental influences have a dominant role in determining character, he sees certain tendencies or dispositions of human nature interacting with these external forces. It is Mill's dispositional view of human nature, one by which humans naturally seek growth, that gives his theory its developmental flavor; in all his writing Mill is consistent in his developmental account.

Mill's qualitative hedonism is a developmental theory of the good. His undeniably basic commitment to self-development is rooted in his substantive conception of the nature of humans as beings with higher faculties who seek to grow and expand these faculties. Because of the structure of the moral sciences and arts, the same principles of human nature govern the moral sciences that correspond to ethics and political philosophy, and thus these principles and the conception of happiness inform all these arts.

Mill makes the same pronouncements about the happiness of creatures with a seeking nature in different contexts. Emphasized always is the claim that we have intellectual faculties and social sympathies that need fulfillment for us to be happy. All the practical moral arts, including ethics and political philosophy, are geared to promoting the end of happiness in their different arenas. We must be competent self-developed agents to be able to both enjoy the appropriate good and measure this value competently. Since each level of the moral arts and sciences presupposes and is deduced from the prior, more basic levels, it should not come as a surprise that the same conception of self-development, embedded in the views of the happiness appropriate for creatures with our nature, plays several roles. Thus different levels both use and presuppose the same conception without conflict.

Mill's view of self-development is the same in *Utilitarianism, On Liberty, Representative Government,* and other writings on social and political philosophy. *On Liberty* provides one central illustration of the hinge between different realms of the moral arts and sciences, in particular the hinge between utility and the good for humans in the realms of ethics and social philosophy. Mill thinks that utility is the foundation of all the moral arts and sciences. Utility grounds not only ethics but also social and political philosophy. *On Liberty* is one of Mill's primary writings in social philosophy, but in it he quite explicitly links his ethics and social philosophy by means of his notions of utility, involving essentially self-development. Having just set down his principle of liberty, a cornerstone of his social philosophy and his ethical theory as well, he says, "It is proper to state that I forego any advantage which could be derived to my argument from the idea of abstract right, as a thing independent of utility. I regard utility as the ultimate appeal on all ethical questions; but it must be utility in the largest sense, grounded on the permanent interests of man as a progressive being" (18:224). These "permanent interests of man as a progressive being" are interests in mental and moral development. In the rest of this essay Mill argues for the development of generic intellectual and social capacities and for autonomy and individuality. Chapter 2, "Of the Liberty of Thought and Discussion," is on one level an eloquent argument for the importance of free discussion and freedom of expression for the development of our intellectual powers. Unless we have an intense desire to seek the truth and reflect critically on important matters, as well as the mental powers obviously presupposed by such a search, we will not continue developing mentally. This dynamic process feeds on itself; the more we use our mental powers, the more we develop them and want to use them. In Chapter 3, "Of Individuality, as One of the Elements of Well-Being," Mill argues for individuality and autonomy, along with the development of generic human capacities, as necessary for human happiness. Each person has a special combination of abilities that is partly discovered and partly created in the process. It is this notion of individuality that I take up in Chapter 7.

7

Liberalism and Individualism

I have argued that Mill's introduction of quality into a more expansive view of the good and the consequent switch from the Benthamite felicific calculus to the judgment of competent agents to measure value do not have the dire consequences so often claimed. It may appear that, though we have come a great distance, I have a good deal farther to go in exonerating Mill. I now must come to grips with a new set of issues and criticisms that confront Mill's principles of the good not in the abstract but in a social context. Unlike Bentham's theory, which can be flatly applied without much thought to milieu, Mill's competent agents and their judgments are crucially dependent on and connected to their social environment, which certainly complicates the requirements of the theory. The very strength and appeal of the theory that does not ignore the social reality in which any plausible moral theory must do its work could also be its Achilles heel.

In looking at this new group of issues, we should keep in mind the kind of objectivity to which Mill's theory aspires. When Mill maintains that developed moral agents rank pleasurable experiences according to their value, he does not mean that they are making a discovery that the world contains things that are valuable independent of human consciousness. On the contrary, Mill's denial of this claim is a crucial element in his dispute with intuitionism. Intuitionists are wedded to the claim that there are eternal moral verities, that the natural world is so constructed that it contains value external to the human mind, and that humans discover value by focusing their reason and intuition. The process of gaining knowledge of the right and the good is a process of discovering these self-evident moral truths. If these claims of intuitionism were correct, that is, if moral agents merely use their special intuitive faculties to discover what is good and obligatory, then intuitionism would be an objective theory in a way that Mill's utilitarianism does not aspire to. But it is precisely because Mill holds that these central claims of intuitionism are false that he castigates intuitionism most severely. Because there are no such ontologically objective values waiting to be discovered by intuition, what passes for these in intuitionist theories are actually the subjective feelings and prejudices of the judge, uncorroborated by public or social mechanisms or by rational procedures. Mill, eschewing what he takes to be false claims about ontologically objective value, builds into his theory such objectivity as he thinks is available in a world without value as part of its metaphysical furniture. Mill's conception of value builds instead on a view of human nature and of humans as developing, seeking, and growing beings.

Mill's commitment to liberty and individual development is one of the most exoteric themes of his moral and political philosophy. But the linkages between his commitment to liberty and development and his conception of utility and principles of the good are not as commonly recognized. Mill's transformed conception of utility necessitates a new method of value measurement which relies heavily on the judgment of competent agents and thus essentially rests on a doctrine of human development and self-development. The procedure for measuring value elicits the preferences of agents who are competently acquainted with all the satisfactions under consideration and who produce a preferential ranking of all these satisfactions which considers both quantity and quality. If competent agents decidedly prefer or judge to be more valuable one pleasurable experience, then according to Mill that experience has the best chance of being the more valuable experience. Thus more valuable experiences are those that are preferred by agents competent to adjudicate, and such agents, according to Mill, are those who are developed in certain specifiable ways. This preferential ranking by judges who are in a position to know is the foundation of Mill's approach to value measurement. For people to become competent agents, they must undergo a process of development and self-development and be socialized and nurtured into rational and benevolent agents.

Value measurement relies on moral agents in their social environment; the measurement procedure uses moral agents who are socialized and educated by the society to which they belong and who are thus to a significant extent social products of that society. Mill does not underestimate the degree to which a society can shape the characters of its members, although his goal is socialization to increase welfare and allow all to reach their full potential. Mill's competent judges are rational and benevolent agents who have been provided with an initial set of social standards and then asked to evaluate and choose those pleasures and projects worth pursuing both individually in the private sphere and socially in the realm of public choice. He thus specifies the sort of agents who make these choices, explaining how they are to be educated for this task. He specifies how they are to make these choices, using social, public standards in a rational and benevolent fashion. He specifies that they are to evaluate and choose what maximizes the satisfaction of all those who have an interest in the situation, treating all impartially.[1]

Rational and benevolent social agents use public procedures for evaluation. Previously I focused on the microlevel of Mill's theory in order to clarify and defend its foundations. This is where Mill begins, because of his associationism, but it is not where he ends. When Mill discusses value he has in mind not only microlevel pleasures and pains but also, on a higher level, worthwhile human lives.

I begin examining some implications of Mill's reliance on competent agents by looking at some common objections to his social and political philosophy. These objections range from general expressions of concern about the objectivity of moral judgments to more particular charges against Mill's liberalism. If Mill's qualified judges are creations of the society in which they happen to be raised, and if the standards they learn during their education and to some extent continue to accept and apply are reflections of the preexisting

---

[1]It must be kept in mind here that this procedure is outlined for choices of the good, not the right. Whereas choices of the good are clearly maximizing, choices of the right may be made differently in Mill's theory and may be only indirectly maximizing. To decide this, we need to settle the dispute between act and rule utilitarian interpretations.

and dominant values of their society, critics can express skepticism about the objectivity of the learned standards and about the socialization that induces people to adopt them as their own.

Some critics deny Mill's claim that the evaluative standards are merely starting points for expertise and instead argue that agents are considerably more class- and culture-bound than Mill believes. Mill is often accused of being a liberal ideologist, and left-wing critics are commonly skeptical about the objectivity claims made on behalf of these social standards, arguing that they are merely the standards of the upper middle class of Mill's day cloaked as more objective judgments.[2] Moreover, it is claimed that Mill's liberalism leads him to acquiesce to inequitable access to developmental opportunities and to accept that the majority of members of his society will never have the chance to lead autonomous lives. The source of the standards and the control of the socialization process become of focal interest, since developed agents are the basis of value measurement and have such special status as both source and judge of human satisfaction.

Individualism and liberty are highly valued by Mill and closely connected in his view with development. Critics, on the other hand, see tension between that thrust of his theory that seems to demand equality of opportunity for all members of society to develop the entire spectrum of their human capacities and the realities of the inequitable social and economic conditions of his time, which Mill accepted at least in the short term and yet which severely limited the potential for development of many members of his society. This charge is particularly serious for Mill because of his theory's dependence on development to produce moral agents. Mill's competent judges are autonomous agents who progressively widen and increase their capacities for happiness in the course of choosing the patterns of their lives. One set of objections takes issue with Mill precisely because of his focus on individual development and attributes to him a form of liberal individualism. These criticisms tie in his philosophy with a long line of liberal thinkers who are seen as building their theories on a narrow and demeaning conception of human

[2]This is a common criticism. Two recent examples are G. G. Brenkert, "Marx's Critique of Utilitarianism," in *Marx and Morality*, ed. Kai Nielsen and Steven C. Patten, *Canadian Journal of Philosophy, Supplementary Volume* 7 (1981): 203–204; Graeme Duncan and John Gray, "The Left against Mill," in *New Essays on John Stuart Mill and Utilitarianism*, ed. Wesley E. Cooper, Kai Nielsen, and Steven C. Patten, *Canadian Journal of Philosophy, Supplementary Volume* 5 (1979): 206.

nature. A classic indictment of liberalism along these lines is propounded by Robert Paul Wolff: "Liberalism views man as a rationally calculating maximizer of pleasure and minimizer of pain."[3] According to Wolff, this stance has profound implications for relations among people: "If the simple psychological egoism of liberal theory is correct, then each individual must view others as mere instruments in the pursuit of his private ends. . . . But always I seek my own pleasure. . . . For me, other persons are obstacles to be overcome or resources to be exploited" (141). Wolff reserves his strongest criticisms for Bentham, but he has this to say about Mill.

> In the more sophisticated versions of liberal philosophy, the crude picture of man as a pleasure maximizer is softened somewhat. Mill recognizes that men may pursue higher ends than pleasure . . . and he even recognizes the possibility of altruistic or other-regarding feelings of sympathy and compassion. Nevertheless, society continues to be viewed as a system of independent centers of consciousness, each pursuing its own gratification and confronting the others as beings standing-over-against the self, which is to say, as *objects*. The condition of the individual in such a state of affairs is what a different tradition of social philosophy would call 'alienation'. (142)

Mill's view of humans, according to Wolff, can be contrasted with traditions that are fundamentally social and communitarian, traditions that see that "man is by nature a social being . . . social in the sense that his essence, his true being, lies in his involvement in a human community" (142).

A similar objection is put by G. G. Brenkert, who also makes somewhat of an exception for Mill, excusing him from some of the worst flaws of utilitarian liberalism. Yet Brenkert claims that a general powerful Marxist objection applies to Mill's version as well:

> In order to determine which actions or rules will promote the greatest good, utilitarianism makes reference to individuals who define themselves and manner of life privately.
> . . . It assumes that individuals are private individuals . . it also consists in a certain unacceptable view of individuals, their goods, and their relation to the social and general good. . . .
> . . . Marx holds that a position is egoistic if it assumes or implies that the individuals involved are private individuals, as opposed to social individuals. . . . they are also egoistic simply by virtue of the

[3]Robert Paul Wolff, *The Poverty of Liberalism*, (Boston, 1968), 141.

fact that their individualities, their desires and ends, are privately rather than socially defined. . . . each individual's desires and interests are ultimately subjectively determined. . . . each individual is the best or final judge of his own interests. . . . the relations in which individuals stand to one another are incidental to, rather than constitutive of, what they are. . . . Thus, individuals view themselves as divided and opposed; they do not, in general, closely identify or experience a harmony of interests with others; they view others and society instrumentally.

Marx's objection to the private individual is that such an individual embodies a mistaken or alienated relation between individuals themselves and society.

As opposed to the private individual, Marx's theory demands a social individual whose interests coincide with the general good and whose affective life permeates and is permeated by the affective lives of others. Marx's social or moral individual is one whose very existence, activity, spirit, and wealth are essentially bound with others and the community. . . . Consequently, one's relations with others and the community are much closer, much more intimate, than on the private individual model.[4]

According to this line of criticism, liberalism takes people to be competitive, egoistic, atomistic, anomic, alienated, and separate from their fellows and their social environment. Even when they do not chase after their own self-centered goals without consideration to others' needs, their efforts at cooperation are stilted or stunted, grudgingly embraced as part of a negotiating strategy rather than an organic, harmonious process. According to this picture, people have to work at recognizing others' interests, in contrast with other political traditions in which people belong naturally to deep social networks and communities.

Both Wolff and Brenkert concede that such objections are primarily directed at Bentham and other utilitarian predecessors of Mill and that they have blunted or limited force against Mill's views. But since Mill is a major figure of the liberal tradition, it is important to emphasize just how little application these objections have to his views.

It is clear at the outset that Mill's individualism assumes social beings, not isolated individuals lacking deep social bonds as charged above. This criticism has some applicability to Bentham, whose narrow portrayal of human nature in fact focused Mill's disagree-

[4]Brenkert, "Marx's Critique of Utilitarianism," 198–201.

ment with Benthamism and his break with its orthodoxy (10:91–97). Mill develops an account of human nature in which social relations and sociality are essential components and competitive egoism is frowned on:

> In the comparatively early state of human advancement in which we now live, a person cannot indeed feel that entireness of sympathy with all others, which would make any real discordance in the general direction of their conduct in life impossible; but already a person in whom the social feeling is at all developed, cannot bring himself to think of the rest of his fellow creatures as struggling rivals with him for the means of happiness, whom he must desire to see defeated in their object in order that he may succeed in his. The deeply rooted conception which every individual even now has of himself as a social being, tends to make him feel it one of his natural wants that there should be harmony between his feelings and aims and those of his fellow creatures. . . . few but those whose mind is a moral blank, could bear to lay out their course of life on the plan of paying no regard to others except so far as their own private interest compels. (10:233)

> As little is there an inherent necessity that any human being should be a selfish egotist, devoid of every feeling or care but those which centre in his own miserable individuality. . . . Genuine private affections, and a sincere interest in the public good, are possible, though in unequal degrees, to every rightly brought up human being. (10:216)

> As between his own happiness and that of others, utilitarianism requires him to be as strictly impartial as a disinterested and benevolent spectator. In the golden rule of Jesus of Nazareth, we read the complete spirit of the ethics of utility. To do as one would be done by, and to love one's neighbour as oneself, constitute the ideal perfection of utilitarian morality. . . . utility would enjoin, first, that laws and social arrangements should place the happiness, or . . . the interest, of every individual, as nearly as possible in harmony with the interest of the whole, and secondly, that education and opinion, which have so vast a power over human character, should so use that power as to establish in the mind of every individual an indissoluble association between his own happiness and the good of the whole . . . also that a direct impulse to promote the general good may be in every individual one of the habitual motives of action, and the sentiments connected therewith may fill a large and prominent place in every human being's sentient existence. (10:218)

According to Mill, the firm line his critics draw between individuality and sociality, between the private individual and the public individual, is misleading and inaccurate. Individuality and sociality are not contradictory but complementary notions, and the development of one's individuality is inextricably tied to and must be balanced by the development of one's sociality. They are two aspects of the same whole, a developed being, and if they do not grow together, or if one outweighs the other, then one's development is to this extent hindered.

Although some left-wing critics of liberalism are rightly concerned that many liberal theories place too much emphasis on the individual and individual liberty at the expense of community and sociality, this is not a feature of Mill's theory. The individualist elements in Mill can be overemphasized by libertarian interpretations, but such interpretations are distorted. Mill is concerned with individuality and sociality equally. Some communitarian theories would emphasize social being and community to the extent of denying entirely the importance of the individual and the private sphere; Mill's theory would be excluded from this circle. But it would require a separate, convincing argument to establish that such a radical undermining of the individual and the private is desirable.

Mill's brand of individualism is in itself quite innocuous and consists of tenets shared by a variety of ethical and political theories. Mill's most compact and straightforward presentation of his views on individuality is found in *On Liberty*. His theory does not embrace possessive individualism; he does not regard humans as primarily acquisitors or consumers, in Macpherson's terminology.[5] Property rights do not occupy the central place in Mill's theory that they enjoy in many other forms of liberalism. In Mill's view, people do not live to acquire property, and too much focus on property is demeaning and can interfere with the increase in welfare that actually results from human development. Thus Mill's theory does not promote acquisitiveness and Lockean property rights, nor does it assume isolated individuals lacking social bonds. Mill's individualism is centered around the value he places on the individual as the generator, focus, and appraiser of value.[6] Value is located in each and every individual; whatever value groups have flows only from the value of its members. Each and every individual has deep value and must be respected and treated in a manner appropriate to

[5]C. B. Macpherson, *The Life and Times of Liberal Democracy* (Oxford, 1980), 22–43; *Democratic Theory: Essays in Retrieval*, (Oxford, 1973), 199.
[6]See Duncan and Gray, "The Left against Mill," 215.

such a bearer of worth, allowing particular, unique patterns of value to emerge and flourish (18:266).

Mill's theory is developmental to its core. The developmental process is structured to create a person of character, for cultivation not only develops each person's cognitive and affective faculties but also develops a person of particularity of thought and feeling. To be in control or possession of one's life and powers, to be accustomed to making and carrying out one's own choices, to have one's ideas and activities and projects be an expression of one's own particularity are essential aspects of Mill's individualism. "A person whose desires and impulses are his own—are the expression of his own nature, as it has been developed and modified by his own culture—is said to have a character" (18:264). Such individuality is a product of learning. Humans are not born with individuality, and it is indeed a characteristic that must be carefully nurtured before it can be manifested. Mill's developed agents are not the assured products of any socialization process; they appear only when the distinctive human faculties are allowed and encouraged into maturation and not blocked from emerging. Mill uses organic metaphors to describe this unfolding: "Human nature is . . . a tree, which requires to grow and develope itself on all sides, according to the tendency of the inward forces which make it a living thing" (18:263).

Developed agents continue to grow after maturation and expand their natures and potentials as long as this is encouraged. The notions of development and individuality are dynamically related, for development creates an individual character and the encouragement of individuality is needed for continued development. Although almost all people have the potential to become developed beings if their social circumstances permit, the developmental path of each is unique and diversity of character and lifestyle inevitable. Society can (and ought to) create conditions for potential to develop, but it cannot, except through coercion, create uniform characters in its members. Society therefore must take care to provide different people with the proper media for their growth:

> Such are the differences among human beings in their sources of pleasure, their susceptibilities of pain, and the operation on them of different physical and moral agencies, that unless there is a corresponding diversity in their modes of life, they neither obtain their fair share of happiness, nor grow up to the mental, moral, and aesthetic stature of which their nature is capable. (18:270)

Associated with his rejection of mechanical modes of viewing human development and his use of natural metaphors is Mill's linkage of individuality and spontaneity. In concentrating on the spontaneous individual as his model, Mill highlights the requirement that our activities and attachments flow naturally from our being and are not forced on us from the outside(18:261). In this way we have the greatest chance of achieving a balance of happiness, of leading happy and worthwhile lives, and of bringing happiness to others. But we cannot maintain and express our individuality unless we are in an atmosphere of security and freedom which allows us to formulate life plans and follow through on them. Freedom is also linked to the flourishing of individuality. *On Liberty* is an impassioned plea for the liberty that will promote the individuality required for self-development and for the appreciation of more valuable pleasures and pursuits.

Mill is apprehensive about the prevalent dead weight of custom; he sees people being pressured to conform to customary activities and ideas rather than to work out their own convictions and ways of life. Living in society does place constraints on behavior, but "it is not by wearing down into uniformity all that is individual in themselves, but by cultivating it and calling it forth, within the limits imposed by the rights and interests of others, that human beings become a noble and beautiful object of contemplation" (18:266).

Mill's distinction between self-regarding and other-regarding actions is relevant here; individuality should be afforded full scope and play only within the self-regarding sphere of actions that primarily concern the individual. Thus our individual experimentation and expression may be curtailed if its free play would harm others or violate their rights or interfere with their vital interests. To work out the right balance here is one of the most profound issues facing Mill's philosophy. I have more to say about this when I examine the right to liberty of self-development in Mill's system, which I argue can actually work to constrict the private sphere of self-regarding actions and private liberty more than strongly libertarian interpretations of Mill would acknowledge. But "it is desirable that in things which do not primarily concern others, individuality should assert itself" (18:261).

Mill argues eloquently for both liberty of expression and liberty of experimentation in living. These freedoms are needed to help individuals discover what patterns of life best suit their natures and to let them live out these patterns unobstructed. By realizing their natures and coming into their powers, they learn to appreciate even more what satisfactions are worthy and their lives as a whole yield them a supreme measure of happiness and fulfillment: "there should be different experiments of living. . . . free scope should be given to varieties of character, short of injury to others" (18:260–61). Value comes not simply from living this life but from choosing it. Unless we choose our own pleasures and activities, we cannot completely appreciate and understand their value and we miss an opportunity to exercise our powers and in so doing to amplify them. As John Gray puts it:

> According to Mill's theory of qualitative hedonism, the higher pleasures are found in forms of life and activity whose content is distinctive and peculiar in each case, but which necessarily involve the exercise of generically human power of autonomous thought and action. It is these forms of life, distinctively human but peculiar in each case, that Mill sees as expressing individuality.[7]

Although Mill's notion of self-development is broader than that of autonomy, the point applies. I use the notion of self-development to denote the development and exercise of higher cognitive and affective faculties, whereas Gray is more concerned with their autonomous exercise once they are developed. The range of valuable activities and pursuits is quite extensive in Mill's view, but the value of all satisfactions is lowered if they reflect the values of others rather than being freely chosen and expressive of the character of the agent:

> Where, not the person's own character, but the traditions or customs of other people are the rule of conduct, there is wanting one of the principal ingredients of human happiness, and quite the chief ingredient of individual and social progress.
>
> . . . to conform to custom, merely *as* custom, does not educate or develope in him any of the qualities which are the distinctive endowment of a human being. . . . The human faculties of perception, judgment, discriminative feeling, mental activity, and even moral preference, are exercised only in making a choice. He who does anything because it is the custom, makes no choice. He gains no practice either in discerning or in desiring what is best. The mental and moral . . . powers are improved only by being used. . . .

[7]Gray, *Mill On Liberty,* 70.

. . . He who lets the world . . . choose his plan of life for him, has no
need of any other faculty than the ape-like one of imitation. He who
chooses his plan for himself, employs all his faculties. (18:261–62)

Within this range of alternatives available to seekers of valuable
sources of happiness, not only is valued lowered if the activity is not
followed as a result of autonomous choice, but the value of an activity can be raised if it is the result of such choice: "If a person
possesses any tolerable amount of common sense and experience,
his own mode of laying out his existence is the best, not because it is
the best in itself, but because it is his own mode" (18:270). This
explains, in part, why the path of self-development is an individual
one, why even when individuals have reached a certain level of self-
development they can act only as guides to others, not as authorities. Someone with a certain measure of development who tries
to act as more than a guide and imposes judgments of value on
others thereby paradoxically undermines that claim to development. This point, I argue shortly, is significant in the context of
representative government and economic democracy and undercuts
the argument that Mill's theory leads to elitism. "All he can claim
is, freedom to point out the way. The power of compelling others
into it, is . . . inconsistent with the freedom and development of all
the rest" (18:269)

Mill's conception of individuality stands up rather well under
scrutiny. But other controversies arise from his form of liberalism.
Most commentators have situated the vulnerability of Mill's argument in a conflict or tension among different values or goals of his
political philosophy. The result is a variety of criticism whose motif
is that Mill's individualism is an admirable value to which Mill
unfortunately can pay only lip service. Alternatively, Mill's goal or
principle of individual development is said to clash with other principles of his liberalism, and again unfortunately the goal of development emerges from these conflicts somewhat the worse for the en-
counter.

Commentators such as C. B. Macpherson and Amy Gutmann
question the extent to which Mill's goal of the most complete development of all members of society, consistent with the like development of all others, is compromised or effectively outweighed by his
toleration of economic and power inequalities. Macpherson has advanced various versions of these themes in his writings. In *Life and*

Times of Liberal Democracy, he puts the problem as the clash between two meanings of liberal democracy. Macpherson asserts that Mill intends by liberal democracy "a society striving to ensure that all its members are equally free to realize their capabilities."[8] But, according to Macpherson, this goal does not quite jibe with Mill's acceptance of a capitalist market economy which allows "freedom of the stronger to do down the weaker by following market rules" (1). This acceptance of market rules is no longer necessary, in Macpherson's view, for the survival of liberal values. In fact, he argues that the durability of a later form of liberal democracy requires that the self-development goal gain ascendancy over capitalist market principles (1). Macpherson argues that such an enduring form of liberal democracy would be of the later participatory democracy form rather than the earlier developmental form which he ascribes to Mill. Whether he is correct in this last assertion, he has accurately pinpointed what is often seen as the weak point of Mill's liberalism, the conflict between its free market economic goals and its political and moral ideals.

According to Macpherson, the tensions among the principles of Mill's liberalism are reflected plainly in Mill's ambivalence toward the claims of the poor and the working class of his society. He recognizes the misery of their living conditions and he "was morally revolted by the life they were compelled to lead." He recognizes that liberal democracy "could contribute to human development" and that the "good society is one which permits and encourages everyone to act as exerter, developer, and enjoyer of the exertion and development, of his or her own capacities" (47–48). Thus also, according to Macpherson, "Mill had been deeply troubled by the incompatibility he saw between the claims of equal human development and the existing class inequalities of power and wealth. Although he did not identify the problem accurately, and so was unable to resolve it even in theory, he did see that there was a problem and try to deal with it" (49). Furthermore, "the greatest aggregate happiness was to be got by permitting and encouraging individuals to develop themselves. . . .

But at the same time . . . Mill recognized that the existing distribution of wealth and of economic power made it impossible for

[8]C. B. Macpherson, *The Life and Times of Liberal Democracy,* 1. See also Macpherson, *Democratic Theory.*

most members of the working class to develop themselves at all, or even to live humanly" (52). Mill also

> found the actual prevailing distribution of the produce of labour wholly unjust. He found the explanation of that unjust distribution in an historical accident, not in the capitalist principle itself. . . .
>
>   In thus putting the blame on the original feudal forcible distribution of property, and the failure of subsequent property law to rectify it, Mill was able to think that the capitalist principle was not in any way responsible for the existing inequitable distributions of wealth, income, and power. (55)

Mill, Macpherson claims, failed to see the conflict between the capitalist principle itself and values of self-development.

Writing from within the liberal tradition, Amy Gutmann attempts in *Liberal Equality* a synthesis of liberal values that are commonly perceived as being in conflict. She contends that what she calls the participatory and redistributionist ideals of liberalism, far from being theoretically incompatible, are rather both necessary and mutually dependent. "The task of integrating democratic participation and equal distribution," she argues, "is one that is both possible and necessary to the spirit of a liberal egalitarian theory of justice."[9] Gutmann scrutinizes Mill's theory and suggests that it is somewhat flawed:

> The opportunities with which Mill appeared most concerned were educational in the broad sense: opportunities for self-development. Political participation was for him an essential component of that opportunity for self-development. This concern with broadening participatory opportunities, and thereby rendering them more nearly equal, is what I take to be the heart and strength of Mill's theory from the perspective of liberal egalitarianism. . . .
>
>   . . . The major weakness of Mill's theory from this perspective is its principled indeterminacy on questions of economic distribution . . .
>
>   . . . the theoretical basis of his argument is also weak. We are never told how much inequality of distribution is compatible with his goal of human self-development through expanding participatory opportunities. . . . Mill's theory therefore does not sufficiently examine what the relationship should be between his participatory goal, intended to achieve a broader distribution of the higher pleasures, and the nature of economic distribution within a society. Nevertheless, he does succeed in presenting one of the strongest liberal arguments for

[9]Amy Gutmann, *Liberal Equality* (Cambridge, 1980), 202–3.

expanding opportunities for everybody to participate in the economic as well as in the political institutions of society. (13)

The gauntlet is thrown down. I would like to sharpen the challenge by pointing out ways in which self-development is particularly important for Mill and illustrating just how fundamental is his theoretical commitment to self-development. A lot hangs on this for Mill, for each stage of my argument has illuminated the fundamental role of self-development in Mill's moral theory. Judgments of utility are the evaluative basis of all our practical reasoning about the ends of the art of life. Estimations of utility figure in all our practical reasoning about ends not only of morality but also of self-interest, beauty, and nobility. But we cannot fully or accurately make judgments of value unless we reach a certain level of self-development. If we reach this point, we are Mill's competent agents.[10]

When considering the tensions within Mill's liberalism, we should not overlook two related points of interest about Mill's transformed conception of utility and method of value measurement. The first point is methodological: Mill's theory requires developed or competent agents even to get off the ground and to be able to do the evaluations on which the theory rests. The second point is that to deny someone the educative experience or opportunity of development is to deny that person the status of moral agency or of complete or full moral agency. This is not to deny that they are full moral persons with rights.

On the first point, an objection immediately arises: even in a society with extreme disparities of developmental opportunities,

---

[10]I leave aside the question of the relationship between principles of good and principles of right; whatever the precise connection, in Mill's theory principles of right must be grounded in some way on utility, and thus the ability to measure utility is indispensible. There is a growing literature on this question; see David Lyons, "Mill's Theory of Morality," *Nous* 10 (1976): 101–20; "Human Rights and the General Welfare," *Philosophy and Public Affairs* 6 (1977): 113–29; "Liberty and Harm to Others," in *New Essays on John Stuart Mill and Utilitarianism*, ed. Cooper, Nielsen, and Patton, 19; D. G. Brown, "Mill on Liberty and Morality," *Philosophical Review* 81 (1972): 133–58; "What Is Mill's Principle of Utility?" *Canadian Journal of Philosophy* 3 (1973): 1–12; "Mill's Criterion of Wrong Conduct," *Dialogue* 21 (1982): 27–44; David Copp, "The Iterated-Utilitarianism of J. S. Mill," in *New Essays on John Stuart Mill and Utilitarianism*, ed. Cooper, Nielsen, and Patten, 75–98; L. W. Sumner, "The Good and the Right," in *New Essays on John Stuart Mill and Utilitarianism*, ed. Cooper, Nielsen, and Patton, 99–114; Jan Narveson, *Morality and Utility*.

where few have reached even a minimal level of development of distinctively human faculties, there are still some few who are capable of judging value. The existence of even a small number of competent agents is enough, it can be objected, to fulfill the methodological requirement. Two responses are in order here. First, it may be that these few would ease the methodological strain, but the measurement procedure would then be elitist. I return to issues of elitism in Chapters 8 and 10. The second response is methodological. In Mill's well-known treatment of liberty of thought and discussion in *On Liberty*, one of his many arguments is that freedom of discussion affords society the best chance of reaching the complete truth on a subject (18:252–54). Often a commonly accepted opinion is not so much false as just a portion of the truth, and full intellectual debate is the best means of ensuring that the other part of the truth emerges. What is needed, claims Mill, is a "collision of adverse opinions," which comes about through the participation of many disputants (18:258). The most extensive and active participation in these debates is desirable, not only because of its beneficial effects on the participants, but also because it aids the search for truth. A parallel argument can be formulated for ensuring that correct value choices and measures are made. The most widespread and active involvement in debates about and choices of public goods is the best procedure for ensuring correct value choices (*Representative Government*, 19:405, 424–25, 433). So, although a small elite of competent agents may suffice to meet the minimal methodological requirements, we can greatly increase the chances that the best values are chosen by widening the field of competent participants.

An extreme conclusion from the second point is that, unless someone has reached a certain level of development, he or she cannot judge the value of enjoyment at all and cannot be said to be a competent agent at all. This position denies entirely the status of moral agency to those who have not undergone development. Its proponents might use an analogy with wine evaluation to argue that someone who has not gone through a wine-evaluation training process is not competent to evaluate wines at all. Such untrained people might claim to make aesthetic judgments about wines, but since they have not learned to make the necessary discriminations and to appreciate some wines above others they can only be expressing personal preferences rather than considered aesthetic judgments. This extreme position is, however, implausible when applied to judgments of value of pleasure and satisfaction; the analogy between evaluations of wine and of pleasure does not hold up well. Few of us have sufficient experience or training to adopt the status of expert wine judges. But almost all humans in the course of normal life development achieve some measure of development of intellect and feeling and some ability to make choices. It is more accurate to think of competency in value judgment as an ability that develops by degrees, or in stages, and to conceive of moral agents as having more or less competence. Still, this interpretation does not remove the pressure from Mill's theory; although moral agency can evolve by degrees, it is nevertheless the case that the theory requires moral agents who have achieved a substantial degree of competence. The theoretical pressure remains not to deny people the opportunity to develop themselves into such agents.

Mill argues in *On Liberty* that unless one's critical intellectual powers are developed one cannot cling to intellectual convictions as living truths but only as dead dogma. The same rationality and benevolence are in operation in judgments of the good and the right. On some interpretations of Mill, moral action consists solely of following the rules of right; when we make judgments of the good we are outside the sphere of morality. Thus it could be asked, on this view, whether moral agency is involved in making judgments of good. This interpretation would mean that when we are deciding what rule of duty to follow we are acting as moral agents, but when rules conflict and we must break the conflict by appeal to utility, thereby deciding what is best, we are no longer acting as moral agents. This last point strains credulity. We are acting as moral agents on both occasions. Similarly, in our conduct, we can only follow moral principles blindly if we have not subjected them to critical scrutiny and freely and rationally accepted them. But again, such scrutiny can only be carried out by agents with developed intellectual and affective powers who know how to examine critically the moral rules commonly adopted to decide whether they merit continued acceptance.

A traditional interpretation maintains that Mill's competent judges of value of pleasures are simply those who have *experienced* the whole gamut of satisfactions to be ranked.[11] But I have argued that

---

[11]Such a view might come from a superficial reading of the relevant passage in *Utilitarianism*; see 10:211.

Mill's competent moral agents are actually much more than simply experienced; they are prepared by a thorough education to make their choices. Although much goes into this educative experience, almost everybody, in Mill's view, has the potential to attain developed status, and it is usually their social circumstances that determine whether their potential unfolds. Since Mill thinks that people naturally strive to exercise and develop their abilities, if these abilities remain undeveloped the explanation is usually found in their social circumstances, in some combination of the absence of social conditions necessary for development and the presence of impedimental forces (10:213–17).

People whose potentials have not been released, from Mill's perspective, lead lives exhibiting less value than do those who have had developmental opportunities. Mill sees such a situation as a waste by utilitarian reckoning in several respects. In the self-regarding domain, those people without developmental opportunity blindly follow the value dictates of the rest without searching out the satisfactions most appropriate to themselves. Those pleasurable experiences they do choose for themselves Mill judges as of lower value, as not being the ones they would choose had they had a broader education. Mill makes these judgments in part by comparing the pleasures chosen by the developed, but he also contends that a necessary component of the most valuable satisfactions, or a factor that raises the value of a satisfaction, is its character of being freely chosen by a person of developed abilities. To all these arguments for development must be added the decreased happiness and often massive misery that is the usual lot of those without the social resources to reach their full human capacity. Often the same social conditions that serve to deny people developmental opportunities do double duty in denying them the means to meet the basic needs of a decent life.

Mill's liberty principle commits him to allow a sphere of personal freedom to those who have not developed themselves, and so he cannot be construed as an elitist in the self-regarding domain. His strong antipaternalism commits him to forbid choices to be made by others "for the person's own good." I have still to examine whether Mill's theory is elitist in the province of public or other-regarding activities. Mill may justly be denominated an elitist in the public sphere if he holds that the choices of the developed can be judged more worthy of societal pursuit. This elitism can take various forms. An extreme form is that in which those not yet developed are not allowed to participate in public choices, when in fact they are undeveloped because they have not had the opportunity to develop even though their society has the means and resources to encourage such developmental opportunities. Or they may be allowed only limited participation in the public domain, for example, if the choices of the developed are given more weight (19:473). Mill can escape the charge of elitism if all are allowed full participation in the public sphere, but this position could give rise to a different set of problems. If a significant segment of society is allowed to participate even though they are not competent judges of public values, then the social choices are defective (19:436). In fact, the possibility of defective choices caused by premature extension of the suffrage did worry Mill.

These considerations show that Mill's ideal is full participation of all adult members of society, where all members have had the opportunity to attain the status of at least threshold competence. From this perspective, I contend that Mill's form of utilitarianism, with its essential dependence on developed, competent moral agents to measure value, inclines his political theory toward a form of radical egalitarianism.

8

Liberty of Self-Development

In the previous chapter I considered some strands connecting self-development with themes in Mill's liberalism. In this chapter I argue that, according to the fundamental tenets of Mill's theory, people have a right to liberty of self-development and thus are harmed and their rights infringed if their social circumstances bar them from developing themselves. Further, I believe that Mill considers harmful not only active interference with this liberty but also to some extent the failure to provide reasonable social conditions and resources necessary for the attainment and exercise of self-development. He asserts that certain interests of people are so fundamental or vital that they are enshrined as moral rights and protected from encroachment: "When we call anything a person's right, we mean that he has a valid claim on society to protect him in the possession of it, either by the force of law, or by that of education and opinion. If he has what we consider a sufficient claim, on whatever account, to have something guaranteed to him by society, we say that he has a right to it" (10:250).

The justification or grounding for rights is found in utility. If we ask why society ought to protect rights, Mill answers, "I can give him no other reason than general utility." Utility gives not only the grounding for these essential rights, but also their criterion, for we are here confronting "the extraordinarily important and impressive kind of utility" (10:250–51). The utility is so impressive because the interests are so essential. What are those interests that are so vital that they are to be protected as rights?

HARM AND RIGHTS

People obviously have a vital interest in not being harmed physically and in being protected from physical harm. But beyond this obvious vital interest, Mill seems to have in mind two other interests so vital that they merit enshrinement as rights. Mill first names security as "to every one's feelings the most vital of all interests" and "this most indispensable of all necessaries, after physical nutriment" (10:251). He then says that "the moral rules which forbid mankind to hurt one another (in which we must never forget to include wrongful interference with each other's freedom) are . . . vital to human well-being." (10:255), and he speaks of "the moralities which protect every individual from being harmed by others, either directly or by being hindered in his freedom of pursuing his own good" (10:256). From these passages it seems that Mill is naming liberty, specifically liberty of self-development, as a vital human interest that must be protected as a right.[1] My argument thus far has been intended to show how in Mill's theory the good (and the pursuit of it) is tied to the development and exercise of one's higher human powers.

It may be objected that Mill is not committing society to much beyond preventing actual interference with this liberty, which leaves untouched people who do not have the social and economic resources to develop themselves. In other words, it could be objected that Mill is speaking here of the traditional liberal notion of a negative right to liberty, which in this context does not have much bite. The traditional liberal distinction between negative and positive rights holds that negative rights make it morally incumbent on other people simply not to interfere with these rights, or to avoid acting in some way, whereas positive rights make it morally incumbent on others to take positive action to fulfill these rights. Thus a negative right to liberty of self-development requires society not to

---

[1]On these issues of harm, vital interests, and rights, see John Gray, *Mill on Liberty*, 48–57; Fred Berger, *Happiness, Justice and Freedom*, 124–225.

interfere with someone's developmental attempts, whereas a positive right might require society to do much more—to take steps to ensure that social conditions are such that everyone can undergo development. Positive rights to liberty might require that society take active steps to educate its members and to ensure that everyone has at least the minimum of food, clothing, and shelter necessary to realize themselves. Positive rights are part of an egalitarian theory of justice, and to leave them out is to miss the core of Mill's liberalism. This is one reason why libertarian interpretations of Mill such as that offered by John Gray are so misguided.[2] I am speaking here of the notions of positive and negative *rights*, not of the notions of positive and negative *liberty*. I argue that Mill maintains that people have both positive and negative rights to negative liberty. Positive liberty is not part of Mill's framework. He believes that people have natural tendencies to enjoy and exert their higher powers, that they do not have to be coerced into doing so. Conditions must, however, be such that these natural tendencies can flourish. There is a distinctly Aristotelian cast to Mill's views, one closely related to John Rawls's Aristotelian principle according to which "other things equal, human beings enjoy the exercise of their realized capacities (their innate or trained abilities), and this enjoyment increases the more the capacity is realized, or the greater its complexity."[3]

Mill does not see these two further vital interests as creating simply negative rights. Security is generally taken as the model of a negative right, yet Mill does not see it so, for when he describes its protection he uses language of positive action. He says that security "cannot be had, unless the machinery for providing it is kept unintermittedly in active play. [We have a claim on our fellow-creatures] to join in making safe for us the very ground-work of our existence. . ." (10:251). Society must engage in positive action to "lay the groundwork" for the protection of the right to security. Speaking of rights in general, Mill says that, "if we desire to prove that anything does not belong to him by right, we think this done as soon as it is admitted that society ought not *to take measures* for securing it to him" (10:250, emphasis added). Similarly, Mill sees society as taking an active role in the development of its members and not just

2See John Gray, *Mill on Liberty*, 52–53.
3John Rawls, *A Theory of Justice* (Cambridge, 1971), 426.

standing back and allowing some, who have the means, to develop themselves.

The distinction between negative and positive rights itself rests on a view that is also controversial—the view that the distinction between acting and omitting to act is, under certain circumstances, morally relevant.[4] It is not necessary to resolve this deeper philosophical problem in order to argue that Mill does not hold the distinction between negative and positive rights, between acting and failing to act in the realm of rights, to be systematically morally relevant. He does not, although in his writing the distinction may come into play in particular circumstances.

Several objections arise here. It can be objected that this position, muting the difference between acting and failing to act, jars with Mill's liberty principle, according to which "the sole end for which mankind are warranted, individually or collectively, in interfering with the liberty of action of any of their number, is self-protection. That the only purpose for which power can be rightfully exercised over any member of a civilized community, against his will, is to prevent harm to others" (*On Liberty*, 18:223). The key is harm to others—our liberty cannot be interfered with unless such interference prevents harm to others. The objection considered here builds on the point that fulfillment of positive rights of liberty of others is supposed to be a greater interference of liberty than is fulfillment of negative rights. It is one thing to be required to refrain from interfering with others; it is something more demanding to require that we act to help others or to ensure that social conditions are such that others can exercise their right to self-development. Behind this objection is the view that, although we may do harm by actually interfering with the developmental efforts of others, we cannot plausibly be said to harm people by failing to do something, in this case by failing to promote conditions that encourage self-development. I take up this question in more detail in my critique of Gray's interpretation of Mill. But whether there is any general merit in the distinction relied on by this objection, it does not help the objector here. To see this we have only to examine Mill's statements on how we may harm others. For Mill the distinction between acting

[4]James Rachels argues that the distinction between active and passive euthanasia is not morally relevant; See *The End of Life* (Oxford, 1986), 106–28.

and failing to act does not converge with the distinction between
harming and not harming:

> The most marked cases of injustice . . . are acts of wrongful aggres-
> sion, or wrongful exercise of power over some one; the next are those
> which consist in wrongfully withholding from him something which
> is his due; in both cases, inflicting on him a positive hurt, either in the
> form of direct suffering, or of the privation of some good which he had
> reasonable ground, either of a physical or of a social kind, for counting
> upon. (10:256)

Just as fulfilling our duties sometimes requires positive action
rather than refraining from action, so we can harm someone not
only by active aggression but also by withholding or failing to take
morally required positive action. One can be harmed by being de-
prived of a good through the failure of some others to act as well as
by being aggressed against. Two examples Mill gives of harming
through failing to act are breach of friendship and breach of promise:
"Few hurts which human beings can sustain are greater, and none
wound more, than when that on which they habitually and with full
assurance relied, fails them in the hour of need; and few wrongs are
greater than this mere withholding of good" (10:256).

Objectors may grant that one may harm by failing to act but argue
that these are examples of particular relations between harmer and
harmed; it may still be doubted that duties to take positive steps can
fall on members of society because there are not particular relations
in these cases between harmer and harmed. It may be held that,
contrary to Mill's words, the duties involved are duties of beneficence, which are examples of imperfect obligations—those not
owed to particular persons or demanded on particular occasions. In
delineating these two types of obligation, Mill says,

> [Duties of imperfect obligation are] those in which, though the act is
> obligatory, the particular occasions of performing it are left to our
> choice; as in the case of charity or beneficence, which we are indeed
> bound to practise, but not towards any definite person, nor at any
> prescribed time. . . . duties of perfect obligation are those duties in
> virtue of which a correlative *right* resides in some person or persons;
> duties of imperfect obligation are those moral obligations which do
> not give birth to any right. (10:247)

One may still ask how those not yet fully developed can have rights
to this liberty when one cannot specify particular persons with cor-

responding duties. Such rights would seem to demand that members of society in general have the correlative duties, and it would seem implausible that certain persons have rights if one cannot be more specific about on whom the correlative duties fall. But this argument does not work. The objection runs that the right to liberty of self-development must be connected with a duty of imperfect obligation—that is, that it is not a genuine right—because one cannot specify which particular members of society have the duties. But this objection turns things around. Whether a duty is one of perfect or imperfect obligation depends, not on whether one can specify particular persons who have duties, but on whether one can specify particular persons who have rights. I began by specifying such persons who have rights. So there are duties of perfect obligation, and thus the right to liberty of self-development is not owed as charity. The objection is wrong on another count, as well. We can specify those persons in whom a correlative duty lies: all adult citizens of a society who have the power to effect and enact laws and social policy. This specification also gives the conditions under which the duty is fulfilled.

Henry Shue amplifies some of these insights. As part of a complex argument designed to undermine the traditional distinction between negative and positive rights, he maintains that the right to security, which is usually taken as a paradigm of a negative right, actually contains elements commonly associated with positive rights.[5] Shue's argument illuminates much of what is wrong with one contemporary examination of Mill, that of John Gray.

Self-Development vs. Autonomy:
In Defense of Mill

Recent work on Mill's ethical theory has clarified its sophisticated structure, which includes a theory of justice. The theory of justice sets out the place of principles of justice, or rights. One central right within Mill's system is the right to liberty. One important component of this right, I have been arguing, is the right to liberty of self-development. Mill can be most plausibly construed as holding that the liberty to develop one's individuality and one's intellectual, mor-

[5]Henry Shue, *Basic Rights* (Princeton, 1980), 37.

al, and affective capacities and to exercise these powers once developed is the sort of vital interest that is the foundation of a right. In *Utilitarianism* Mill asserts that certain interests of people are so fundamental or vital that they are to be enshrined as rights and protected from encroachment. The justification for rights is found in utility; we are here confronting "certain social utilities which are vastly more important, and therefore more absolute and imperative, than any others are as a class" (10:259). The two rights that Mill picks out as most basic are the rights to security and to liberty. John Gray interprets Mill's right to liberty as a right to autonomy.[6] I propose to examine this interpretation, and in so doing to shed light on the substance of and conditions surrounding this basic right as well as its place within Mill's ethical theory.

Several aspects of Gray's treatment of the right to autonomy bear scrutiny, and some of these are troubling and problematic. I postpone looking at Gray's discussion of the substance of the right, that is, of what constitutes autonomy, and how well it fits over self-development in Mill. His stance on the conditions surrounding this right presents a useful starting point. Several elements present themselves as posing puzzles and problems. First, Gray insists that the right to autonomy comes into play only at the stage at which the agent's powers are to some degree developed. Second, he contends that the right to autonomy is a negative right only. Both claims pose difficulties, I argue, because they are faithful neither to Mill nor to most current treatments of autonomy. The central effect of both argumentative thrusts is to place on Mill's theory a restrictive elitist and libertarian emphasis that violates the spirit of his liberalism, shifting his political philosophy away from the collectivist, social democratic pole and toward the libertarian individualist pole of the continuum of liberalism.

Gray is forceful and clear in claiming that the right to autonomy appears only at a particular stage in development and is not present from childhood: "Crucially, unlike security, the moral right to autonomy is possessed, not by all men, but only by those possessing in some minimal degree the capacities of an autonomous agent: it comes into play only at what I have termed the third tier of Mill's hierarchical utilitarianism" (55). The three-tiered structure Gray refers to is as follows:

[6]Gray, *Mill on Liberty*.

First we have the utility principle in its role as an axiological principle specifying happiness alone as of intrinsic value. . . . Next, we have utility in its applications to human beings, whose generic powers allow for happy and wretched lives whose qualities are (so far as we know) peculiar to our species. . . . Third, there are the applications of the utility principle to reflective and civilized men in whom the capacities for an autonomous life have been developed and to whom the higher pleasures are accessible. (46)

Gray points to "Mill's exclusion of children, the mentally unbalanced and backward peoples from the sphere of application" of the principle of liberty to buttress his exclusion of certain classes of humans (78).

Let me start my examination by looking at some current discussions of autonomy, with a view to isolating Gray's departure from these. Other scholars agree with Gray that a full-fledged right to autonomy does not come into being until certain human capacities are developed. What is distinctive about Gray's treatment is its silence on the issue of the rights status of those who are not yet in the sacred circle. I claim that the right to liberty of self-development is best seen as a continuum consisting of the right to attain this status and the right to exercise these capacities unimpeded once developed; others express the same substantive point in different language. But none of these writers ignore, as Gray does, the prior status of those reaching for the development of their capacities but not yet there. I argue that the heart of this right is cut out if we do not acknowledge this prior moral status. We cannot just leave people to develop autonomy and exclude them from the status of rights bearer if they do not make it on their own. Prior moral status must be seen as the early stage of the right.

Joel Feinberg's prominent and influential treatment of the prior status of developing autonomous persons illuminates the source of Gray's mistake.[7] Feinberg distinguishes adult and children's rights and notes that one subgroup of the latter is children's autonomy rights-in-trust:

When sophisticated autonomy rights are attributed to children who are clearly not yet capable of exercising them, their names refer to rights that are to be saved for the child until he is an adult, but which

[7]Joel Feinberg, "The Child's Right to an Open Future," in *Ethical Principles for Social Policy*, ed. J. Howie (Carbondale, 1983), pp. 97–122.

can be violated in advance, so to speak, before the child is even in a position to exercise them. Violations guarantee now that when the child is an autonomous adult, certain key options will already be closed to him. While he is still a child, he has the right to have these future options kept open until he is a fully formed self-determining agent capable of deciding among them. (98)

Rights-in-trust are not any weaker for their name, and violations carry with them all the seriousness of violations of rights in general. Feinberg notes that the stage before the attainment of status as rights bearer could without loss of his point be referred to as a stage of a right. He refers to Locke's argument on the same question. Locke calls all human rights adult rights but explains that children cannot yet exercise some of them: "Thus we are born free as we are born rational; not that we have actually the exercise of either; age that brings one, brings with it the other too."[8] According to Feinberg, Locke's argument expresses the same points in different terms. Children's rights-in-trust, Feinberg continues, can be grouped under the "right to an open future." Such rights must be "held in trust" for the child. Autonomy rights "sit . . . side by side with the right to walk freely down the public sidewalk as held by an infant of two months, still incapable of self-locomotion. One would violate that right in trust now, before it can even be exercised, by cutting off the child's legs" (98–99). The child's right to an open future carries with it duties on parents to raise children in ways consistent with autonomous development and duties on the state to protect those rights-in-trust (112).

Lawrence Haworth argues along similar lines that children have a strong interest in the development of their autonomous capacities and are harmed if these are not promoted. Parents and the state have duties to carry out this development and can violate children's rights if development is neglected or distorted.[9]

What can be gleaned from these discussions is that one cannot simply leave children to develop into autonomous adults if luck will have it and protect their rights only if good fortune thus shines on them. Their rights are violated if they are not permitted and nur-

---

[8]John Locke, *Second Treatise*, sec. 61; quoted in Feinberg, "Child's Right," 98–99, n. 1.

[9]Lawrence Haworth, *Autonomy: An Essay in Philosophical Psychology and Ethics* (New Haven, 1986), 126.

tured into this status, violated by parents and by the state that does not promote autonomy though resources permit. To make too strong an analogy between children and adult workers in nineteenth-century Britain would be misleading and insulting to the latter. Mill is usually careful to treat these cases separately, and he has different things to say about children and adult workers of his time. But the argument is important for the similarities it reveals in their conditions. They are both reaching for autonomous status, although adult workers are much farther along and in most cases have reached the threshold of competence to participate in public choices. The key point to be drawn from Feinberg's discussion is that rights (or rights-in-trust) are violated if children and adult workers do not attain the status of autonomous beings because not permitted or not nurtured, except in those rare cases where normal autonomy is not possible because of handicap. The right to attain the status of autonomy gets equal billing with the right to exercise autonomy once attained.

Gray's analysis is clearly not in accord with these current accounts of autonomy. Still, he might argue that his account is faithful to Mill, pointing for evidence to Mill's apparent exclusion of children and "backward peoples" from the sphere of application of the principle of liberty. But further investigation shows that Mill's comments do not support Gray's argument but rather lend weight to its alternative. Mill's statement of the liberty principle and its surrounding conditions is as follows:

> That principle is, that the sole end for which mankind are warranted, individually or collectively, in interfering with the liberty of action of any of their number, is self-protection. That the only purpose for which power can be rightfully exercised over any member of a civilized community, against his will, is to prevent harm to others. His own good, either physical or moral, is not a sufficient warrant. (18:223)

Then come the comments on children and "backward peoples":

> This doctrine is meant to apply only to human beings in the maturity of their faculties. We are not speaking of children. . . . Those who are still in a state to require being taken care of by others, must be protected against their own actions as well as against external injury. For the same reason, we may leave out of consideration those backward states of society in which the race itself may be considered as in its nonage. (224)

It is apparent that Mill's comments here do not sustain the point Gray needs to make. Mill's remarks are consistent with the claim that children do not have a full-fledged right. This claim is agreed to on all sides, but it does not support Gray's view in particular. Mill is saying only that paternalism is justified in the case of children. He does not allow any and all restrictions of liberty in the case of children, only interventions for their own good. Those who hold that children have a prior moral status also hold that paternalistic intervention is not necessarily a violation of the right-in-trust; indeed they hold that children must be coerced and treated paternalistically as part of the process that makes them autonomous agents. This kind of paternalism is fully consistent with holding that children have a right-in-trust.[10]

For Gray to make his point he must show, not that Mill's principle of liberty allows paternalism in the case of children, but a quite different point. He must show that the principle of liberty *disowns* children from moral status prior to their attainment of full rights and that the principle is consistent with the claim that there is no violation of children's rights or rights-in-trust if they are not nurtured into development. But Mill does in fact argue that children's rights are violated if they are not developed. [11]

That Mill's claim that children are subject to paternalism is not a denial that they have prior moral status before they acquire the full right is even clearer when we look at the rest of the passage in *On Liberty*. He does not deny that children have prior moral status. Why does the liberty principle not apply to children and to "backward people," and under what conditions would it apply?

> Despotism is a legitimate mode of government in dealing with barbarians, provided the end be their improvement. . . . Liberty, as a principle, has no application to any state of things anterior to the time when mankind have become capable of being improved by free and equal discussion . . . But as soon as mankind have attained the capacity of being guided to their own improvement by conviction or persuasion . . . compulsion . . . is no longer admissible as a means to their own good, and justifiable only for the security of others. (18:224)

It is not entirely clear from this passage whether Mill is speaking only of ancient societies as "backward" or instead includes under-

---

[10]See, e.g., Feinberg, "Child's Right," 113.

[11]Haworth, *Autonomy*. Haworth explains how paternalistic coercion to foster future autonomy is part of the developmental process.

developed societies of his time. In either case, the assumption that members of underdeveloped countries are "backward" and are like children is not just false, it is embarrassingly false. Contemporary anthropological, economic, and sociological studies have enlightened our sensitivity to cultural diversity; we no longer equate economic development with intellectual and moral development. Human development takes place in all societies, though it manifests itself differently and can be greatly impeded by poverty. But we should focus on Mill's point and not on his false statement of the facts. The key is capacity for improvement, which is the basis of the right to attain the status of autonomy—and children and those in underdeveloped nations have this capacity.

If further evidence is needed, it comes from Mill's discussion of children's right to be educated. Education, of course, is one of the main vehicles for achieving the capacities on which autonomy is founded:

> Is it not almost a self-evident axiom, that the State should require and compel the education, up to a certain standard, of every human being who is born its citizen? . . . to bring a child into existence without a fair prospect of being able, not only to provide food for its body, but instruction and training for its mind, is a moral crime, both against the unfortunate offspring and against society; and . . . if the parent does not fulfill this obligation, the State ought to see it fulfilled, at the charge, as far as possible, of the parent. (18:301–02)

This passage establishes that children have a right to an education. It specifies directly that parents and the state have obligations toward the child; it does not specify directly that children have rights. Yet all the elements for rights assessment are there. From the tenor of Mill's comments it is hard to read the children's interests involved as less weighty than those that form the foundation of rights. And there are definite persons (children) with those vital interests. These two elements, the weightiness of the interests that the state is obligated to protect and the existence of assignable individuals to whom obligations are owed, are sufficient to warrant the interpretation that children have rights to an education. Mill argues here and elsewhere that the corresponding obligation falls on both parents and society. In Mill's theory the notion of protection or guarantee is part of the notion of a right. How a right may be effectively guaranteed is, however, an empirical question with answers that vary across different societies and with changes in social relations. In

Mill's society, parents were seen as primarily responsible for their children's education, whereas in our society the state has taken on a much more active role in education and assumed a larger share of the correlative duty. As Mill sets it out, parents have the primary obligation and the state is there to enforce and to step into the breach when this parental role is not fulfilled. In *Representative Government* he claims that society has a duty to educate its citizens (19:470). In the passage from *On Liberty* it may appear that parents have this duty because they have brought the child into the world, and thus the child's right may seem to rest only on this particular relation of child to parent. But closer inspection shows that there is more to the child's right. It is a "moral crime" against children if they are not rendered capable of providing for themselves materially and if their mental powers are not nurtured and developed. This vital interest of the child is not generated by its particular relation to its parents; it is the basis of a claim that is socially guaranteed and protected. The child has this right not merely qua child of a set of parents but qua human child in the social world with capacities that require development and nurturance. This is the early stage of the right to liberty of self-development.

The issue of a child's right to an education is but one source of evidence that Mill takes a full-fledged right to be preceded by a right-in-trust, a right to attain the status. Gray's argument that the right to autonomy appears only at a certain stage of development does not allow us to make sense of Mill's most fundamental commitment, the development of all members of society of their capacities to lead meaningful lives. Mill is unmistakably concerned to protect the rights of those lucky enough in their social placing to already have achieved a fair degree of development. But his commitment to development applies to everyone, and Gray's argument does not take account of the vital interests of the rest. If the right to autonomy comes into being when development is to some degree achieved, children and some adult workers are cut off from social protection and guarantees to their chance, yet Mill's theory clearly does elaborate such protections and guarantees. When this denial of prior moral status is combined with an analysis of the right to autonomy as a negative right, one not requiring positive action and intervention, the elitist thrust of Gray's interpretation is compounded and his picture of society gets even more inconsistent with Mill's liberalism.

I turn now to Gray's claim that the right to autonomy is a negative right. His remarks on this topic are not quite as unequivocal as those on pre-development rights, but on balance this does seem to be his view. Human vital interests, Gray says, "are satisfied when men refrain from invading one another's autonomy and from undermining one another's security."[12] Furthermore,

> autonomy is abridged not only when actions are prevented by some external obstruction such as forcible restraint or the threat of legal punishment, but, more fundamentally, when the pressure of public opinion is such that certain options are not even conceivable, or, if conceivable, not treated as genuine candidates for viable forms of life. (77)

External obstruction and the pressure of public opinion are both violations of a negative right; they are violations that result from actual interference with rights holders. Gray offers this example: "Human beings failed to be autonomous if—as was the case of women in traditional marriage arrangements, according to Mill—they lacked the opportunity to develop wills of their own and to act on them"(78). We see here hints that more than a negative right may be needed for autonomy to develop, but Gray only claims that lack of opportunity may lead to lack of development. He does not suggest that a rights violation has occurred or that anything should be done about the lack of opportunity he describes. Overall, then, he sticks to a negative rights account of autonomy. He does not see that positive action may be required to effectively guarantee rights of autonomy. More fundamental still, his argument depends on a distinction between acts and omissions which is not defended and to my knowledge has never been successfully defended.

Millian rights are socially embedded, and they can be fully understood only in their social context. One can begin with Mill's argument that the protection of a right is part of the concept of a right. Mill's language, in one of the central passages in which he explains his concept of a right, is compelling and unmistakable: "To have a right, then, is, I conceive, to have something which society ought to defend me in the possession of" (10:250). To have a right is to have a justification for societal protection—not merely a justification that one hopes potential violators will listen to, which would empty it of

---

[12]Gray, *Mill on Liberty*, 52.

its point if that were all the backing it had. It is to have a justification to demand (and get) protection from society against potential and actual violators.[13]

Henry Shue's analysis also recognizes the centrality of protection for rights.[14] It is commonly supposed that our rights to physical security are fulfilled as long as other people refrain from certain actions or omit to act in ways that would result in a violation of these rights; that is, the right to physical security places correlative duties on others to refrain from attacking the rights bearer. But Shue correctly points out that, at least in a violence-ridden society, such omissions are not sufficient to guarantee these rights. Individuals can ensure that they do not infringe others' rights merely by refraining from attack, but for the rights bearer this is cold comfort. The rights holders are entitled to guarantees of social backup for their rights to security, backup that will require positive steps:

> For example, at the very least the protection of rights to physical security necessitates police forces; criminal courts; penitentiaries; schools for training police; lawyers, and guards; and taxes to support an enormous system for the prevention, detection, and punishment of violations of personal security. All these activities and institutions are attempts at providing social guarantees for individuals' security so that they are not left to face alone forces that they cannot handle on their own. (37–38)

Shue sees that social guarantees of rights lead to corresponding duties to make institutional arrangements to do this effectively.

> Being socially guaranteed . . . is the aspect that necessitates correlative duties. A right is ordinarily a justified demand that some other people make arrangements so that one will still be able to enjoy the substance of the right even if—actually, especially if—it is not within one's own power to arrange on one's own to enjoy the substance of the right. (16)

This analysis of rights puts the element of guarantee or protection foremost. Along with Mill, Shue holds that protection is part of the notion of a right. But, as Shue makes explicit, this view cannot be taken to mean that a right bearer is entitled to protection against

[13]See David Lyons, "Introduction," in *Rights*, ed. David Lyons (Belmont, 1979), 4; and "Human Rights and the General Welfare," in ibid., 181–82.
[14]See Shue, *Basic Rights*, 13.

any and all possible threats, only against "standard threats." The question of how rights may be protected is an empirical one, and answers vary across different societies with different social relations posing different standard threats to rights. Various arrangements for rights protection are possible and viable, but this fact does not invalidate the claim that protection is built into the idea of a right. The measures required to secure the right to security in a Trappist monastery are different from those needed in New York City. Shue is also correct to emphasize that rights are not adequately secured until the necessary institutional arrangements are in place. This is one way that rights, for Shue and Mill, are deeply interconnected with social relations and structures.[15]

As Mill says, rights protection requires that "the machinery for providing it is kept unintermittedly in active play" (10:251). Without institutional arrangements, rights protection is an empty notion. But institutional arrangements, which require positive action, are also necessary for rights traditionally thought of as negative such as security. Thus the idea of social protection of rights gains a different flavor from that conveyed by Gray's account. Rights are backed by society, and rights holders and potential violators are not left to square off on their own. But since the guarantor is society, neither are individuals left to guarantee, in most instances, on their own, although they must individually ensure they do not violate. The corresponding duties are collective, as we see below.[16]

According to Mill, rights are located in a social nexus. Their social setting dictates that their protection involve institutional arrangements, and so even those rights traditionally conceived of as negative—those requiring as the first line of defense that potential violators not interfere with the rights holder—necessitate positive actions to set up machinery of protection as a second line of defense. Once we see that institutional guarantees are called for by rights, we can see that virtually every right may require positive action to

[15]Russell Hardin, *Morality within the Limits of Reason*, 79. He also points out the role of institutional arrangements in rights protection.

[16]Nathan Brett, "Two Concepts of Rights," presented at the Canadian Philosophical Association, Winnipeg, May 1986, also has a helpful discussion of many of these points. Another illuminating discussion of negative and positive rights as they relate to these questions is found in Jan Narveson, "Rights and Utilitarianism," in *New Essays on John Stuart Mill and Utilitarianism*, ed. Cooper, Nielsen, and Patten, 137–60.

fulfill it, and thus the distinction between positive and negative rights is further called into question.

At bottom, the concern to hold the line between positive and negative rights involves a concern about the costs and restrictions to individuals and societies of guaranteeing rights. It may appear at first glance that the cost of guaranteeing negative rights is much less than that of guaranteeing positive rights. But in many cases this is not so. I may find the cost or restriction of refraining from acting in order to avoid rights violation equally painful or more painful than that of acting. The distinction between acting and not acting is dubious as a morally relevant feature. And it cannot be relied on as a systematic indicator of cost either. It can be equally burdensome to control oneself or to rouse oneself to action, depending on circumstances. Self-control is a burden, too. The point is that a burden or cost to duty holders cannot be analyzed adequately according to whether they are required to act or to omit to act. A violent man may find it difficult to control his anger and refrain from assaulting his wife and children. Until he gets his anger under control, the burden of omitting to act is as onerous as the burden of acting in many other circumstances. Self-control is terribly difficult for most people under many conditions, yet it often requires not acting when one is inclined to do so. Thus the adequate explanation of cost must be in terms of other features of the situation.

This concern to draw the line at negative rights relies on other misconceptions of the way our duties to act must be fulfilled as well. Proponents of this view often have a particular libertarian model of duty fulfillment in mind, a model that is excessively atomistic and individualist.[17] The social world is conceived of as a series of individual transactions in which each of us makes our way by tending our own garden. Our duties are fulfilled as long as we do not invade someone else's garden, and we have the right to tend our own in perfect peace. But what of those unfortunates without a garden (though there is land available) or without gardening skills? The libertarian argues that it is too much of a burden for me to drop my gardening every time some positive action would set someone else up in gardening. If I spend too much time and energy helping others (on this model such actions are seen merely as helping others, not as

[17]Brett "Two Concepts of Rights," has a good discussion of this libertarian model of rights.

part of duty fulfillment), then my own talents and projects suffer. There are likely to be many such interruptions, so no one is ever left in peace to garden. With the costs of duty fulfillment on this model so high, the libertarian feels justified in drawing the line at negative rights: in such a way we preserve the peace of those engaged in gardening, and we cannot be required to take positive steps for others.

This picture is one in which some individuals constantly approach other individuals with demands for action to fulfill individually their rights to liberty of gardening. But the picture is hardly realistic. Many duties to act are to be fulfilled by collective, not individual, action in which each individual is expected to do a part, not the whole job. If the unfortunates have the right to garden, the rest of us fulfill our duties collectively by together setting up institutions to teach gardening and to distribute available land to those without resources. We each fulfill many correlative duties by taking part in such collective action to set up the right social policies. We do not each have to help each and every unfortunate; our duty is to see, with others who are in a position to enact policies, that effective mechanisms are set up and maintained. We fulfill many of our positive duties by so acting as responsible citizens. In such cases, individual-to-individual interaction is not expected or called for. One way to read Mill's comments on our obligations to take part in cooperative ventures is that such actions set up the institutional machinery necessary for general rights protection. As Mill says, a person has duties "to bear his fair share in the common defence, or in any other joint work necessary to the interest of the society of which he enjoys the protection" (18:225).[18]

So even rights traditionally conceived of as negative are attended by positive action for their fulfillment. But the right to autonomy requires even more positive action and intervention than this. Gray focuses his concern on the right to autonomy of those above the threshold of competence, and many of the duties attendant to these

---

[18]Brett says, "Omissions do not *always* cost less (in terms of one's freedom) than actions. . . . the extent to which an individual's options will be limited by a rule against (unwilling) interaction with others will depend upon that individual's desires and needs. . . . On the other hand, the actions which provide for the protection of other persons (and, in particular, their liberty), may cost very little. It may be sufficient that I pay taxes to support a police system which provides this protection" (ibid., 12–13).

rights are of nonintervention, of allowing the rights holder to exercise autonomy unimpeded. The right to develop into autonomous
status, however, is a far different situation. More must be done and
more active steps taken by duty bearers to guarantee rights. The
right to attain the status of development, held by children and by
adults who have been blocked by poverty, requires exposure to educative experiences; education requires much positive action to
achieve its goals. These requirements are clear from the standard
view of development of human capacities, including autonomous
capacities. The right to autonomy is as pointless if the obligation of
positive intervention is denied as it is pointless if pre-development
moral status is denied. Lawrence Haworth explains the necessity of
positive intervention if autonomous status is to be reached:

> The child's interest in becoming autonomous mandates noninter-
> ference with him; so far, the right to an open future is a negative right.
> But securing the child's future autonomy requires positive action as
> well and may require coercion. For his capacity to live autonomously
> to be developed, he needs, among other things, the sorts of formal and
> informal educational experiences that nurture both an ability to think
> critically and an ability to act on the results of such thought.[19]

Terence Qualter provides the political context for Mill's recognition
of the need for positive intervention as well as for noninterference
for the full protection of rights.

> The social consequences of laissez-faire gradually led some to appreci-
> ate that while liberty is the absence of legal restraint, it may also be
> more than that. . . . This wider definition of freedom began to emerge
> in the middle of the nineteenth century with the increasing awareness
> of the extent to which poverty, ignorance, economic dependence, job
> insecurity, or lack of access to information could all be barriers to
> freedom. John Stuart Mill was one of the first to expand on the notion
> of the law as an instrument for widening opportunities for freedom.[20]

I have put off scrutiny of the substance of the right as Gray sees it,
the conception of autonomy in play, in order to examine the conditions Gray thinks surround the right. But such questions are also in
order. Gray thinks that one might ask whether Mill even held a

[19]Haworth, *Autonomy,* 127.
[20]Terence Qualter, *Conflicting Political Ideas in Liberal Democracies* (Toronto,
1986), 96–97.

notion of autonomy: "The reader may reasonably doubt if the apparatus of terms and distinctions I have sketched has any basis in
Mill's writings but, though the reservation is not unreasonable in
that these distinctions are not in any sense derived from Mill's work,
it is groundless if it implies that nothing in Mill's writings corresponds to them."[21]

My argument is that Gray is looking in the wrong direction for a
dispute. It is reasonable to grant that the promotion of autonomy is
in full accord with the spirit of Mill's commitments. My concern is
again with what Gray's conception of autonomy leaves out. He offers only part of the picture. Mill's conception of self-development is
broader than Gray's autonomy, and Gray's narrow account has consequences for the picture of liberalism that results.

What is Gray's conception of autonomy? He works through four
conceptions of freedom: negative freedom, rational self-direction,
autarchy, and autonomy. Negative freedom is freedom of action
from forcible or coercive intervention. Freedom as rational self-direction or self-determination allows rational deliberation on available options. "This conception . . . could properly be used of a slave
or an agent acting under coercion, providing only that he succeeds in
acting in accordance with his own rational policies." Autarchy combines negative freedom and rational self-direction and is stronger
than either of the them. An autonomous agent has all the capacities
of an autarchic agent, and in addition "an autonomous agent must
also have distanced himself in some measure from the conventions
of his social environment and from the influence of the persons
surrounding him. His actions express principles and policies which
he has himself ratified by a process of critical reflection." Such
agents have second-order desires and volitions that ratify first-order
desires. Agents fail to be autarchic if their behavior is compulsive or
governed by another. Heterarchic agents lack wills of their own.
Gray refers to the discussions of H. G. Frankfurt and Joel Feinberg in
order to clarify his own position. Gray notes that Frankfurt has
defined a wanton as one who does not care about her will and lacks
second-order desires and volitions.[22] According to Gray, hetero-
nomous agents can choose rationally and have wills of their own but

[21]Gray, *Mill on Liberty*, 78.

[22]Ibid., 76. Gray refers here to H. G. Frankfurt's discussion in "Freedom of the Will,
and the Concept of a Person," *Journal of Philosophy* 68 (1971): 5–20.

are influenced by custom or public opinion. Gray claims that "In Frankfurt's idiom, an autonomous agent is one who has a will of his own, who has subjected his volitions to a sustained critical evaluation, who has the opportunity to translate his will into action, and whose will is free."[23] Gray quotes from Joel Feinberg to sum up: "I am autonomous if I rule me, and no-one else rules I."[24]

Gray's analysis is that Mill was pessimistic about the rule of custom in his society, a rule leading to an abundance of heteronomy. To combat this environment, Mill's individuality is supposed to encourage authenticity: having "desires and projects [of one's] own."[25] We humans have a range of possibilities that are to be discovered and expressed in our lives, and our greatest happiness comes about through such choice and experimentation to seek our own nature.

Gray's picture of autonomy does not capture the complete essence of human development for Mill. Individuality and intellectual cultivation have a central place in Mill's account, but Gray's analysis leaves out much that is important. Moral development always accompanies mental development for Mill. To hear him tell it, mental development without an accompaniment of moral development is a caricature of development. A person who is highly developed in critical capacities, including self-determination, but who lacks social bonds is not held up as ideal—quite the opposite:

> When people who are tolerably fortunate in their outward lot do not find in life sufficient enjoyment to make it valuable to them, the cause generally is, caring for nobody but themselves. . . . Next to selfishness, the principal cause which makes life unsatisfactory, is want of mental cultivation. . . . A cultivated mind—I do not mean that of a philosopher, but any mind to which the fountains of knowledge have been opened, and which has been taught, in any tolerable degree, to exercise its faculties—finds sources of inexhaustible interest in all that surrounds it. . . . It is possible, indeed, to become indifferent to all this . . . but only when one has had from the beginning no moral or human interest in these things, and has sought in them only the gratification of curiosity. . . .
> . . . As little is there an inherent necessity that any human being should be a selfish egotist, devoid of every feeling or care but those which centre in his own miserable individuality. (10:215–16)

[23] Ibid., 76–77. Gray again refers to Frankfurt, "Freedom of the Will", 5–20.
[24] Ibid., 77. Gray quotes from Joel Feinberg, *Social Philosophy* (Englewood Cliffs, N.J., 1973), 15–17.
[25] Ibid., 79.

These comments should temper the enthusiasm of those who interpret Mill as the classic exponent of individualism without noticing what is for him its natural companion—sociality and fellow feeling. Those who pursue projects out of curiosity rather than attachment and commitment equally receive not praise but scorn:

> Utility would enjoin . . . that education and opinion, which have so vast a power over human character, should so use that power as to establish in the mind of every individual an indissoluble association between his own happiness and the good of the whole. . . . a direct impulse to promote the general good may be in every individual one of the habitual motives of action" (10:218).

There are no qualms expressed here about the force of public opinion pushing sociality on the self-absorbed egotist happily pursuing self-centered projects.

There is much overlap between modern treatments of autonomy and parts of Mill's self-development. Mill stresses intellectual development, which is the core of rational and critical reflective powers necessary to reach the level of autonomy. He stresses the centrality of liberty of choice and of self-determination. His views on individuality fit well with the component of authenticity, backing our first-order desires and our projects and commitments. But, although Gray holds up autonomous people as the pinnacle of Mill's system, the autonomous person he sets out does not fit Mill's ideal for humanity. Mill's ideal person is one who has achieved a balance and harmony, a wholistic combination of intellectual, moral, and affective development, of individuality and autonomy with sociality, attachment, and caring. Many theories suggest that we must choose between the supposedly conflicting ideals of individualism and sociality, of autonomy and caring. This suggestion is so at odds with an acceptable view of human functioning and flourishing that the amount of attention it gets is amazing. When taken to an extreme without a proper balance, either individualism and autonomy or nurturing, caring, and sociality result in a distorted and deformed psyche. There is no inconsistency in recognizing, as Mill does, the need for a healthy dose of both in a happy human life. Hence his condemnation of the person who has developed intellectual and autonomous capacities but neglected the moral and social side. Autonomy without sociality is not Mill's ideal but his horror.

The contrast between these two pictures of human development and social life, between Gray's autonomy and Mill's self-development, is striking. I have argued that Gray's interpretation of autonomy departs from Mill's views in several important ways. Gray interprets the right to autonomy as held only by those who have attained a threshold of autonomy. He claims that the right to autonomy is negative, and he holds to a narrow conception of autonomy that ignores moral development and social attachment. In Gray's view, the right to autonomy is held only by an elite. Since there is no prior moral status, although it would be good if all members of society were fortunate enough to have the chance to attain the threshold, they have no right to attain this status. Arrangements to allow all to reach this status fall into the category of benefiting others rather than of fulfilling duties corresponding to rights. In addition, since the right is negative, corresponding duties are all of the sort of nonintervention. No one is called on to take positive action to fulfill the right. Positive action again falls into the category of benefiting others rather than of carrying out a duty. We do not have definite duties to construct policies and institutions with the goal of nurturing autonomy. Finally, we can fulfill the ideal of humanity even if we are entirely without social connections and attachments and without fellow feeling. We can pursue our lives in self-absorbed splendor, swept along by a sense of curiosity and adventure but devoid of attachment and commitment. Though we care not a whit for anyone else, as long as our lives exhibit and manifest our autonomous and intellectual capacities we are the ideal of humanity.

I argue that the view of the right to liberty of self-development is a more plausible interpretation of Mill. All have the right to liberty of self-development, and fulfillment of the corresponding obligations necessitates positive action as well as nonintervention. The positive actions include cooperative ventures to establish and maintain social institutions. Rights are thoroughly embedded in a social context, and the sociality of agents is combined with their individuality. This is not a right of an elite but one held by all.

It is hard to overlook the fact that Mill's most fundamental commitment is to the self-development of all, not to the protection of autonomy of a developed elite. The most plausible reading of the text and spirit of Mill is that all people are harmed if they are denied the opportunity to develop themselves to the extent social resources permit. Mill claims that all people have the right to develop themselves, or, more strictly, the right to the opportunity to develop themselves. It is thus incumbent on others and on society to provide social guarantees of this right, and these guarantees involve both guarantees of noninterference with developmental attempts and also allocation of social resources, which requires positive action, to give all a decent opportunity to realize their unique potential. Mill calls for the right for all to attain the status of development and to exercise their human faculties once this status is attained.

ELABORATIONS ON SELF-DEVELOPMENT

In Mill's writings the distinction between negative and positive rights and liberties is blurred. Although our liberty to self-development has to be protected from interference, the conditions of noninterference connected with the traditional notion of negative liberty do not capture the conditions Mill thinks are required. The point Mill makes is similar to C. B. Macpherson's claim that we must take "the basic criterion of democracy to be that equal effective right of individuals to live as fully as they may wish. This is simply the principle that everyone ought to be able to make the most of himself, or make the best of himself."[26] Macpherson discusses the conditions necessary for development. The degree of development of human abilities that occurs is essentially bound up with social conditions, and these can operate primarily as enabling or impeding forces, to promote or to obstruct human development. Macpherson's key claim is that power "must be measured in terms of impediments to the use and development of . . . human capacities" (40).

Macpherson is putting the role of impediments in the strongest possible way, and here he parts company with Mill, who measures utility according to judgments of developed agents. Nevertheless, Mill shares with Macpherson the awareness that the goal of development is a sham if society does not act at least to reduce impediments. Macpherson lists impediments that are to some extent under the control of social policy, and that can be left in place or reduced by social choice. Along with "lack of protection against invasion by others" he cites "lack of adequate means of life" and "lack of access to the means of labour" (59–60). For the two latter, society must act

[26]C. B. Macpherson, *Democratic Theory*, 51.

positively to see to it that the requisite resources are provided to its members.

Further clarification should be made. Mill's moral theory, with its use of competent judges lies between theories that use ideal observers like R. M. Hare's archangels, who have "superhuman powers of thought, superhuman knowledge and no human weaknesses,"[27] and those that simply accept all kinds of human satisfactions as equally valuable without critical scrutiny. The first kind of theory leaves us the problem of having to use our human faculties to figure out what an archangel would value, and actual-satisfaction accounts face the objection put so forcefully by Mill that they may be deemed "doctrine worthy only of swine." Avoiding both extremes, Mill's method of value measurement uses actual humans who have undergone a process of development—a process we can reasonably expect societies with a certain level of material resources to provide. These judges are authoritative yet fallible; they are in the best position to assess value but they can be mistaken and shown to be so. Their preferences do not make the satisfactions they favor valuable; what makes these satisfactions valuable are their good-making properties, features of the experiences themselves which the judges can pick out as providing reasons for their preferences. Ultimately, the most valuable satisfactions are those that stretch human capacities to their fullest. Mill is interested in ways of life that develop human nature to its limit, and so his ultimate criterion is whether a way of life does this. Thus competent agents can be wrong because they can be mistaken about or unaware of the potential of human nature or human capacities and powers. Mill in fact believes that the human race can be much improved, and he speaks of "what the human species may be made" (10:216). Suppose, for example, that if people were to practice a particular kind of meditative technique they could transform themselves; not only would their mental powers be sharpened, but they would view themselves as part of a vast unity, connected with all their fellow creatures. From the vantage point of their vastly changed perspective and increased powers, they would regard their former pursuits and enjoyments as greatly inferior to their present appreciations and could see that their earlier judgments of value were mistaken.

Because of Mill's views on education, his theory does not face a

[27]R. M. Hare, *Moral Thinking*, 44.

serious problem of circularity, although competent agents are not entirely able to escape the influences of their culture and class. In the educational process students are not simply trained to adopt a set of values; rather, they develop their cognitive and affective powers and their benevolence. In particular, they are trained to use their cognitive capacities as critical tools, not just presented with models of truth to be accepted on authority. Mill is passionately opposed to rote learning of any sort, including rote learning of the "proper" values. The result of this educational process is a rational agent similar to those at the center of many contemporary theories, except that Mill's rational agents are strongly benevolent. If we are unable to design an educative process that enables agents to be thus critical and rational, we have a serious problem that affects almost every moral theory, not only Mill's. The criticism that Mill's competent agents are firmly class- and culture-bound vastly underestimates the power of critical human capacities to transcend their surroundings. Reform is based on this capacity.

Although Mill thinks that the judgments of competent agents will tend to converge over time, and that they will agree on a range of acceptable values, he does not look for more agreement than this for the immediate future. This is one of the reasons that he advocates democratic procedures for choices of public or social values. Mill places great emphasis on the fact that people have different talents and capacities, which ensures that even the most highly developed agents do not value the same set of satisfactions or pursuits for themselves. Their sympathetic connections encourage them to put themselves in others' shoes, and they may come to agree on sets of satisfactions for persons of particular talents. Thus, although an intellectually inclined agent can come to see that one set of satisfactions may be appropriate for those of artistic inclinations, this agent need not want this set for herself. A competent agent can have at least the minimal qualifications to make these general judgments without being qualified to the degree of those devoted to art, who can make much finer discriminations within the set.

That Mill's writings contain both egalitarian and elitist trends is evident. The ends of Mill's theory are egalitarian, whereas the means of achieving these ends are partly elitist. This pattern follows that of Book 6 of the *Logic*, where Mill argues that the province of art is to articulate ends, whereas that of science, in this case sociology, psychology, political economy and ethology, is to help in the formulation of social policies to achieve these ends. Mill's end is egalitarian—the equal opportunity for all to develop and use their human faculties. In its political and economic applications, this end requires that people learn from those who are more developed, and thus, according to Mill, it requires a certain amount of elitism. As we see in Chapter 10, however, this elitist tendency is outweighed by other considerations.

It has also been objected, mistakenly, that Mill's qualitative hedonism impels us toward elitism. If quality of satisfactions matters, runs the objection, it could matter so much that a society might choose to put all its resources into developing the capacities of the few most talented and ignore the rest. It should be apparent why this argument does not touch Mill's position. Mill's theory is built around rights, and all have a right to liberty of self-development, a right that is explicitly violated in the suggested scenario. There are good reasons for having this right, but in any case it is purely desert-island thinking to suppose that the misery of those whose capacities are thwarted could in any real society be outweighed by the elevated enjoyments of the few. Mill believed that almost all people were capable of leading intellectually and emotionally satisfying lives, and the fact that even the most advanced industrial societies fall short of the simple justice needed to apply resources so all can have their chance is no reason to abandon the goal. There is still another reply to this objection. The objection presupposes that developed agents are like Gray's autonomous agents, not like Mill's developed agents. Development is of moral and affective capacities, not just of intellectual ones. If "developed" agents reveal their lack of concern for and connection to those less fortunate members of their society by supporting elitist developmental resource allocations, they by these very actions undermine their claim to this developed status. Thus such elitist advocacy is self-defeating. It should be remembered as well that the denial of this elitist alternative does not require the most talented to "sacrifice" their talents by spending all their time helping others; they can fulfill their duties collectively.

Mill's argument for egalitarianism does not suggest that all can equally attain the status of competent agents, at least not all to the same degree. Mill recognizes that, even under optimal conditions, people differ in natural talents and in the extent to which they choose to exercise them, although he does believe that almost all would become competent agents to a significant extent. I have presented considerations in support of the egalitarian argument: that to deny people educative opportunities is to deny them the status of complete moral agency; and that people have a right to liberty of self-development.

The issue raised in this chapter is how to balance the same right—the right to liberty of self-development—of all members of a community. This is the right to develop one's human faculties and to exercise these faculties once developed. Mill's argument is that we all have a vital interest in our freedom to pursue our own good. Those on the developmental frontier do not have a different right from those who have not had the chance to develop their talents. All have the same right. Since this is a right within a utilitarian theory, it is a strong though not absolute right, and the theory has the means of using the principle of utility to arbitrate conflicts. Some libertarians worry about the restraints on the most highly developed; some left-wing theorists worry that the right is empty for the poorest members of the society. But the question is how to mediate conflicts of the same right, not how to weigh two different considerations of liberty and self-development.

These deliberations give us another perspective on the significance of development in Mill's theory. But they do not resolve all of the problems, for Mill does not always clearly specify what ought to be done when vital interests conflict. The vital interest in the freedom to develop oneself, for example, might conflict with the rights to freedom of the already developed. Nor does Mill tell us what to do if property rights conflict with redistributive policies that may be required to allow more equal opportunity for self-development. The right to attain this status of development are the right to exercise these talents once attained form a continuum of the same right. I have argued that development is fundamental to Mill's theory as well as to his view of human welfare. Thus the right to liberty of self-development must be weighed more heavily in these conflicts than has generally been recognized. As we look at the application of Mill's theoretical commitments to concrete social situations, we should remember that Mill's conceptions of value and of human nature are more basic in his system than are economic market relations. His theoretical commitments would impel him to change his economic theory rather than his value theory if the two were in conflict. And, in fact, Mill does move away from a commitment to the free market and toward a form of utopian socialism in his later thought. These are issues for chapter 10.

9

Liberty and Harm to Others

The right to liberty of self-development is prominent in Mill's ethical theory and theory of justice. Although this book is primarily concerned with Mill's views on utility and the good, our right to liberty to pursue our self-development and become competent judges of the good takes us into the territory of rights, obligation, and justice. A full-fledged examination of the philosophical problems within this territory would take me too far afield, but a sketch of questions surrounding this particular right, central to my argument, is in order.

The right I am concerned with is the one Mill eloquently defends in *On Liberty*. Several key passages in that essay and in *Utilitarianism* provide most of what I need to cast light on this right. In *Utilitarianism* Mill grounds rights within a utilitarian system on vital interests. In *On Liberty* interests (especially vital interests) and harms are connected. Many, though by no means all, of the problems traditionally associated with Mill's doctrine of liberty dissolve if we take the discussions of these two essays together, for then we can view the principle of liberty and the right it defends as embedded in Mill's theory of justice. It is doubtful that all the problems of interpretation can ever be resolved, but this route is, I believe, the most helpful and promising. One set of problems that should be addressed focuses on two questions about harm: (1) what is Mill's conception of harm? and (2) does Mill's principle of liberty permit restrictions of liberty of conduct that causes harm to others, or, more broadly, can liberty be restricted to prevent harm to others? The first question must be dealt with before the second.

The principle of liberty says that liberty can be restricted only to prevent harm to others. Problems of interpretation and defense of the principle arise partly because Mill gives it different formulations in the course of *On Liberty*. One formulation has led many commentators down a garden trail into a bog—the interpretation of the principle of liberty in terms of self-regarding and other-regarding conduct: "The only part of the conduct of any one, for which he is amenable to society, is that which concerns others. In the part which merely concerns himself, his independence is, of right, absolute" (18:224).[1] The problems that ensue if we take this line are obvious: unless we can isolate a sphere of action that affects only self, the liberty principle is without teeth. But in real life few of our actions can be so isolated. C. L. Ten says, "According to the traditional interpretation, self-regarding actions have no effect on others against their wishes; they only affect the agents and consenting adults."[2] Since we are not atomistic individuals and do not live isolated from others, self-regarding actions on this view are trivial and severely restricted—hence the lack of teeth to the principle. But, says Ten, "Mill readily and explicitly admits that self-regarding conduct affects others, and this admission is fatal to the traditional interpretation" (11).

J. C. Rees, according to Ten, sets out the line of interpretation that leads out of the bog: "Rees maintains that self-regarding actions do not affect the interests of others. He claims that there is for Mill a distinction between merely 'affecting others' and 'affecting the interests of others' and that in some crucial passages when he is stating his principle, Mill uses the notion of interests rather than that of effects"[3] (11). Rees is exactly right, and when we look at passages in which Mill expands on the principle of liberty we see that his explication is in terms of interests. Gray also sees that we need to move from talk of self- and other-regarding conduct to talk of interests to make headway:

[1]David Lyons notes the bog this formulation can and has led to; see "Liberty and Harm to Others," 4.
[2]C. L. Ten, *Mill on Liberty* (Oxford, 1980), 10.
[3]See J. C. Rees, "A Re-Reading of Mill on Liberty," *Political Studies* 8 (1960).

Ever since *On Liberty* was published, the commonest line of criticism of his argument has been that it presupposes what does not exist—a domain of purely self-regarding actions which non-trivially affect only the agent and no one else. If this is so, then Mill's principle cannot do the job he had in mind for it—that of securing a determinate and important area of human life from liberty-limiting invasion.[4]

Berger sees the same thing. He claims that the theme of *On Liberty* is

> the doctrine of the importance to human well-being of individual self-development, or, as I prefer to call it, autonomy. . . .
>
> [*On Liberty*] is aimed at providing a rule of conduct for society that is designed to protect what Mill regards as a vital interest of persons—autonomous development and activity. . . . people have a right to individuality. Mill's theory of liberty, then, is an application of his theory of justice.[5]

In the background is Berger's analysis of what it is to have a right in Mill's theory. He claims that "Mill held that someone has a right to act in a certain way or be treated by others in a certain way if and only if society has a duty, specified by a rule, to protect the person's interest in acting in that way, or to be treated in that way" (230).

It is best to avoid the route of self-regarding and other-regarding conduct in explaining Mill's principle of liberty. The language of harms and interests dominates his discussion. We make headway by seeing harm as the invasion of or injury to interests. The interests Mill refers to in *On Liberty* and *Utilitarianism* are the same, and in *Utilitarianism* he explicitly makes these the foundation of his theory of justice. That Mill has a theory of justice has recently been convincingly argued by Berger (123–226), who contends that the central theme of *On Liberty* is not the usual negative thesis attributed to Mill but his defense of the right of individual self-development or autonomy. Berger notes Mill's description in the *Autobiography* of his intention in *On Liberty* to examine "the doctrine of the rights of individuality."[6] This is the positive aspect of the negative theme *On Liberty* explicitly defends, and "the principle [is] stated in terms meant to rule out certain *grounds* for interfering

---

[4]Gray, *Mill on Liberty*, 49.
[5]Berger, *Happiness, Justice and Freedom*, 229.
[6]Berger, *Happiness, Justice and Freedom*, 229, quoting Mill, 1:260.

with the freedom of others, or to rule out certain kinds of conduct as fit objects of social control" (229). If we see how Mill explains harm in terms of interests and note that interests, especially vital interests, ground rights, the positive defense of the right to liberty of self-development is clarified.

After his introduction of the principle of liberty in *On Liberty*, Mill shows that he regards harm and injury to interests as two sides of the same coin. He straightforwardly ties his principle of liberty to notions of utility or, as he puts it, "utility in the largest sense, grounded on the permanent interests of man as a progressive being" (18:224). Mill makes it plain that he is concerned with a weighing of interests, which is what one would expect from a utilitarian:

> Those interests, I contend, authorize the subjection of individual spontaneity to external control, only in respect to those actions of each, which concern the interest of other people. . . . In all things which regard the external relations of the individual, he is *de jure* amenable to those whose interests are concerned, and if need be, to society as their protector. (18:224–25)
>
> The fact of living in society renders it indispensable that each should be bound to observe a certain line of conduct towards the rest. This conduct consists first, in not injuring the interests of one another; or rather certain interests, which . . . ought to be considered as rights. As soon as any part of a person's conduct affects prejudicially the interests of others, society has jurisdiction over it, and the question whether the general welfare will or will not be promoted by interfering with it, becomes open to discussion. (18:276)

On the other hand, fair competition may damage interests but not warrant interference. In such cases interests are not violated (18:293).

The connections among harm, injuries to interests, and violations of rights are thrown into further into relief in the final chapter of *On Liberty*. There Mill reformulates the principle of liberty into two maxims, and these maxims are expressed in the language of interests:

> The maxims are, first, that the individual is not accountable to society for his actions, in so far as these concern the interests of no person but himself. . . . Secondly, that for such actions as are prejudicial to the interests of others, the individual is accountable, and may be subjected either to social or to legal punishment, if society is of the opinion that the one or the other is requisite for its protection. (18:292)

Immediately following his formulation of the maxims, in his initial explanation prior to a detailed exploration of case applications,
Mill moves from the language of interests to the language of rights.
None of this is surprising when we consider the treatment of rights
and justice in *Utilitarianism*. Once we see that harm is restricted in
Mill's theory to injury or damage to interests, that it does not stretch
to cover effects of actions generally, we are on the right road. But
interests are still a rather broad class, and we need to see more
explicitly how interests are to be weighed if the principle of liberty is
to have practical action-guiding efficacy. Some commentators, including Gray, move to restrict the relevant interests to those vital
interests that give birth to rights. But this restriction limits the class
of relevant interests too severely. The principle of liberty protects
our vital interest in liberty, including liberty of self-development,
and in Mill's system these vital interests give rise to a right. Since
we have a right to liberty, it is apparent that this right can be overrid-
den or outweighed only by strong countervailing interests. But these
countervailing interests cannot be restricted in every case to those
vital interests which ground rights, as Gray claims. In most cases
the interests that ground rights can be outweighed only by other
vital interests grounding rights, but not always. Mill says that "justice is a name for certain moral requirements, which, regarded collectively, stand higher in the scale of social utility, and are therefore
of more paramount obligation, than any others; *though particular
cases may occur in which some other social duty is so important, as
to overrule any one of the general maxims of justice*" (10:259, emphasis added). If such cases can occur, then the countervailing interests cannot be limited to those that give rise to rights, since rules
that set out rights are all rules of justice. So the net of relevant
interests must be cast somewhat wider than those protected by
rights. The sense of interests Mill has in mind is not a special sense
but the ordinary sense. Since those interests embodied in rights are
the weightiest, it is relatively rare for them to be outweighed by
interests not so embodied, but it can happen. The right to liberty is
one of the strongest in Mill's theory, but it is not absolute, nor
indeed is any secondary principle in his system absolute. The general apparatus of his moral theory can be called on when this right
conflicts with other moral principles. The principle of liberty can be
understood as defending a right to liberty, and conflicts are decided
in accordance with the general method for deciding conflicts of
rights with other secondary moral principles.

Mill's conception of harm should now be somewhat clearer. But there are also controversies over whether Mill's principle of liberty restricts liberty only in cases where conduct causes harm to others or, more broadly, whether it restricts liberty in order to prevent harm to others. D. G. Brown contends the former, David Lyons the latter.

Brown expresses Mill's principle of liberty as the principle that the "liberty of action of the individual ought prima facie to be interfered with if and only if his conduct is harmful to others."[7] Brown formulates Mill's principle in this fashion because, even though Mill uses the expression "to prevent harm to others" in his first presentation of the liberty principle, this does not, according to Brown, reveal Mill's intent. Brown thinks that, rather, "Mill consistently writes and argues as if he had specified, not that interference with the conduct should prevent harm to others, but rather that the conduct itself should be harmful to others" (135). To back up his claim that Mill's principle is concerned only with conduct that causes harm to others, and not with the broader category, Brown quotes Mill: "A person may cause evil to others not only by his actions but by his inaction, and in either case he is justly accountable to them for the injury."[8] Brown's central interpretive claim then follows:

> I take it Mill implies here a rough identification of harming, injury, and causing evil, and uses the notion of causing evil by inaction to argue that these terms have a wider extension than one might think. He seems to imply both that not preventing evil can in some circumstances be causing evil by inaction . . . and that it is the only way of causing evil by inaction. (144–45)

This implication, claims Brown, brings Mill serious trouble: it is questionable whether Mill's arguments "could stretch the category of 'causing evil to others' to cover the whole range of conduct that Mill actually includes" (145).

Since Mill includes examples that seem to fit better a harm-prevention than a harmful-conduct principle, and since his initial presentation is in terms of harm prevention, we could be led at this juncture to reconsider whether Mill's principle is not best seen as a harm-prevention principle. But Brown persists in his line of argument that Mill's principle is actually one about harmful conduct, even though his examples cannot be accommodated by and conflict

---

[7]D. G. Brown, "Mill on Liberty and Morality," 135.
[8]Brown, "Mill on Liberty and Morality," 144, quoting Mill, 18:225.

with such a principle. If Mill's examples are in tension with a harmful-conduct interpretation, one wonders what to make of Brown's claim that Mill "consistently writes and argues as if he had specified" such a principle. If Mill uses inappropriate examples, it is not plausible to take him as arguing consistently for such a principle. This of course is not to let Mill off the hook for his slipshod mode of expression, but if we are to choose between the sins of inconsistency and of lax expression, the latter is preferable. Brown goes on to examine whether a harmful-conduct principle can accommodate the two types of cases offered by Mill, what are called (by Lyons) cooperation and good-samaritan examples. Mill speaks, under the first set, of being justified in compelling an agent "to perform certain acts of individual beneficence, such as saving a fellow-creature's life" (18:225). Brown reacts to this type of example by claiming that failure to perform such good-samaritan acts does not naturally fit a case of causing harm:

> If I do not save a fellow creature's life, or do not protect the defenseless against a third party, even in circumstances in which I could be required to do so, it does not follow that in every such case I cause harm to the neglected person or to anyone at all. It is sufficient to preclude such an inference, and in general to preclude any inference from not preventing evil to causing evil, to consider the agency of other people. A drowning man may have jumped or may have been pushed, and quite ordinary circumstances may require us to assign the agency of some other person than myself as the cause of the evil. (145)

Examples of cooperation, according to Brown, are even more difficult to assimilate to causing harm to others. Mill gives examples of bearing a fair share of the "joint work necessary to the interest of the society of which he enjoys the protection" and of "sacrifices incurred for defending the society or its members from injury and molestation" (18:225; 276). Brown claims that causing harm does not stretch far enough in such cases:

> There can be no guarantee that joint works necessary to the interest of society will not include institutional care for the mentally defective, urban redevelopment, or foreign aid to countries whose economic condition might otherwise lead to war. I cannot see how refusal to cooperate in such efforts toward alleviation of existing problems could be shown to constitute causing harm to others. (146)

Brown further contends that even a harm-prevention principle cannot extend to all Mill's examples. Although this broader principle might explain some of the above examples, "even the general prevention of harm would not stretch to cover a fair share of every joint work necessary to the interest of society" (146). Brown does not defend this central claim that harm prevention cannot cover such cases; he simply states that this is the case—and ends with an assessment: "It seems to me that we have duties to help other people which go beyond the avoidance of harming them; that the performance of such duties can legitimately be extracted from us, very commonly in our roles as citizens and taxpayers; and that such exactions are not permitted by Mill's main principle" (158).

David Lyons takes the other route, defending Mill's principle of liberty as a general harm-prevention principle and effectively criticizes Brown's analysis in the process.[9] While taking full note of the difficulties Mill creates for himself through careless presentation, Lyons manages to give a sympathetic and convincing reading. He reads Mill's principle of liberty as arguing that "the prevention of harm to other persons is a good reason, and the only good reason, for restricting behavior" (6). Lyons lists what Mill takes to be examples of warranted interference with liberty according to the liberty principle. This principle would allow control in cases of conduct harmful to others, but beyond this, as we have seen, the principle also has good-samaritan and cooperative-venture requirements. Lyons notes Brown's argument that these latter two examples are not in accord with the liberty principle as Brown sees it but contends that his own reading is more plausible:

> On the reading I propose, freedom may be limited only for the purpose of preventing harm to other persons, but the conduct that is interfered with need not itself be considered harmful or dangerous to others. Such a principle both conforms to Mill's definitive statement and accommodates his examples. The cooperation and good samaritan requirements that Mill refers to could not be justified on the ground that they prevent conduct that causes harm to others; but it can be argued that such regulations nevertheless work in other ways to prevent harm to others. (4)

Lyons explains that "harm to others can be prevented not just by interfering with acts that can be said to cause, or that threaten to cause, harm to other persons" (5). He first tackles the application of the principle of liberty to good-samaritan examples. In such exam-

---

[9]Lyons, "Liberty and Harm to Others," 1–21.

ples, a person who is injured or in danger can be saved further harm through the aid of another.

> It makes no difference here what, if anything, can be said to cause the harm or danger. If the Principle of Liberty says flatly (as on my reading it does) that the prevention of harm to others justifies interfering with my liberty, then it might justify interfering with my liberty in this sort of case. I might be required to come to another's aid, in order to prevent harm to him, even if I may not be said to have caused the harm that he will suffer if I should fail to help him when I can. . . . harm to others can be prevented not only by interfering with, preventing, or otherwise suppressing harmful and dangerous conduct but also by requiring, or otherwise eliciting helpful, harm-preventing conduct. (5)

Next Lyons turns to cooperation requirements, which at first glance do not seem to be cases of preventing harm. How can giving evidence in court be construed as preventing harm? The answer recalls the need for institutional arrangements to protect rights. Giving evidence "is needed as part of an institution that helps to prevent harm. . . . the point of such a rule is not to interfere with conduct that would independently be characterized as harmful or dangerous to others, but is rather to redirect behaviour so as to help create a social practice that will help prevent harm" (7). Lyons sees that Mill recognizes the need for institutional arrangements to secure members of society from harm. Since harm is often injury to vital interests grounding rights, this point is closely allied to my argument that institutional arrangements (and the steps required to set them up) are needed for adequate rights protection. Brown's narrow construal of the principle of liberty allows only intervention with conduct that is itself harmful; this again is cold comfort for those on whom preventable harm has fallen because adequate steps were not taken to prevent injury to their interests, even though the agent who could have prevented the injury did not actually engage in harmful conduct. Such a case is similar to the complaint of one whose rights have not been adequately protected because proper institutional arrangements have not been made. The narrow construal confuses the activities needed to protect rights and prevent harm through institutions and social arrangements with activities that go beyond rights protection or harm prevention to benefit others; it tries to veto such activities as are needed for rights securement or harm prevention because it falsely labels such activities as extending beyond the realm of rights protection and harm prevention. Sometimes failure to help is failure to prevent harm, and these cases are not to be construed as failure to promote benefits beyond rights securement. As Lyons puts it, "we are speaking here only of preventing harm and not of using coercion to promote benefits in general" (7). The need for institutional arrangements and social practices also applies to cooperative ventures. Cooperation requirements "may well provide the *only* means of preventing or eliminating some significant harms, such as malnutrition and starvation, emotional disturbances, illness and disease, vulnerability to attack, homelessness, and so on. In fact, it is difficult to think of major social problems that might be dealt with just be limiting conduct that causes or threatens to cause harm to others" (7–8). Thus Lyons concludes that the general harm-prevention interpretation of the principle of liberty is superior. Mill did distinguish between preventing or eliminating harm and increasing benefits, but the line does not fall where Brown draws it. Mill's cooperation and good-samaritan requirements are justified on the grounds that they prevent harms, not on the basis that they increase benefits.

> The Principle of Liberty permits some 'trade-offs', but it never sanctions the imposition of burdens on some for the sake of others' positive benefits. No benefits beyond harm-prevention can justify coercion under the Principle of Liberty. The trade-offs it allows are these: loss of liberty . . . in order to prevent or eliminate greater harm to others. (16)

The implications of this interpretation are far-reaching. The right to liberty does not exclude obligations to take part in cooperative social ventures. An egalitarian theory of justice and a balance of individuality and sociality are the results.

IO

Applications of the Theory

The roads of Mill's argument all lead back to human development. I have sought to underscore the indispensability of this concept as a preliminary to my investigation of how well Mill follows through on this theoretical commitment. The test of Mill's commitment is his stance on opportunities of development of the working class of nineteenth-century Britain. As we have seen, Mill lucidly recognizes the effects on the lives of the working class of the deficiency of chances to develop themselves and pursue meaningful lives. His extensive discussions of representative democracy and economic democracy are a good entry to an exploration of the adequacy of his synthesis of liberal values, which has often appeared conflictive. In assessing his success, we must look at development not as an all-or-nothing characteristic that one either has or does not have but as a characteristic that admits of degree. Adult workers have developed their rational and social skills at least to a minimum, and the question is how to increase and refine these powers.

REPRESENTATIVE GOVERNMENT

Considerations on Representative Government is a balancing act in which Mill tries to equilibrate the goals of participation and development in the political sphere against those of competent government.[1] His faith in the wisdom of the already competent elite clashes with his aim of developing all people's potential through participation in the democratic political process. Mill is unequivocal about the power of democratic political institutions as agents of "national education." Participation in political life is one of the main tools in the arsenal of a social policy of expanding developmental opportunities.

One of the central tests of a good government is "the degree in which it tends to increase the sum of good qualities in the governed, collectively and individually; since, besides that their well-being is the sole object of government, their good qualities supply the moving force which works the machinery." Government can increase the welfare of people by acting as an "agency of national education." We judge governments as good in part because of "the degree in which they promote the general mental advancement of the community, including under that phrase advancement in intellect, in virtue, and in practical activity and efficiency" (19:390–93).

Mill devotes Chapter 3 of *Representative Government* to an extensive argument that a representative political democracy best fulfills the functions of government, and prominent among these functions is a governmental role in developing members of the community. He concludes that

> the only government which can fully satisfy all the exigencies of the social state, is one in which the whole people participate; that any participation, even in the smallest public function, is useful; that the participation should everywhere be as great as the general degree of improvement of the community will allow; and that nothing less can be ultimately desirable, than the admission of all to a share in the sovereign power of the state. (19:412)

Mill's deliberations lead him to exclude as less than ideal all non-democratic forms of government and to settle on a democracy with "supreme controlling power . . . vested in the entire aggregate of the community" as the model. Self-protection is one of the principal reasons for extension of the suffrage to the working class, because

---

[1]See Dennis Thompson *John Stuart Mill and Representative Government* (Princeton, 1976). My overall analysis differs in some ways from Thompson's because of my analysis of Mill's qualitative hedonism and his views on self-development.

only members of the working class themselves can air their perspective and stand up for their interests in the public arena. "The rights
and interests of every or any person are only secure from being
disregarded, when the person interested is himself able, and habitually disposed, to stand up for them." But democratic government is
also exemplary because it extends to working people participation in
public choices and educates them and broadens their perspective.
The effect of this participation is improvement and development,
and thus an increase in social welfare as a whole. Mill claims that
"the general prosperity attains a greater height, and is more widely
diffused, in proportion to the amount and variety of the personal
energies enlisted in promoting it." Democracy's real strength resides
in its aptitude for encouraging and harnessing the energies of active
and energetic characters. These are the mainstay of social improvement and progress: "Now there can be no kind of doubt that the
passive type of character is favoured by the government of one or a
few, and the active self-helping type by that of the Many" (19:403–
10).

Intellectual, practical, and moral excellence are all fostered by
active participation in public life (19:407). Accepting some public
responsibility is one of the best avenues for deepening people's social feelings and teaching them to look beyond their narrow self-
interests.

> It is not sufficiently considered how little there is in most men's
> ordinary life to give any largeness either to their conceptions or to
> their sentiments. Their work is a routine; not a labour of love, but of
> self-interest in the most elementary form, the satisfaction of daily
> wants; neither the thing done, nor the process of doing it, introduces
> the mind to thoughts or feelings extending beyond individuals.
> (19:411)

Public service and activity cuts through this routine and takes individuals beyond themselves:

> He is called upon, while so engaged, to weigh interests not his own; to
> be guided, in case of conflicting claims, by another rule than his
> private partialities; to apply, at every turn, principles and maxims
> which have for their reason of existence the common good. . . . Where
> this school of public spirit does not exist, scarcely any sense is enter-
> tained that private persons, in no eminent social situation, owe any
> duties to society, except to obey the laws and submit to the govern-

ment. There is no unselfish sentiment of identification with the public. Every thought or feeling, either of interest or of duty, is absorbed in the individual and in the family. The man never thinks of any collective interest, of any objects to be pursued jointly with others, but only in competition with them, and in some measure at their expense. A neighbour, not being an ally or an associate, since he is never engaged in any common undertaking for joint benefit, is therefore only a rival. Thus even private morality suffers, while public is actually extinct. (19:412)

The advantage of representative government is

that which most widely diffuses the exercise of public functions; on the one hand, by excluding fewest from the suffrage; on the other, by opening to all classes of private citizens, so far as is consistent with other equally important objects, the widest participation in the details of judicial and administrative business; as by jury trial, admission to municipal offices, and above all by the utmost possible publicity and liberty of discussion, whereby not merely a few individuals in succession, but the whole public, are made, to a certain extent, participants in the government, and sharers in the instruction and mental exercise derivable from it. (19:436)

From these remarks, development would seem to have the field, the only question being how to remove as quickly as possible all impediments to society-wide development. In a sense Mill does make this case, but his reformism leads him to introduce several brakes and cautionary measures into the process. Development as a value encompasses two very different elements that Mill is anxious to protect but does not balance in any determinate way.[2] In Chapter 5 I argued that two elements—experience and judgment—are incorporated in the developmental process. People gain experience in the public domain through active participation in political choices, but from Mill's perspective this is only part of the picture. It is just as important for those developing themselves to learn to exercise judgment so that their participation does not lead to defective choices. The conflictive elements of liberalism reappear here under a new guise, because this second element mandates learning standards from those who are already competent. Although Mill aspires to make competence a function of education, not of class or property,

[2]Both Dennis Thompson, ibid., and Amy Gutmann, *Liberal Equality*, discuss this lack of balance.

the majority of those already developed in nineteenth-century Britain were, as Mill sees it, of the middle or upper class, whereas most of those who were still developing were of the working class. Mill assumes that the already competent members of the middle class who are to help others become competent are able to put aside their class interests and make social choices grounded on the interests of all, and in the process help members of the working class become competent.

We are also left with the theoretical problem of balancing political competence and participation so as best to extend and promote development. On this point, it is helpful to keep in mind that in Mill's view this balancing problem is only a problem of the interim; once the members of society are developed, this embarrassment disappears. Development carries competence with it; once the majority of members of society have attained a reasonably developed status, there is no longer a worry that defective social choices will result from the input of less than fully competent actors. Until this time, Mill can argue that participation and competence need to be balanced and protected. The problem is to keep the level of participation as extensive and active as possible. But once all actors are developed, they are thereby competent, and competence no longer needs protection against the participation of the less fully competent. Still, individuals' development can be hampered if they lack active participation, and social choices suffer from a lack of infusion of energy if all do not participate. So participation requires protection and nurturance, even after competence is assured.

In these terms, it becomes apparent that Mill's theory is more acute than his understanding of the dynamics of his own society; his beliefs about the working class cloud his judgment and interfere with the execution of his goals. In *Participation and Democratic Theory*, Carole Pateman is critical of Mill for "not tak[ing] his own arguments about participation seriously enough."[3] The elitist trend in Mill's thought prompts him to be overly protective of the interests of the middle class at the expense of working-class advancement and to exaggerate the dangers of involvement of the developing working class in the public domain. His plea for the development of all in Chapter 3 is offset by his argument of Chapter 6 on the dangers of representative government.

[3]Carole Pateman, *Participation and Democratic Theory* (Cambridge, 1970), 31.

In addition to the problem of defective social choices from premature participation, Mill is at pains to emphasize the dangers of giving too much power at too early a stage to those he sees as not yet ready to make social choices for the welfare of all. Two evils of representative government are "first, general ignorance and incapacity, or, to speak more moderately, insufficient mental qualifications, in the controlling body; secondly, the danger of its being under the influence of interests not identical with the general welfare of the community" (19:436). He adds, "One of the greatest dangers . . . of democracy, as of all other forms of government, lies in the sinister interest of the holders of power: it is the danger of class legislation; of government intended for (whether really effecting it or not) the immediate benefit of the dominant class, to the lasting detriment of the whole" (19:446).

Although the working class of Mill's society was far from dominant, the dangers of class legislation he refers to are examples of working-class legislation that could result if the suffrage was extended to the working class without adequate checks and balances. The middle and upper classes were actually dominant, but Mill is not concerned that they might abuse their political power. He is worried that the middle class might be forced by working-class inspired legislation to bear an unduly large or the entire portion of taxes. Mill also lists other possible examples of abusive class legislation: "legislative attempts to raise wages, limitation of competition in the labour market, taxes or restrictions on machinery, and on improvements of all kinds tending to dispense with any of the existing labour." Inheritance might even be done away with. So a representative government must be designed so as "not to allow any of the various sectional interests to be so powerful as to be capable of prevailing against truth and justice and the other sectional interests combined" (19:442–47).

The well-known phrase "tyranny of the majority" encapsulates Mill's concern that a minority of the wisest and most distinguished could be swept away by the tide of the newly powerful, enfranchised majority. One result of this concern is that Mill pushes for policies such as the weighted ballot and a system of proportional representation that stipulates that all interest groups have a voice in proportion to their numbers. "The virtual blotting out of the minority is no necessary or natural consequence of freedom; . . . far from having any connexion with democracy, it is diametrically opposed to the first principle of democracy, representation in proportion to numbers. It is an essential part of democracy that minorities should be adequately represented" (19:452).

Mill does realize the damaging effects on the working class of debarring them from much of the political and governmental process, but he does not correctly analyze the causes or impact of this exclusion:

> We need not suppose that when power resides in an exclusive class, that class will knowingly and deliberately sacrifice the other classes to themselves: it suffices that, in the absence of its natural defenders, the interest of the excluded is always in danger of being overlooked; and, when looked at, is seen with very different eyes from those of the persons whom it directly concerns. In this country, for example, what are called the working classes may be considered as excluded from all direct participation in the government. I do not believe that the classes who do participate in it, have in general any intention of sacrificing the working classes to themselves. They once had that intention; witness the persevering attempts so long made to keep down wages by law. But in the present day, their ordinary disposition is the very opposite: they willingly make considerable sacrifices, especially of their pecuniary interest, for the benefit of the working classes. . . . nor do I believe that any rulers in history have been actuated by a more sincere desire to do their duty towards the poorer portion of their countrymen. Yet does Parliament, or almost any of the members composing it, ever for an instant look at any question with the eyes of a working man? (19:405)

Mill thus attributes the harmful effects of the denial of suffrage to the working class to a lack of opportunity of self-protection rather than to intentionally sinister class legislation by middle- and upper-class voters. But Mill's optimistic outlook that middle-class voters of his time no longer abused their powers of suffrage to damage workers' interests is not realistic. In historical perspective it can be seen that late nineteenth-century voters were no more enlightened in their use of political power than were their predecessors. If class legislation is a danger, then that danger comes equally from the middle class. In Mill's time, it was the working class who suffered the actual damage of lack of political power.

Mill's real worry, however, is that the educated elite minority might be effectively silenced by the rest, and, although his arguments for proportional representation apply to all minorities, foremost in his mind is the educated middle-class minority:

The natural tendency of representative government, as of modern civilization, is towards collective mediocrity: and this tendency is increased by all reductions and extensions of the franchise, their effect being to place the principal power in the hands of classes more and more below the highest level of instruction in the community. But though the superior intellects and characters will necessarily be outnumbered, it makes a great difference whether or not they are heard. (19:457)

These concerns lead Mill to devise strategies to strengthen the hand of the educated elite under universal suffrage. A plan like Thomas Hare's proportional representation is one. (19:453) Other strategies to increase the power of the educated elite include plural or weighted voting and an educational qualifier on voting rights. But Mill also argues for short-term exclusions from the suffrage which would, in practice, have the effect of barring, often permanently, many working-class people from a voice in government:

I regard it as wholly inadmissible that any person should participate in the suffrage, without being able to read, write, and, I will add, perform the common operations of arithmetic. Justice demands . . . that the means of attaining these elementary acquirements should be within the reach of every person. . . . When society has not performed its duty, by rendering this amount of instruction accessible to all, there is some hardship in the case, but it is a hardship that ought to be borne. If society has neglected to discharge two solemn obligations, the more important and more fundamental of the two must be fulfilled first: universal teaching much precede universal enfranchisement. (19:470)

This part of Mill's argument is weak, but its weakness does not touch the fundamental principles of his theory; rather, the weakness results from shaky and unsupportable empirical generalizations about class characteristics and about the dangers of granting political power to those without basic literacy. It connects the abilities of a rational moral agent too strictly with literacy. Certainly the standard model of education begins with basic literacy, but Mill himself recognizes that the powers of a competent agent are broader than those of literacy and also may be acquired independently of literacy training. Mill recognizes the positive effects not only of formal education but also of more informal avenues of instruction. Everything from "instruction obtained from newspapers and political tracts . . . institutions for lecture and discussion, the collective deliberations on questions of common interests, the trade unions, the political agitation, all serve to awaken public spirit, to diffuse variety of ideas among the mass, and to excite thought and reflection in the more intelligent."[4] Instead of viewing two processes (gaining understanding through basic literacy training and gaining understanding through education in the political sphere) as working together toward a common goal, Mill here makes one a precondition of the other.

Mill does not have good reasons for thinking that the damage of premature suffrage would be greater than the damage of debarment from the political power and educative experience of the suffrage. In effect, such a policy would have permanently barred most adult members of the working class, since campaigns for education would have been aimed at the children of the working class. The damage to the disenfranchised working class resulting from their lack of social and political power, including the power of suffrage, was palpable and massive; it is hard to justify counting this actual harm as less weighty than the uncertain or possible harm of granting suffrage to the uneducated.

The more interesting question arises at a more basic level of Mill's theory. His political theory requires us to weigh different elements of competence and participation. A significant question is whether the necessity of balancing signals a flaw in the theory or is evidence of its flexibility and realism. Every moral theory requires some sort of balancing; Mill's is not unique. Mill's theory gives more guidance in this balancing than others—a balancing guided by welfare and by the centrality of the commitment to human development. If extensive development is our stated goal, then, although there is a range of weightings of competence and participation by reasonable people, still much can be ruled out as unacceptable. The fundamental value of development and the actual damage done to individuals and to society by the presence of large numbers of people who have not achieved a measure of development of their potential weigh heavily on the acceptability of alternatives.

Mill's anxieties about premature universal suffrage have not withstood the tests of time and sociological study. The harm done to those excluded from their just share of power cannot begin to be outweighed by the harms, if any, of political participation of the

<hr/>

[4]See, e.g., Mill, *Principles of Political Economy*, chap. 7, "On the Probable Futurity of the Labouring Classes," 3:763–64.

uneducated. To insist that they acquire basic education before they acquire a vote is to do them a double injustice, for the power inequities that a social policy of political participation is presumably trying to rectify usually arise from the same forces that have prevented people from getting an education. Mill's recommendations for qualifying universal suffrage would have the effect that most adult workers of his society would not have the opportunity to participate in the political process and derive the benefits of participation for which he argues so eloquently. Without the chance to participate, development is short-circuited. Once we understand this consequence, we can see the weakness of Mill's weighting of participation and competence. He undervalues participation and places such severe restrictions on it that for many people it would never come into play. Even if Mill's concerns about too extensive participation of those developing had more grounding, the most this case would justify is a social policy that nourishes competence and participation in tandem, not one that delays participation indefinitely until other conditions have been met. It is more reasonable to design policies that rectify both injustices of lack of education and disenfranchisement at the same time. Both literacy campaigns and political participation are forms of education that promote development.

The flaws in Mill's argument arising from his unsupportable apprehensions about universal suffrage and his consequent recommendations to qualify and restrict his overall policy are easy to see from a vantage point one hundred years hence. But his basic theory is sound, and the flaw is located in the unsound application of his principles. This misapplication exemplifies a common criticism which claims that liberalism has good values that it eliminates or overrides in practice. But the flaw of Mill's argument lies not in a weak theoretical base but in inadequate sociological evidence on the effects of different social policies in achieving the goals of the theory. In the *Logic,* Mill sets out the general relation between art (including morality) and science, noting that after we have chosen our ends of morality we need a thorough scientific study to discover the means to achieve our ends:

> Suppose that we have completed the scientific process only up to a certain point. . . . If, in this imperfect state of the scientific theory, we attempt to frame a rule of art, we perform that operation prematurely. Whenever any counteracting cause, overlooked by the theorem, takes place, the rule will be at fault: we shall employ the means and the end

will not follow. . . . there is nothing for it but to turn back and finish the scientific process which should have preceded the formation of the rule. (8:945)

ECONOMIC DEMOCRACY

When we examine Mill's views on developmental opportunities for the working class in the sphere of economic activity, a pattern similar to that in the political area emerges. In studying the impact on the development of working-class people of their position in the economic life of their society, we can consider Mill's positions on a range of issues—property rights and the legitimacy of private property, the justification for government regulation of and intervention in economic activities, and the desirability of alternative economic structures such as worker cooperatives. Mill the liberal economist who has a healthy respect for the free market strains against Mill the utopian socialist who values worker-run collective industrial enterprises, in part because of the developmental impact of involvement in such activities. Mill's economic theory raises many questions; my discussion focuses on the role of development of competent agents through involvement in the economic arena. Here again Mill exhibits a deep commitment to development yet is unable fully to follow through on this goal when he weighs it against other goals and values. The improvement of the working class and the claims of labor must find their proper place in their balance with existing rights of private property and economic efficiency and productivity.

On questions of the claims of labor, Mill's repugnance at the material conditions of working people and their dearth of opportunities to use their human gifts of rationality and autonomy is coupled with insight about the power of economic democracy to unleash these. Mill sees the working class of his day as being in a transitional phase from a state of poverty and dependence to one of independence. He hopes that workers advance concurrently both in their economic status and in rationality and sociality. Here the main object of his scrutiny is the effect on laborers of their working conditions. In his time, the economy was in transition from an agricultural to an industrial base.

I cannot think that they will be permanently contented with the condition of labouring for wages as their ultimate state. . . . In the present stage of human progress, when ideas of equality are daily spreading more widely among the poorer classes . . . it is not to be expected that the division of the human race into two hereditary classes, employers and employed, can be permanently maintained. (3:766–67)

Mill's solution to the deplorable conditions of the working class projects new forms of economic relations that would serve, among many things, to immerse workers in an educational environment in their everyday workplaces. He looks to democratic economic institutions formed on association or partnership relations of two basic types: partnerships of workers and capitalists, and workers' cooperative associations. He particularly notes the benefits of association for the social feelings:

But if public spirit, generous sentiments, or true justice and equality are desired, association, not isolation, of interests, is the school in which these excellences are nurtured. The aim of improvement should be not solely to place human beings in a condition in which they will be able to do without one another, but to enable them to work with or for one another in relations not involving dependence. . . . the relation of masters and workpeople will be gradually superseded by partnership, in one of two forms: in some cases, association of the labourers with the capitalist; in others, and perhaps finally in all, association of labourers among themselves. (3:768–69)

These benefits are to be attained without sacrificing the property rights of owners of capital (3:775). Moreover, this school of the workplace is not to operate at the expense of economic efficiency, rather, it would enhance it. Mill outlines this transformation of economic relations:

Associations, . . . by the very process of their success, are a course of education in those moral and active qualities by which alone success can be either deserved or attained. As associations multiplied, they would tend more and more to absorb all work-people, except those who have too little understanding, or too little virtue, to be capable of learning to act on any other system than that of narrow selfishness. As this change proceeded, owners of capital would gradually find it to their advantage, instead of maintaining the struggle of the old system with work-people of only the worst description, to lend their capital to the associations; to do this at a diminishing rate of interest, and at last, perhaps, even to exchange their capital for terminable annuities. In this or some such mode, the existing accumulations of capital might honestly, and by a kind of spontaneous process, become in the end the joint property of all who participate in their productive employment: a transformation which, thus effected, (and assuming of course that both sexes participate equally in the rights and in the government of the association) would be the nearest approach to social justice, and the most beneficial ordering of industrial affairs for the universal good, which it is possible at present to foresee. (3:793–94)

Mill does not think that economic productivity and efficiency would be compromised by partnership associations. On the contrary, he takes as a crucial determinant of the productivity of an enterprise the degree of interest felt in it by each of the involved parties (*Principles of Political Economy*, 2:107). Interest in or individual benefit from work is crucial, and the common relation of owner and worker fails badly on this account. Although these trends are only speculative until actual experience has been their trial, Mill does not see how such new structures could be less efficient than the typical owner-worker arrangement. He expects the test of time to show that cooperatives are at least as productive as the traditional workplace structures.

As with the case of political democracy, the goal of development must be balanced internally among its elements and externally against other ends. In the economic realm the value of economic partnerships for development must be balanced against good economic management and the property rights of owners. These balancings have also been the occasion for challenges. In the economic arena, workers gain experience through participation in economic associations, and they learn judgment from those who have more competence, in this case owners, managers, or other workers who have knowledge of economic enterprises. The immediate rejoinder from left-wing critics is obvious: Mill is chided for his naivete in thinking that owners would voluntarily relinquish their power in favor of partnership with workers or even share their knowledge with workers. Moreover, worker cooperatives are not as easy to establish as Mill thinks.

There is much truth to these charges, but the enduring appeal of this participatory goal is not easy to dismiss. And it should be noted that Mill's insight that participation is essential for development has been validated by recent theoretical and empirical work on democratic processes; the results of this study highlight the potentially radical implications of his views.

In *Participation and Democratic Theory*, Carole Pateman lauds Mill for his emphasis on the educative purpose of participation and his insight that participation in the realm of industry can have a profound developmental effect even as she criticizes him for not fully following through on his insights. She also points out the radical implications of taking participatory opportunities seriously:

> If such participation in the workplace is to be possible then the authority relationship in industry would have to be transformed from the usual one of superiority–subordination (managers and men) to one of co-operation or equality with the managers (government) being elected by the whole body of employees. . . . Society can be seen as being composed of various political systems, the structure of authority of which has an important effect on the psychological qualities and attitudes of the individuals who interact within them.[5]

Mill sees that participation is a necessary element of the developmental process. What Pateman's work brings home is that participation must be genuine to be efficacious, and to be genuine it must involve a profound change in workplace relations. Mill's speculation that participation in democratic political and economic institutions is useful in developing the active character he holds as ideal has been borne out by evidence, as Pateman points out:

> John Stuart Mill argued that an "active" character would result from participation. . . . If one is to be self-governing in, for example, one's workplace, then certain psychological qualities are clearly necessary. For example, the belief that one can be self-governing, and confidence in one's ability to participate responsibly and effectively, and to control one's life and environment would certainly seem to be required. These are not characteristics that would be associated with "servile" or "passive" characters and it is reasonable to suggest that the acquisition of such confidence, etc., is part, at least, of what the theorists of the participatory society saw as the psychological benefits that would accrue through participation. . . . Now one of the most important positive correlations that has emerged from empirical investigations into political behaviour and attitudes is that between participation and what is known as the sense of political efficacy or sense of political competence. . . . People who have a sense of political efficacy are more likely to participate in politics than those in whom this feeling is lacking and it has also been found that underlying the sense of political efficacy is a sense of general, personal effectiveness, which involves self-confidence in one's dealings with the world. (45–46)

[5]Pateman, *Participation and Democratic Theory*, 34–35.

Not surprising, then, participation is a process that gains momentum and builds on itself; it is an important stimulus to the sense of general well-being that leads to further, broader, more active involvement in and control of one's environment. Does participation in economic structures help? Pateman presents strong evidence that workplace participation is useful in bringing about this sense of political efficacy (50–52). Workplace structures do have an impact on the psychological characteristics of workers:

> It seems clear from this evidence that the argument of the participatory theory of democracy that an individual's (politically relevant) attitudes will depend to a large extent on the authority structure of his work environment is a well-founded one. Specifically, the development of a sense of political efficacy does appear to depend on whether his work situation allows him any scope to participate in decision making. (53)

The authenticity of the participation is very much a factor in its effectiveness for development. The key element is control: "the amount of control that the individual [is] able to exercise over his job and job environment" (56).

Besides presenting results of social scientific studies on worker participation, Pateman takes an illuminating look at the concept of participation, distinguishing its different kinds: pseudo, full, and partial participation. The last two kinds nicely coincide with Mill's two stages of partnership, that between capitalist and workers, and that among workers in a collective endeavor. Workers are not just participating in a vacuum; they are participating in decisions about their work. The crucial determinant of whether participation is partial or full lies in the difference between merely influencing decisions and having full, equal power with others to decide a course of action.

Following P. H. Partridge, Pateman explains that "'influence' is applicable to a situation where individual A affects individual B, without B subordinating his wishes to those of A. . . . the final power of decision rests with the management, the workers if they are able to participate, being able only to influence that decision. Because they are 'workers' they are in the (unequal) position of permanent subordinates; the final 'prerogative' of decision making rests with the permanent superiors, with management" (69–70).[6]

[6]See P. H. Partridge, "Some Notes on the Concept of Power," *Political Studies* 11 (1963): 107–25.

Pateman contrasts this partial participation with full participation in which "there are not two 'sides' having unequal decision making powers, but a group of equal individuals who have to make their own decisions about how work is to be allocated and carried out" (70–71). In this full participation, each has equal decision-making power.

What often passes for participation in contemporary experiments in work reform is in reality what Pateman labels pseudo-participation—persuasion surreptitiously substituted for decision making. Here owners or management try to create a sense of worker participation to persuade workers to accept decisions that have already been made. Workers in reality have no control over the decision, and the developmental impact is minimal.

Mill's argument is that competent moral agency requires a process of development and self-development composed of experience and judgment. One's work environment can provide an arena for such training. But in the sphere of work, the experience translates into participation, and participation is the exercise of control over decisions in that arena. If the decision-making control is removed, the participation becomes counterfeit. So a presupposition of workplace participation is a fundamental reorganization of work relations. Several parallels can be drawn between these points and other related arguments. The essentiality of autonomy in personal or self-regarding decisions affecting one's life is paralleled in the work sphere by the importance of the element of control over decisions about one's work environment. A similar pattern in the political sphere is found here in Mill's clarity about the ideal coupled with indeterminacy about how this is to be attained.

The utopian socialist persona of Mill appears in his postulation of an economy of producer and consumer cooperatives as both the ideal and the probable result of economic relations of his time. Just as Mill thought that the path to political democracy must be guarded by protective policies such as weighted voting and minimum educational qualifications, so he thought that the goal of industrial economic democracy must also be protected. Mill sees owner-worker partnerships and small-scale worker co-operatives as the interim structures that will prepare workers for full economic democracy. Participatory activity and development of judgment are the two internal components that need to be balanced; here again, because increasing participation means increasing power, cautionary measures are needed to ensure that workers are not empowered before they have the expertise to make wise decisions. In the balancing of development of workers' powers against external values of economic efficiency and property rights, Mill does not seem as worried that economic democracy could have a devastating impact as he is worried about political democracy. In the political realm Mill seems, from a twentieth-century vantage point, to have been unduly pessimistic about the effects of universal suffrage; from the same vantage point he seems unduly optimistic about the prospects for success of full economic democracy. He accepts too easily that a gradual evolution of economic structures and relations would accommodate universal development, economic productivity and efficiency, and rights of private property. As a result, he gives us little indication of how to weigh these ends when they are not all easily accommodated, as now seems the case.

Mill does not think that economic productivity and efficiency will be compromised by partnership associations. On the contrary, he takes as a crucial determinant of the productivity of an enterprise the degree of interest felt in it by each involved party. Although interest in our individual benefit from work is so crucial, the common relation of owner and worker fails badly on this account. In response to a common objection against socialism that workers under this system would be tempted to shirk, Mill answers:

> The objection supposes, that honest and efficient labour is only to be had from those who are themselves individually to reap the benefit of their own exertions. But how small a part of all the labour performed in England, from the lowest paid to the highest, is done by persons working for their own benefit. . . . a labourer for hire . . . has no personal interest in the matter at all. (2:204–5)

When we add the efficiency of large-scale production and the fact that under socialism policies of universal education would be followed, the advantages of this system for increased efficiency are pronounced. Although these trends are only speculative until tried by experience, Mill does not see how such structures could be less efficient than the typical owner-worker structure. This is the case even apart from the question of the justice of such structures.

Mill expects the test of time to show cooperatives to be at least as productive as the traditional workplace structures:

> From the progressive advance of the co-operative movement, a great increase may be looked for even in the aggregate productiveness of

industry. . . . The other mode in which co-operation tends, still more efficaciously, to increase the productiveness of labour, consists in the vast stimulus given to productive energies, by placing the labourers, as a mass, in a relation to their work which would make it their principle and their interest—at present it is neither—to do the utmost, instead of the least possible, in exchange for their remuneration. It is scarcely possible to rate too highly this material benefit, which yet is as nothing compared with the moral revolution in society that would accompany it: the healing of the standing feud between capital and labour; the transformation of human life, from a conflict of classes struggling for opposite interests, to a friendly rivalry in the pursuit of a good common to all; the elevation of the dignity of labour; a new sense of security and independence in the labouring class; and the conversion of each human being's daily occupation into a school of the social sympathies and the practical intelligence. (3:791–92)

Mill maintains that owners will see it in their interest to include their workers as partners, because they will recognize that exclusion reduces while inclusion increases workers' interest in their work and that participation will amply repay them through increased productivity. Economic efficiency will take care of itself. The development of workers also must be ordered against private property rights of owners, but here too Mill's solution seems overly simple and optimistic: workers will buy out owners in the long run, removing the injustices of the present form of capitalism without thereby violating any rights of owners:

Eventually, and in perhaps a less remote future than may be supposed, we may, through the co-operative principle, see our way to a change in society, which would combine the freedom and independence of the individual, with the moral, intellectual and economical advantages of aggregate production; and which, without violence or spoliation, or even any sudden disturbance of existing habits and expectations, would realize, at least in the industrial department, the best aspirations of the democratic spirit, by putting an end to the division of society into the industrious and the idle, and effacing all social distinctions but those fairly earned by personal services and exertions. (3:793)

A thorough analysis of why Mill's projections on this point have not come to pass would take us too far afield. Because, as Macpherson and others have emphasized, Mill did not accurately understand the full impact of a capitalist market economy, he took it that historical accident, rather than integral elements, caused the problems

facing the fledgling cooperative movement of his day. He did not
hold the capitalist principle itself responsible.

Whereas Mill sees the centrality of autonomy in some contexts—
particularly in the personal sphere, where autonomy is control or
power over the plan of one's life—and begins to extend the analysis
into the public sphere with his insights about participation, he does
not extend the analysis far enough in the case of rights of private
property. He does not see clearly that, although it may be in the
owners' interests in some respects to extend partnership to workers—in that increased interest increases productivity and profit—
there is another side to this coin. Increasing partnership and participation, if it is not to be pseudo-participation, means increasing
power and control vested in workers to make meaningful decisions
about their work. But owners also have a strong interest in maintaining their power and control and may not be as willing as Mill
suggests to trade this even for increased profit. Even less may they be
willing to give it up entirely by selling their capital to workers'
cooperatives. With the increasing success of worker associations
comes an inevitable, not accidental, backlash against cooperatives in
the form of state interference. Mill does not squarely face such conflicts.

These problems are not Mill's alone. It is instructive to end this
discussion with a look at the proposals of C. B. Macpherson, one of
Mill's most penetrating critics. Macpherson claims that the difficulty with participatory democracy "is not how to run it but how to
reach it."[7] Two conditions seem necessary. The first is a change in
consciousness such that people view themselves not as consumers
but as "exerters and enjoyers of the exertion and development of
their own capacities" (99). This echoes Mill. The second is a reduction of social and economic inequality, a goal also shared by Mill.
But the vicious circle that Macpherson sees in this scheme is that
"we cannot achieve more democratic participation without a prior
change in social inequality and in consciousness, but we cannot
achieve the changes in social inequality and consciousness without
a prior increase in democratic participation" (100). Mill's mistake
was to expect an orderly progression in both conditions together,
which has not happened. Instead, we must look for "loopholes"
anywhere in the circle and grab onto them. But an interesting con-

[7]C. B. Macpherson, *Life and Times of Liberal Democracy*, 98.

clusion is that many of Macpherson's loopholes are Mill's as well. Macpherson hopes, for example, that local and community movements and movements for industrial democracy will have the desired impact. Mill may look like a naive liberal, but it is difficult to find other solutions.

Mill offers us one of the richest of ethical and political theories, challenging and frustrating in its complexity and in its refusal to back away from the messiness of social and political reality. In all his work Mill defies easy analysis or categorization, instead enriching and expanding the theories of his predecessors until they threaten to burst the familiar boundaries of utilitarianism and liberalism. But if ethical and political life are as complex as they seem, we need a theory as sophisticated as Mill's to encompass them.

Bibliography

Abrams, M. H. *The Mirror and the Lamp: Romantic Theory and the Critical Tradition.* London: Oxford University Press, 1981.

Amerine, Maynard A., and Edward B. Roessler. *Wines: Their Sensory Evaluation.* San Francisco: W. H. Freeman, 1976.

Anschutz, R. P. *The Philosophy of J. S. Mill.* London: Oxford University Press, 1963.

Arneson, Richard. "Mill versus Paternalism." *Ethics* 90 (July 1980): 470–89.

Arrow, Kenneth. *Collected Papers of Kenneth J. Arrow: Social Choice and Justice, Volume I.* Cambridge: Belknap Press, 1983.

August, Eugene. *John Stuart Mill: A Mind at Large.* New York: Charles Scribner's Sons, 1975.

Bain, Alexander. *John Stuart Mill. A Criticism: With Personal Recollections.* London: Longmans, Green, 1882.

Barry, Brian. *Political Argument.* London: Routledge & Kegan Paul, 1970.

Bayles, Michael, ed. *Contemporary Utilitarianism.* Garden City: Doubleday, 1968.

Becker, Lawrence. *Property Rights.* Boston: Routledge & Kegan Paul, 1977.

Beebe-Centre, J. G. *The Psychology of Pleasantness and Unpleasantness.* New York: Van Nostrand, 1932.

Benn, Stanley I. "Freedom, Autonomy and the Concept of a Person." *Proceedings of the Aristotelian Society* 76 (1976): 109–30.

——. "Freedom and Persuasion." *Australasian Journal of Philosophy* 45 (1967): 259–75.

Bentham, Jeremy. *The Collected Works of Jeremy Bentham: An Introduction to the Principles of Morals and Legislation,* ed. J. H. Burns and H. L. A. Hart. London: Athlone Press, 1970.

——. *Jeremy Bentham's Economic Writings,* 3 vols., ed. W. Stark. London: George Allen & Unwin, 1954.

———. *The Theory of Legislation.* London: Kegan Paul, Trench, Trubner, 1931.

Berger, Fred. *Happiness, Justice, and Freedom: The Moral and Political Philosophy of John Stuart Mill.* Berkeley: University of California Press, 1984.

———. "John Stuart Mill on Justice and Fairness," in *New Essays on John Stuart Mill and Utilitarianism,* ed. Wesley E. Cooper, Kai Nielsen, and Steven C. Patten. *Canadian Journal of Philosophy, Supplementary Volume* 5 (1979): 115–36.

Berlin, Isaiah. *Four Essays on Liberty.* London: Oxford University Press, 1969.

Billings, John R. "J. S. Mill's Quantity-Quality Distinction." *Mill News Letter* 7 (Fall 1971): 6–16.

Bowring, John, ed. *The Works of Jeremy Bentham,* 10 vols. New York: Russell and Russell, 1962.

Bradley, F. H. *Ethical Studies* 2d ed. London: Oxford University Press, 1962.

Brandt, Richard. *A Theory of the Good and the Right.* Oxford: Clarendon Press, 1979.

Brenkert, G. G. "Marx's Critique of Utilitarianism," in *Marx and Morality,* ed. Kai Nielsen and Steven C. Patten. *Canadian Journal of Philosophy, Supplementary Volume* 7 (1981): 193–220.

Brett, Nathan. "Two Concepts of Rights." Paper presented at the Canadian Philosophical Association, Winnipeg, May 1986.

Broad, C. D. "Certain Features in Moore's Ethical Doctrines," in *The Philosophy of G. E. Moore,* 2 vols., ed. P. A. Schlipp. La Salle, Ill.: Open Court, 1968.

Bronaugh, Richard N. "The Utility of Quality: An Understanding of Mill." *Canadian Journal of Philosophy* 4 (December 1974): 7–25.

Brown, D. G. "Mill on Liberty and Morality." *Philosophical Review* 81 (1972): 133–58.

———. "Mill's Act-Utilitarianism." *Philosophical Quarterly* 24 (1974): 67–68.

———. "Mill's Criterion of Wrong Conduct." *Dialogue* 21 (1982): 27–44.

———. "What Is Mill's Principle of Utility?" *Canadian Journal of Philosophy,* 3 (1973): 1–12.

Burge, Tyler. "Individualism and the Mental," in *Midwest Studies in Philosophy:* vol. 4: *Studies in Metaphysics,* ed. P. A. French, E. E. Vehling, and H. K. Wettstein, pp. 73–121. Minneapolis: University of Minnesota Press, 1979.

———. "Other Bodies," in *Thought and Object,* ed. Andrew Woodfield. Oxford: Clarendon Press, 1982: 97–120.

Burston, W. H. *James Mill on Philosophy and Education.* London: Athlone Press, 1973.

Coleridge, S. T. *Biographia Literaria,* 2 vols., ed. J. Shawcross. London: Oxford University Press, 1962.

Cooper, Wesley, E., Kai Nielsen, and Steven C. Patten, eds. *New Essays on John Stuart Mill and Utilitarianism, Canadian Journal of Philosophy, Supplementary Volume* 5 (1979).

Copp, David. "The Iterated-Utilitarianism of J. S. Mill," in *New Essays on John Stuart Mill and Utilitarianism,* ed. Wesley E. Cooper, Kai Nielsen, and Steven C. Patten. *Canadian Journal of Philosophy, Supplementary Volume* 5 (1979). 75–98.

Cowan, J. L. *Pleasure and Pain.* London: St. Martin's Press, 1968.

Cowling, Maurice. *Mill and Liberalism.* Cambridge: Cambridge University Press, 1963.

Cupples, Brian. "A Defence of the Received Interpretation of J. S. Mill." *Australasian Journal of Philosophy* 50 (August 1972): 131–37.

Dahl, Norman O. "Is Mill's Hedonism Inconsistent?" *American Philosophical Quarterly*, Monograph No. 7, 1973: 37–54.

Devlin, Patrick. *The Enforcement of Morals*. London: Oxford University Press, 1965.

Donagan, Alan. *The Theory of Morality*. Chicago: University of Chicago Press, 1977.

Donner, Wendy. "Gray's Autonomy: In Defence of Mill," in *Ethics and Basic Rights*, ed. Guy Lafrance, pp. 117–30. Ottawa: University of Ottawa Press, 1989.

——. "John Stuart Mill's Concept of Utility." *Dialogue* 22 (September 1983): 479–94.

——. "Mill on Liberty of Self-Development." *Dialogue* 26 (Summer 1987): 227–37.

——. Review of *Conflicting Political Ideas in Liberal Democracies*, Terence Qualter (Methuen, 1986). *Canadian Philosophical Reviews* 7 (July 1987).

——. Review of *The Limits of Utilitarianism*, ed. Harlan B. Miller and William H. Williams (Minneapolis: University of Minnesota Press, 1982). *Mill News Letter* (Winter 1983): 20–26.

——. Review of *Morality within the Limits of Reason*, Russell Hardin (Chicago: University of Chicago Press, 1988). *Canadian Philosophical Reviews* 10 (March 1990): 112–15.

Dummett, Michael. *Voting Procedures*. Oxford: Clarendon Press, 1984.

Duncan, Graeme, and John Gray. "The Left against Mill," in *New Essays on John Stuart Mill and Utilitarianism*, ed. Wesley E. Cooper, Kai Nielsen, and Steven C. Patten. *Canadian Journal of Philosophy, Supplementary Volume* 5 (1979): 203–29.

Dworkin, Gerald. "Is More Choice Better Than Less?" in *Ethical Principles for Social Policy*, ed. J. Howie, pp. 78–96. Carbondale: Southern Illinois University Press, 1983.

——. "Paternalism," *Monist* 56 (1972): 64–84.

Dworkin, Ronald. *Taking Rights Seriously*. Cambridge: Harvard University Press, 1978.

Edwards, Rem B. "Do Pleasures and Pains Differ Qualitatively?" *Journal of Value Inquiry* 9 (Winter 1975): 270–81.

——. "Narveson on Qualitative Hedonism." *Mill News Letter* 16 (Winter 1981): 6–10.

——. *Pleasures and Pains: A Theory of Qualitative Hedonism*. Ithaca: Cornell University Press, 1979.

Elster, Jon. "Sour Grapes—Utilitarianism and the Genesis of Wants," in *Utilitarianism and Beyond*, ed. Amartya Sen and Bernard Williams, pp. 219–38. Cambridge: Cambridge University Press, 1982.

Feinberg, Joel. "The Child's Right to an Open Future," in J. Howie, ed., pp. 97–122. *Ethical Principles for Social Policy*, (Carbondale: Southern Illinois University Press) 1983.

——. *Rights, Justice and the Bounds of Liberty*. Princeton: Princeton University Press, 1980.

——. *Social Philosophy.* Englewood Cliffs, N.J.: Prentice-Hall, 1973.

Frankfurt, H. G. "Freedom of the Will, and the Concept of a Person." *Journal of Philosophy* 68 (1971): 5–20.

Frey, R. G., ed., *Utility and Rights.* Minneapolis: University of Minnesota Press, 1984.

Garforth, F. W. *Educative Democracy: John Stuart Mill on Education in Society.* New York: Oxford University Press, 1980.

——. *John Stuart Mill's Theory of Education.* Oxford: Martin Robertson, 1979.

Glover, Jonathan. *Causing Death and Saving Lives,* Harmondsworth: Penguin, 1977.

Goodman, L. A., and H. Markowitz, "Social Welfare Functions Based on Individual Rankings," *American Journal of Sociology* 58 (1952): 257–62.

Graff, J. A. "Mill's Quantity-Quality Distinction: A Defence." *Mill News Letter* 7 (Spring 1972): 14–18.

Gray, John. *Mill on Liberty: A Defence.* London: Routledge and Kegan Paul, 1983.

Griffin, James. *Modern Utilitarianism. Revue Internationale de Philosophie* 141 (1982).

——. *Well-Being.* Oxford: Clarendon Press, 1986.

Gutman, Amy. *Liberal Equality.* Cambridge: Cambridge University Press, 1980.

——. "What's the Use of Going to School?" in *Utilitarianism and Beyond,* ed. Amartya Sen and Bernard Williams, pp. 261–77. Cambridge: Cambridge University Press, 1982.

Halevy, Eli. *La Formation du radicalisme philosophique.* 3 vols. Paris: Ancienne Librairie Germer–Bailliere, 1901.

——. *The Growth of Philosophic Radicalism.* reprinted Clifton, N.J.: Augustus M. Kelley, 1972.

Hall, E. W. "The 'Proof' of Utility in Bentham and Mill." *Ethics* 60 (October 1949): 1–18.

Halliday, R. J. *John Stuart Mill.* London: George Allen and Unwin, 1976.

Hammond, Peter. "Utilitarianism, Uncertainty, and Information," in *Utilitarianism and Beyond,* ed. Amartya Sen and Bernard Williams, pp. 85–122. Cambridge: Cambridge University Press, 1982.

Hardin, Russell. *Morality within the Limits of Reason.* Chicago: University of Chicago Press, 1988.

Hare, R. M. "Ethical Theory and Utilitarianism," in *Utilitarianism and Beyond,* ed. Amartya Sen and Bernard Williams, pp. 23–38. Cambridge: Cambridge University Press, 1982.

——. *Freedom and Reason.* New York: Oxford University Press, 1965.

——. *Moral Thinking: Its Levels, Method, and Point.* Oxford: Clarendon Press, 1981.

Harsanyi, John. *Essays on Ethics, Social Behavior, and Scientific Explanation.* Dordrecht: D. Reidel, 1976.

——. "Morality and the Theory of Rational Behaviour," in *Utilitarianism and Beyond,* ed. Amartya Sen and Bernard Williams, pp. 39–62. Cambridge: Cambridge University Press, 1982.

Hart, H. L. A. "Are There Any Natural Rights?" in *Rights,* ed. David Lyons. Belmont, Calif: Wadsworth, 1979: 14–25.

——. *Law, Liberty, and Morality.* New York: Random House, 1966.

Haworth, Lawrence. *Autonomy: An Essay in Philosophical Psychology and Ethics.* New Haven: Yale University Press, 1986.

Hayek, F. A. *John Stuart Mill and Harriet Taylor: Their Friendship and Subsequent Marriage.* London: Routledge & Kegan Paul, 1969.

Himmelfarb, Gertrude. *On Liberty and Liberalism: The Case of John Stuart Mill.* New York: Alfred A. Knopf, 1974.

Kamm, Josephine. *John Stuart Mill in Love.* London: Gordon & Cremonesi, 1977.

Kretzmann, Norman. "Desire as Proof of Desirability," *Philosophical Quarterly* 8 (1958): 246–58.

Letvin, Shirley. *The Pursuit of Certainty.* Cambridge: Cambridge University Press, 1965.

Lewis, Thomas. *Pain.* New York: Macmillan, 1942.

Locke, John. *Second Treatise of Government,* Indianapolis: Bobbs-Merrill, 1952.

Luce, R. Duncan, and Howard Raiffa. *Games and Decisions.* New York: John Wiley & Sons, 1957.

Lyons, David. *Forms and Limits of Utilitarianism.* Oxford: Clarendon Press, 1965.

——. "Human Rights and the General Welfare," *Philosophy and Public Affairs* 6 (1977): 113–29.

——. "Liberty and Harm to Others," in *New Essays on John Stuart Mill and Utilitarianism,* ed. Wesley E. Cooper, Kai Nielsen, and Steven C. Patten. *Canadian Journal of Philosophy, Supplementary Volume* 5 (1979): 1–19.

——. "Mill's Theory of Morality." *Nous* 10 (1976): 101–20.

——. ed. *Rights.* Belmont, Calif.: Wadsworth, 1979.

Mabbott, J. D. "Interpretations of Mill's *Utilitarianism.*" *Philosophical Quarterly* 6 (1956): 115–20.

McCloskey, H. J. *John Stuart Mill: A Critical Study.* London: Macmillan, 1971.

Mackie, J. L. *Ethics: Inventing Right and Wrong.* Harmondsworth: Penguin, 1979.

Macpherson, C. B. *Democratic Theory: Essays in Retrieval.* Oxford: Clarendon Press, 1973.

——. *The Life and Times of Liberal Democracy.* Oxford: Oxford University Press, 1980.

——. *The Political Theory of Possessive Individualism.* Oxford: Oxford University Press, 1962.

McPherson, Michael. "Mill's Moral Theory and the Problem of Preference Change." *Ethics* 92 (January 1982): 252–73.

Mill, James. *An Analysis of the Phenomena of the Human Mind,* 2 vols. First ed. 1829; second ed. 1869, edited by John Stuart Mill, (London: Longmans, Green, Reader & Dyer reprinted New York: Augustus M. Kelly, 1967.

Mill, John Stuart. *Autobiography,* ed. Jack Stillinger. Boston: Houghton Mifflin, 1969.

——. *The Collected Works of John Stuart Mill,* ed. John M. Robson. 33 vols. Toronto: University of Toronto Press. 1963–91.

——. *The Early Draft of John Stuart Mill's Autobiography,* ed. Jack Stillinger. Urbana: University of Illinois Press, 1961.

——. *Inaugural Address Delivered to the University of St. Andrews.* London: Longman's, Green, Reader, and Dyer, 1867.

———. *Mill's Essays on Literature and Society,* ed. J. B. Schneewind. New York: Macmillan, 1965.

———. "Thoughts on Poetry and Its Varieties," in *Dissertations and Discussions,* 2 vols. John W. Parker & Son, 1859.

Mill, John Stuart, and Harriet Taylor Mill. *Essays on Sex Equality,* ed. Alice S. Rossi. Chicago: University of Chicago Press, 1970.

Miller, Harlan, and William Williams, eds. *The Limits of Utilitarianism.* Minneapolis: University of Minnesota Press, 1982.

Mirrlees, J. A. "The Economic Uses of Utilitarianism," in *Utilitarianism and Beyond,* ed. Amartya Sen and Bernard Williams, pp. 63–84. Cambridge: Cambridge University Press, 1982.

Mitchell, Wesley C. "Bentham's Felicific Calculus," in *Jeremy Bentham: Ten Critical Essays,* ed. Bhikhu Parekh, 168–86 London: Frank Cass, 1974.

Moore, George Edward. *Principia Ethica.* Cambridge: Cambridge University Press, 1966.

Narveson, Jan. *Morality and Utility.* Baltimore: Johns Hopkins University Press, 1967.

———. Review of *Pleasures and Pains,* Rem Edwards (Ithaca: Cornell University Press, 1979). *Mill News Letter* 15 (Winter 1980): 28–31.

———. "Rights and Utilitarianism," in *New Essays on John Stuart Mill and Utilitarianism,* ed. Wesley E. Cooper, Kai Nielsen, and Steven C. Patten. *Canadian Journal of Philosophy. Supplementary Volume* 5 (1979): 137–160.

Neff, Emery. *Carlyle and Mill: An Introduction to Victorian Thought.* New York: Columbia University Press, 1926.

Nielsen, Kai, and Steven C. Patten, eds. *Marx and Morality. Canadian Journal of Philosophy, Supplementary Volume* 7 (1981).

Nozick, Robert. *Anarchy, State and Utopia.* New York: Basic Books, 1974.

———. *Philosophical Explanations.* Cambridge, Mass.: Belknap Press, 1981.

Owen, W. J. B., ed. *Wordsworth and Coleridge: Lyrical Ballads, 1798.* London: Oxford University Press, 1967.

Packe, Michael St. John. *The Life of John Stuart Mill.* New York: Capricorn Books, 1970.

Parekh, Bhikhu, ed. *Jeremy Bentham: Ten Critical Essays.* London: Frank Cass, 1974.

Partridge, P. H., "Some Notes on the Concept of Power," *Political Studies* 11 (1963): 107–25.

Pateman, Carole. *Participation and Democratic Theory.* Cambridge: Cambridge University Press, 1970.

Qualter, Terence. *Conflicting Political Ideas in Liberal Democracies.* Toronto: Methuen, 1986.

Rachels, James. *The End of Life.* Oxford: Oxford University Press, 1986.

Rawls, John. "Social Unity and Primary Goods," in *Utilitarianism and Beyond,* ed. Amartya Sen and Bernard Williams, pp. 154–85. Cambridge: Cambridge University Press, 1982.

———. *A Theory of Justice.* Cambridge: Harvard University Press, 1971.

Rees, J. C. "A Re-Reading of Mill on Liberty." *Political Studies* 8 (1960): 113–29.

Robson, John M. *The Improvement of Mankind.* Toronto: University of Toronto Press, 1968.

———. "J. S. Mill's Theory of Poetry.", *University of Toronto Quarterly* 29 (1960): 420–38.

Robson, John M., and Michael Laine. *James and John Stuart Mill: Papers of the Centenary Conference.* Toronto: University of Toronto Press, 1976.

Ryan, Alan. *John Stuart Mill.* New York: Random House, 1970.

——. *J. S. Mill.* London: Routledge and Kegan Paul, 1974.

——. *The Philosophy of John Stuart Mill,* 2d ed. London: Macmillan, 1988.

Schick, Frederic. *Having Reasons: An Essay on Rationality and Sociality.* Princeton: Princeton University Press, 1984.

——. "Under Which Descriptions?" in *Utilitarianism and Beyond,* ed. Amartya Sen and Bernard Williams, pp. 251–60. Cambridge: Cambridge University Press, 1982.

Schlipp, Paul Arthur. *The Philosophy of G. E. Moore.* Lasalle, Ill.: Open Court, 1968.

Schneewind, J. B., ed. *Mill's Essays on Literature and Society.* New York: Macmillan, 1965.

Schwartz, Pedro. *The New Political Economy of J. S. Mill.* London: Weidenfeld and Nicolson, 1968.

Sen, Amartya. *Choice, Welfare and Measurement.* Oxford: Basil Blackwell, 1982.

——. *Collective Choice and Social Welfare.* San Francisco: Holden-Day, 1970.

Sen, Amartya, and Bernard Williams. *Utilitarianism and Beyond.* Cambridge: Cambridge University Press, 1982.

Sharpless, F. Parvin. *The Literary Criticism of John Stuart Mill.* The Hague: Mouton, 1967.

Shelley, Percy Bysshe. *The Prose Works of Percy Bysshe Shelley,* 4 vols., ed. Harry Buxton Forman. London: Reeves and Turner, 1880.

Shue, Henry. *Basic Rights.* Princeton: Princeton University Press, 1980.

Sidgwick, Henry. *The Methods of Ethics.* London: Macmillan, 1901.

Smart, J. J. C., and Bernard, Williams. *Utilitarianism: For and Against.* Cambridge: Cambridge University Press, 1973.

Smith, James M., and Ernest Sosa, eds. *Mill's Utilitarianism.* Belmont, Calif.: Wadsworth, 1969.

Stephen, Leslie. *The English Utilitarians, Vol. III.* New York: Augustus M. Kelley, 1968.

Sumner, L. W. *Abortion and Moral Theory.* Princeton: Princeton University Press, 1981.

——. "The Good and the Right," in *New Essays on John Stuart Mill and Utilitarianism,* ed. Wesley Cooper, Kai Nielsen, and Steven Patten. *Canadian Journal of Philosophy, Supplementary Volume* 5 (1979): 99–114.

——. *The Moral Foundation of Rights.* Oxford: Clarendon Press, 1987.

——. Unpublished mss on Jeremy Bentham.

Ten, C. L. *Mill on Liberty.* Oxford: Clarendon Press, 1980.

Thomas, William. *The Philosophic Radicals.* Oxford: Clarendon Press, 1979.

Thompson, Dennis F. *John Stuart Mill and Representative Government.* Princeton: Princeton University Press, 1976.

Urmson, J. O. "The Interpretation of the Moral Philosophy of J. S. Mill." *Philosophical Quarterly* 3 (January 1953): 33–39.

Von Neumann, J., and O. Morgenstern. *Theory of Games and Economic Behavior.* Princeton: Princeton University Press, 1942.

West, Henry. "Mill's 'Proof' of the Principle of Utility," in *The Limits of Utilitar-*

ianism, ed. Harlan Miller and William Williams, pp. 23–34. Minneapolis: University of Minnesota Press, 1982.

——. "Preference Utilitarianism vs. Mental State Utilitarianism." Presented to Pacific American Philosophical Association, March 1987.

——. "Reconstructing Mill's 'Proof' of the Principle of Utility." *Mind* 81 (1972): 256–57.

Whewell, William. *Lectures on the History of Moral Philosophy.* Cambridge: Deighton, Bell, 1862.

Willey, Basil. *Nineteenth Century Studies.* New York: Harper and Row, 1966.

Wilson, Fred. "Mill's Proof That Happiness is the Criterion of Morality." *Journal of Business Ethics* 1 (Fall 1982): 59–72.

Wolff, Robert Paul. *The Poverty of Liberalism.* Boston: Beacon Press, 1968.

Wollheim, Richard. "John Stuart Mill and Isaiah Berlin: The Ends of Life and the Preliminaries of Morality," in *The Idea of Freedom.* Oxford: Oxford University Press, 1979. 253–69.

Woodfield, Andrew, ed. *Thought and Object.* Oxford: Clarendon Press, 1982.

Index

Abrams, M. H., 101
Amerine, Maynard, 83–91, 93
Analysis of the Phenomena of the Human Mind, 11, 15, 17–19, 39, 101, 105, 117, 133
Aristotle, 121, 162
Associationist psychology, 4, 9–26, 37–75, 83, 93–97, 113–17, 132–40; complex experiences, 3, 8, 14–23, 66–75, 83; simple sensations, 3, 14–26, 66–70. *See also* Happiness
Autobiography, 3, 97–100, 108–10, 112, 118
Autonomy, 5, 8, 118, 120, 125, 144, 151–52, 157–59, 165–83, 213, 216. *See also* Self-development

Bain, Alexander, 12
Bentham, Jeremy, 1–15, 34–36, 46, 52, 56–68, 79, 89–90, 104, 109, 113–14, 127, 141; dominant account, 23–25, 40–41, 54, 57–61, 66, 83, 92; secondary account, 23–26, 60–66
Berger, Fred, 2, 6, 19–20, 30, 32, 119–20, 124–25, 190
Bowring, John, 11, 13, 24–26, 58
Bradley, F. H., 42–44
Brandt, Richard, 66–67, 79–82
Brenkert, G. G., 144–46

Brett, Nathan, 175–77
Broad, C. D., 84, 90
Bronaugh, Richard, 49–52, 89
Brown, D. G., 2, 10, 155, 193–97
Burge, Tyler, 77–78

Carlyle, Thomas, 100, 104, 109
"Carlyle's *French Revolution*," 104–5
Children, rights of, 166–72
"Civilization," 111
"Claims of Labour," 128
Coleridge, S. T., 98, 101, 105, 109
Collective and cooperative ventures, 127, 177, 194–97, 208–13
Competent agents, 3–6, 9, 20–23, 28–36, 40, 52–56, 65, 83, 90–92, 94, 120–23, 131, 135, 141–43, 155–59, 184–87
Considerations on Representative Government, 7, 126, 130–31, 139, 156, 172, 198–208
Cooper, Wesley, 10, 121, 144, 155, 175
Copp, David, 155
Cowan, J. L., 58–59

Davidson, Donald, 78
Development, doctrine of, 1–6, 18, 36, 45, 91–142, 147–50, 156–59, 170, 198–213

Donagan, Alan, 29
Duncan, Graeme, 144, 148
Dworkin, Ronald, 126

Economic democracy, 7, 152–55, 198, 208–17
Edwards, Rem, 16, 40, 52–56, 76–78
Elitism, 5, 7, 128–31, 152, 156–59, 166, 182, 185–86
Empiricism, 11, 101–2, 121–25

Feinberg, Joel, 167–70, 179–80
Forman, Harry Buston, 102
Frankfurt, H. G., 179–80
Free market, 153–55, 187

Garforth, F. W., 96
Glover, Jonathan, 66
Goodman, L. A., 63–64
Gorovitz, Samuel, 30
Gray, John, 2, 7, 121–22, 144, 148, 151, 161–62, 165–83, 186, 190
Griffin, James, 66–76, 80–82
Gutmann, Amy, 152, 154–55, 201

Halevy, Eli, 57, 61
Hall, E. W., 29–31
Happiness, 9–11, 18–21, 118–25, 131, 134–35, 138–40. *See also* Associationist psychology
Hardin, Russell, 71, 175
Hare, R. M., 71, 184
Hare, Thomas, 205
Harm, 188–97
Haworth, Lawrence, 168, 170, 178
Hedonism, qualitative, 1–21, 28–78, 83, 92, 118–25, 131, 134–41, 151–52, 184–87; correlationism, 49–52; critics of, 41–45; reductionism, 46–52
Hedonism, quantitative, 1–4, 8–15, 24–26, 37, 52–65, 83
Human faculties, 3, 5, 92, 119–20, 126–27, 134–38, 180–83, 200; affective, 96–107, 112, 151, 157, 166, 185–87; intellectual, 107–12, 123, 151, 157, 165; moral, 112–17, 165–66
Human nature, 3–4, 8, 65, 91, 93, 115, 118–25, 131–40, 149–52, 184

Inaugural Address Delivered to the University of St. Andrew's, 39, 106, 111, 117

Individualism, possessive, 6, 130, 138, 140, 145–46, 176–79
Individuality, 5–6, 118, 120–25, 130, 138–52, 165, 180–83, 192
Interpersonal standards, 65, 90–91, 93, 96, 107–13
Intuitionism, 4, 9, 11, 26, 28–36, 95–96, 114–15, 120, 141–42

Lewis, Thomas, 58–59
Liberalism, 5–6, 95, 115, 120, 125–32, 141–59; critics of, 143–48, 152–56, 160–87
Libertarian interpretation of Mill, 166–83, 187. *See also* Gray, John
Liberty, principle of, 7, 142, 158, 166–72, 188–97; harm prevention or harmful conduct principle, 193–97
Locke, John, 148, 168
Luce, R. Duncan, 62–65
Lyons, David, 2, 10, 155, 174, 189, 193–97

Macpherson, C. B., 148, 152–55, 183–84, 216–17
Markowitz, H., 63–64
Mill, James, 2, 8, 11–12, 15, 17–18, 39, 54, 68, 79, 101, 117, 133
Miller, Harlan, 30
Mitchell, Wesley, 26, 57, 61
Moore, G. E., 29–30, 44–45, 84, 90
Moral arts and sciences, 94–97, 131–40, 185–86

Narveson, Jan, 41, 46, 53, 56, 155, 175
Neutralism and the state, 125–31
Nielsen, Kai, 10, 144, 155, 175
Nozick, Robert, 69–78

Objectivity of moral theories, 4, 6, 24, 26–36, 52–65, 93, 141, 144
"On the Definition of Political Economy," 131, 136–37
"On Genius," 110
On Liberty, 111, 122, 127–28, 139, 148–52, 156–59, 166–85, 187–97
Owen, W.J.B., 102–3

Parekh, Bhiku, 26, 57, 61
Participation, economic and political, 7, 153–55, 156–59, 198–217
Partridge, P. H., 212

Pateman, Carole, 202, 211–13
Paternalism, 170
Patton, Steven, 10, 144, 155, 175
Pleasurable experience, 9–23, 37, 41, 44–45, 76–78. *See also* Hedonism
Principles of Political Economy, 206–13

Qualter, Terence, 178

Rachels, James, 163
Raiffa, Howard, 62–65
Rawls, John, 126, 162
Rees, J. C., 189
"Remarks on Bentham's Philosophy," 113–14
Representative government, 7, 126, 130–31, 139, 152, 156, 198–208
Rights, 5, 7, 129, 160–93, 196–97; liberty of self-development, 7, 129, 160–88; negative and positive, 161–65, 173–79, 182–84; social context of, 173–79, 182, 196–97
Robson, John, 100, 102, 104
Roessler, Edward, 83–91, 93
Romanticism, 100–106
Ryan, Alan, 1–2, 29, 31, 118

Saint-Simonians, 109
Schlipp, Paul Arthur, 84
Schneewind, J. B., 100, 105
Sedgwick, Adam, 29, 114
"Sedgwick's Discourse," 114–15
Self-development, 1–7, 36, 40, 45, 91–92, 114–15, 142–52, 153–55, 160–63, 180–83, 187, 198–213. *See also* Autonomy; Development
Self-regarding and other regarding actions, 189–91
Sen, Amartya, 63–65
Sharpless, F. Parvin, 97, 104
Shelley, P. B., 101–5

Shue, Henry, 165, 174–75
Sidgwick, Henry, 28–29
Smith, James, 46
Sociality, 5, 92, 113–20, 143–49, 180–83, 197
Sosa, Ernest, 46–52, 89
Subjection of Women, 130
Sumner, L. W., 10, 66, 68, 79–81, 155
System of Logic, A., 2, 20–23, 37–41, 94–97, 119, 123, 132–36, 185–86, 207–8

Ten, C. L., 189
"Tennyson's Poems," 103–5
Thompson, Dennis, 199, 201
"Thoughts on Poetry and its Varieties," 100–103

Utilitarianism, 39–41, 46–52, 90–91, 115–17, 122, 139, 157, 160–62, 166, 180–81, 188–93
Utility: desire-satisfaction model, 4–5, 60–67, 79–82; mental-state model, 4, 8–9, 22–23, 66–78; principle of, 2, 4, 9–11, 19–23, 28–36, 95, 123, 160–61, 166–67, 181, 187, 191
Utopian socialism, 7, 187, 208–13

Value: good-making characteristics, 3, 10–11, 14–15, 18–23, 36–79, 83–84, 90–92; measurement of by felicific calculus, 3, 5, 9, 14–15, 23–26, 36, 54–60, 83, 92, 141. *See also* Competent agents

West, Henry, 2, 30–31
Whewell, William, 28–36, 115
"Whewell on Moral Philosophy," 115
Willey, Basil, 101
Wolff, Robert Paul, 145–46

Library of Congress Cataloging-in-Publication Data

Donner, Wendy, 1948–
    The liberal self: John Stuart Mill's moral and political
philosophy / Wendy Donner.
      p.   .cm.
    Includes bibliographical references and index.
    ISBN 0-8014-2629-4 (alk. paper)
    1. Mill, John Stuart, 1806–1873. 2. Ethics, Modern—19th century,
3. Political science—Philosophy—History—19th century. I. Title.
B1607.D58 1991
171'.5'092—dc20
                                          91-55065